# The Earthly Paradise by William Morris

## A Poem

## Part IV

I0151169

William Morris was born in Walthamstow, London on 24th March 1834 he is regarded today as a foremost poet, writer, textile designer, artist and libertarian.

Morris began to publish poetry and short stories in 1856 through the Oxford and Cambridge Magazine which he founded with his friends and financed while at university. His first volume, in 1858, The Defence of Guenevere and Other Poems, was the first published book of Pre-Raphaelite poetry. Due to its luke warm reception he was discouraged from poetry writing for a number of years.

His return to poetry was with the great success of The Life and Death of Jason in 1867, which was followed by The Earthly Paradise, themed around a group of medieval wanderers searching for a land of everlasting life; after much disillusion, they discover a surviving colony of Greeks with whom they exchange stories. In the collection are retellings of Icelandic sagas. From then until his Socialist period Morris's fascination with the ancient Germanic and Norse peoples dominated his writing being the first to translate many of the Icelandic sagas into English; the epic retelling of the story of Sigurd the Volsung being his favourite.

In 1884 he founded the Socialist League but with the rise of the Anarachists in the party he left it in 1890.

In 1891 he founded the Kelmscott Press publishing limited edition illuminated style books.  His design for The Works of Geoffrey Chaucer is a masterpiece.

Morris was quietly approached with an offer of the Poet Laureateship after the death of Tennyson in 1892, but declined.

William Morris died at age 62 on 3rd October 1896 in London.

## Index Of Contents

## DECEMBER

Dead lonely night and all streets quiet now,
Thin o'er the moon the hindmost cloud swims past
Of that great rack that brought us up the snow;
On earth strange shadows o'er the snow are cast;
Pale stars, bright moon, swift cloud make heaven so vast
That earth left silent by the wind of night
Seems shrunken 'neath the grey unmeasured height.

Ah! through the hush the looked-for midnight clangs!
And then, e'en while its last stroke's solemn drone
In the cold air by unlit windows hangs,
Out break the bells above the year foredone,
Change, kindness lost, love left unloved alone;
Till their despairing sweetness makes thee deem
Thou once wert loved, if but amidst a dream.

O thou who clingest still to life and love,
Though nought of good, no God thou mayst discern,
Though nought that is, thine utmost woe can move,
Though no soul knows wherewith thine heart doth yearn,
Yet, since thy weary lips no curse can learn,
Cast no least thing thou lovedst once away,
Since yet perchance thine eyes shall see the day.

December came, with mirth men needs must make
E'en for the empty days and leisures' sake
That earth's cold leaden sleep doth bring; so there
Our elders sat within the guest-hall fair,
Not looking older for the snow without;
Cheery enough; remembering not old doubt,
A gnawing pain once, grown too hard to bear,
And so cast by; not thinking of old fear,
That conquering once, e'en with its victory
Must fade away, and, like all things else, die.
Not thinking of much else than that they had
Enough of life to make them somewhat glad
When all went well with them.

Now so it fell
That mariners were there, who 'gan to tell
Mishaps betid upon the winter seas,
Which set some younger men amidst of these
To ask the Wanderers of their voyage vain,
As knowing scarce the tale thereof. Small pain

It gave them now to answer: yet belike
On the old men, their hosts, the thing did strike
In jarring wise, this turning o'er and o'er
Of memories once so bitter sharp and sore:
Wherefore at last an elder said, "Let be,
My masters! if about the troublous sea
Ye needs must hear, hearken a tale once told
By kin of ours in the dim days of old,
Whose thoughts when turning to a peaceful home
Unto this very west of ours must come—
Scarce causelessly meseems when all is said,
And I remember that years bow my head,
And not the trouble of those days of war,
Of loss and wrong that in old stories are."


## THE GOLDEN APPLES

**This tale tells of the voyage of a ship of Tyre, that, against the will of the shipmen, bore Hercules to an unknown land of the West, that he might accomplish a task laid on him by the Fates.**

As many as the leaves fall from the tree,
From the world's life the years are fallen away
Since King Eurystheus sat in majesty
In fair Mycenæ; midmost of whose day
It once befell that in a quiet bay
A ship of Tyre was swinging nigh the shore,
Her folk for sailing handling rope and oar.

Fresh was the summer morn, a soft wind stole
Down from the sheep-browsed slopes the cliffs that crowned,
And ruffled lightly the long gleaming roll
Of the peaceful sea, and bore along the sound
Of shepherd-folk and sheep and questing hound;
For in the first dip of the hillside there
Lay bosomed 'mid its trees a homestead fair.

Amid regrets for last night, when the moon,
Risen on the soft dusk, shone on maidens' feet
Brushing the gold-heart lilies to the tune
Of pipes complaining, o'er the grass down-beat
That mixed with dewy flowers its odour sweet,
The shipmen laboured, till the sail unfurled
Swung round the prow to meet another world.

But ere the anchor had come home, a shout
Rang from the strand, as though the ship were hailed.
Whereat the master bade them stay, in doubt
That they without some needful thing had sailed;
When, lo! from where the cliffs' steep grey sides failed

Into a ragged stony slip, came twain
Who seemed in haste the ready keel to gain.

Soon they drew nigh, and he who first came down
Unto the surf was a man huge of limb,
Grey-eyed, with crisp-curled hair 'twixt black and brown,
Who had a lion's skin cast over him,
So wrought with gold that the fell showed but dim
Betwixt the threads, and in his hand he bore
A mighty club with bands of steel done o'er.

Panting there followed him a grey old man,
Bearing a long staff; clad in gown of blue,
Feeble of aspect, hollow-cheeked and wan,
Who when unto his fellow's side he drew,
Said faintly: "Now, do that which thou shouldst do;
This is the ship." Then in the other's eye
A smile gleamed, and he spake out merrily:

"Masters, folk tell me that ye make for Tyre,
And after that still nearer to the sun;
And since Fate bids me look to die by fire,
Fain am I, ere my worldly day be done,
To know what from earth's hottest can be won;
And this old man, my kinsman, would with me.
How say ye, will ye bear us o'er the sea?"

"What is thy name?" the master said: "And know
That we are merchants, and for nought give nought;
What wilt thou pay?—thou seem'st full rich, I trow."
The old man muttered, stooped adown and caught
At something in the sand: "E'en so I thought,"
The younger said, "when I set out from home—
As to my name, perchance in days to come

"Thou shalt know that—but have heed, take this toy,
And call me the Strong Man." And as he spake
The master's deep-brown eyes 'gan gleam with joy,
For from his arm a huge ring did he take,
And cast it on the deck, where it did break
A water-jar, and in the wet shards lay
Golden, and gleaming like the end of day.

But the old man held out a withered hand,
Wherein there shone two pearls most great and fair,
And said, "If any nigher I might stand,
Then might'st thou see the things I give thee here
And for name—a many names I bear,
But call me Shepherd of the Shore this tide,
And for more knowledge with a good will bide."

From one to the other turned the master's eyes;
The Strong Man laughed as at some hidden jest,
And wild doubts in the shipman's heart did rise;
But thinking on the thing, he deemed it best
To bid them come aboard, and take such rest
As they might have of the untrusty sea,
'Mid men who trusty fellows still should be.

Then no more words the Strong Man made, but straight
Caught up the elder in his arms, and so,
Making no whit of all that added weight,
Strode to the ship, right through the breakers low,
And catching at the rope that they did throw
Out toward his hand, swung up into the ship:
Then did the master let the hawser slip.

The shapely prow cleft the wet mead and green,
And wondering drew the shipmen round to gaze
Upon those limbs, the mightiest ever seen;
And many deemed it no light thing to face
The splendour of his eyen, though they did blaze
With no wrath now, no hate for them to dread,
As seaward 'twixt the summer isles they sped.

Freshened the wind, but ever fair it blew
Unto the south-east; but as failed the land,
Unto the plunging prow the Strong Man drew,
And silent, gazing with wide eyes did stand,
As though his heart found rest; but 'mid the band
Of shipmen in the stern the old man sat,
Telling them tales that no man there forgat.

As one who had beheld, he told them there
Of the sweet singer, who, for his song's sake,
The dolphins back from choking death did bear;
How in the mid sea did the vine outbreak
O'er that ill bark when Bacchus 'gan to wake;
How anigh Cyprus, ruddy with the rose
The cold sea grew as any June-loved close;

While on the flowery shore all things alive
Grew faint with sense of birth of some delight,
And the nymphs waited trembling there, to give
Glad welcome to the glory of that sight:
He paused then, ere he told how, wild and white,
Rose ocean, breaking o'er a race accurst,
A world once good, now come unto its worst.

And then he smiled, and said, "And yet ye won,
Ye men, and tremble not on days like these,
Nor think with what a mind Prometheus' son

Beheld the last of the torn reeling trees
From high Parnassus: slipping through the seas
Ye never think, ye men-folk, how ye seem
From down below through the green waters' gleam."

Dusk was it now when these last words he said,
And little of his visage might they see,
But o'er their hearts stole vague and troublous dread,
They knew not why; yet ever quietly
They sailed that night; nor might a morning be
Fairer than was the next morn; and they went
Along their due course after their intent.

The fourth day, about sunrise, from the mast
The watch cried out he saw Phœnician land;
Whereat the Strong Man on the elder cast
A look askance, and he straight took his stand
Anigh the prow, and gazed beneath his hand
Upon the low sun and the scarce-seen shore,
Till cloud-flecks rose, and gathered and drew o'er.

The morn grown cold; then small rain 'gan to fall,
And all the wind dropped dead, and hearts of men
Sank, and their bark seemed helpless now and small;
Then suddenly the wind 'gan moan again;
Sails flapped, and ropes beat wild about; and then
Down came the great east wind; and the ship ran
Straining, heeled o'er, through seas all changed and wan.

Westward, scarce knowing night from day, they drave
Through sea and sky grown one; the Strong Man wrought
With mighty hands, and seemed a god to save;
But on the prow, heeding all weather nought,
The elder stood, nor any prop he sought,
But swayed to the ship's wallowing, as on wings
He there were set above the wrack of things.

And westward still they drave; and if they saw
Land upon either side, as on they sped,
'Twas but as faces in a dream may draw
Anigh, and fade, and leave nought in their stead;
And in the shipmen's hearts grew heavy dread
To sick despair; they deemed they should drive on
Till the world's edge and empty space were won.

But 'neath the Strong Man's eyes e'en as they might
They toiled on still; and he sang to the wind,
And spread his arms to meet the waters white,
As o'er the deck they tumbled, making blind
The brine-drenched shipmen; nor with eye unkind
He gazed up at the lightning; nor would frown

When o'er the wet waste Jove's bolt rattled down.

And they, who at the last had come to think
Their guests were very gods, with all their fear
Feared nought belike that their good ship would sink
Amid the storm; but rather looked to hear
The last moan of the wind that them should bear
Into the windless stream of ocean grey,
Where they should float till dead was every day.

Yet their fear mocked them; for the storm 'gan die
About the tenth day, though unto the west
They drave on still; soon fair and quietly
The morn would break; and though amid their rest
Nought but long evil wandering seemed the best
That they might hope for; still, despite their dread,
Sweet was the quiet sea and goodlihead

Of the bright sun at last come back again;
And as the days passed, less and less fear grew,
If without cause, till faded all their pain;
And they 'gan turn unto their guests anew,
Yet durst ask nought of what that evil drew
Upon their heads; or of returning speak.
Happy they felt, but listless, spent, and weak.

And now as at the first the elder was,
And sat and told them tales of yore agone;
But ever the Strong Man up and down would pass
About the deck, or on the prow alone
Would stand and stare out westward; and still on
Through a fair summer sea they went, nor thought
Of what would come when these days turned to nought.

And now when twenty days were well passed o'er
They made a new land; cloudy mountains high
Rose from the sea at first; then a green shore
Spread fair below them: as they drew anigh
No sloping, stony strand could they espy,
And no surf breaking; the green sea and wide
Wherethrough they slipped was driven by no tide.

Dark fell ere they might set their eager feet
Upon the shore; but night-long their ship lay
As in a deep stream, by the blossoms sweet
That flecked the grass whence flowers ne'er passed away.
But when the cloud-barred east brought back the day,
And turned the western mountain-tops to gold,
Fresh fear the shipmen in their bark did hold.

For as a dream seemed all; too fair for those

Who needs must die; moreover they could see,
A furlong off, 'twixt apple-tree and rose,
A brazen wall that gleamed out wondrously
In the young sun, and seemed right long to be;
And memory of all marvels lay upon
Their shrinking hearts now this sweet place was won.

But when unto the nameless guests they turned,
Who stood together nigh the plank shot out
Shoreward, within the Strong Man's eyes there burned
A wild light, as the other one in doubt
He eyed a moment; then with a great shout
Leaped into the blossomed grass; the echoes rolled
Back from the hills, harsh still and over-bold.

Slowly the old man followed him, and still
The crew held back: they knew now they were brought
Over the sea the purpose to fulfil
Of these strange men; and in their hearts they thought,
"Perchance we yet shall live, if, meddling nought
With dreams, we bide here till these twain come back;
But prying eyes the fire-blast seldom lack."

Yet 'mongst them were two fellows bold and young,
Who, looking each upon the other's face,
Their hearts to meet the unknown danger strung,
And went ashore, and at a gentle pace
Followed the strangers, who unto the place
Where the wall gleamed had turned; peace and desire
Mingled together in their hearts, as nigher

They drew unto that wall, and dulled their fear:
Fair wrought it was, as though with bricks of brass;
And images upon its face there were,
Stories of things a long while come to pass:
Nor that alone—as looking in a glass
Its maker knew the tales of what should be,
And wrought them there for bird and beast to see.

So on they went; the many birds sang sweet
Through all that blossomed thicket from above,
And unknown flowers bent down before their feet;
The very air, cleft by the grey-winged dove,
Throbbed with sweet scent, and smote their souls with love.
Slowly they went till those twain stayed before
A strangely-wrought and iron-covered door.

They stayed, too, till o'er noise of wind, and bird,
And falling flower, there rang a mighty shout
As the Strong Man his steel-bound club upreared,
And drave it 'gainst the hammered iron stout,

Where 'neath his blows flew bolt and rivet out,
Till shattered on the ground the great door lay,
And into the guarded place bright poured the day.

The Strong Man entered, but his fellow stayed,
Leaning against a tree-trunk as they deemed.
They faltered now, and yet all things being weighed
Went on again; and thought they must have dreamed
Of the old man, for now the sunlight streamed
Full on the tree he had been leaning on,
And him they saw not go, yet was he gone:

Only a slim green lizard flitted there
Amidst the dry leaves; him they noted nought,
But trembling, through the doorway 'gan to peer,
And still of strange and dreadful saw not aught,
Only a garden fair beyond all thought.
And there, 'twixt sun and shade, the Strong Man went
On some long-sought-for end belike intent.

They 'gan to follow down a narrow way
Of green-sward that the lilies trembled o'er,
And whereon thick the scattered rose-leaves lay;
But a great wonder weighed upon them sore,
And well they thought they should return no more,
Yet scarce a pain that seemed; they looked to meet
Before they died things strange and fair and sweet.

So still to right and left the Strong Man thrust
The blossomed boughs, and passed on steadily,
As though his hardy heart he well did trust,
Till in a while he gave a joyous cry,
And hastened on, as though the end drew nigh;
And women's voices then they deemed they heard,
Mixed with a noise that made desire afeard.

Yet through sweet scents and sounds on did they bear
Their panting hearts, till the path ended now
In a wide space of green, a streamlet clear
From out a marble basin there did flow,
And close by that a slim-trunked tree did grow,
And on a bough low o'er the water cold
There hung three apples of red-gleaming gold.

About the tree, new risen e'en now to meet
The shining presence of that mighty one,
Three damsels stood, naked from head to feet
Save for the glory of their hair, where sun
And shadow flickered, while the wind did run
Through the grey leaves o'erhead, and shook the grass
Where nigh their feet the wandering bee did pass.

But 'midst their delicate limbs and all around
The tree-roots, gleaming blue black could they see
The spires of a great serpent, that, enwound
About the smooth bole, looked-forth threateningly,
With glittering eyes and raised crest, o'er the three
Fair heads fresh crowned, and hissed above the speech
Wherewith they murmured softly each to each.

Now the Strong Man amid the green space stayed,
And, leaning on his club, with eager eyes
But brow yet smooth, in voice yet friendly said:
"O daughters of old Hesperus the Wise,
Well have ye held your guard here; but time tries
The very will of gods, and to my hand
Must give this day the gold fruit of your land."

Then spake the first maid—sweet as the west wind
Amidst of summer noon her sweet voice was:
"Ah, me! what knows this place of changing mind
Of men or gods; here shall long ages pass,
And clean forget thy feet upon the grass,
Thy hapless bones amid the fruitful mould;
Look at thy death envenomed swift and cold!"

Hiding new flowers, the dull coils, as she spake,
Moved near her limbs: but then the second one,
In such a voice as when the morn doth wake
To song of birds, said, "When the world foredone
Has moaned its last, still shall we dwell alone
Beneath this bough, and have no tales to tell
Of things deemed great that on the earth befell."

Then spake the third, in voice as of the flute
That wakes the maiden to her wedding morn:
"If any god should gain our golden fruit,
Its curse would make his deathless life forlorn.
Lament thou, then, that ever thou wert born;
Yet all things, changed by joy or loss or pain,
To what they were shall change and change again."

"So be it," he said, "the Fates that drive me on
Shall slay me or shall save; blessing or curse
That followeth after when the thing is won
Shall make my work no better now nor worse;
And if it be that the world's heart must nurse
Hatred against me, how then shall I choose
To leave or take?—let your dread servant loose!"

E'en therewith, like a pillar of black smoke,
Swift, shifting ever, drave the worm at him;

In deadly silence now that nothing broke,
Its folds were writhing round him trunk and limb,
Until his glittering gear was nought but dim
E'en in that sunshine, while his head and side
And breast the fork-tongued, pointed muzzle tried.

Closer the coils drew, quicker all about
The forked tongue darted, and yet stiff he stood,
E'en as an oak that sees the straw flare out
And lick its ancient bole for little good:
Until the godlike fury of his mood
Burst from his heart in one great shattering cry,
And rattling down the loosened coils did lie;

And from the torn throat and crushed dreadful head
Forth flowed a stream of blood along the grass;
Bright in the sun he stood above the dead,
Panting with fury; yet as ever was
The wont of him, soon did his anger pass,
And with a happy smile at last he turned
To where the apples o'er the water burned.

Silent and moveless ever stood the three;
No change came o'er their faces, as his hand
Was stretched aloft unto the sacred tree;
Nor shrank they aught aback, though he did stand
So close that tresses of their bright hair, fanned
By the sweet garden breeze, lay light on him,
And his gold fell brushed by them breast and limb.

He drew adown the wind-stirred bough, and took
The apples thence; then let it spring away,
And from his brow the dark hair backward shook,
And said: "O sweet, O fair, and shall this day
A curse upon my life henceforward lay—
This day alone? Methinks of coming life
Somewhat I know, with all its loss and strife.

"But this I know, at least: the world shall wend
Upon its way, and, gathering joy and grief
And deeds done, bear them with it to the end;
So shall it, though I lie as last year's leaf
Lies 'neath a summer tree, at least receive
My life gone by, and store it, with the gain
That men alive call striving, wrong, and pain.

"So for my part I rather bless than curse,
And bless this fateful land; good be with it;
Nor for this deadly thing's death is it worse,
Nor for the lack of gold; still shall ye sit
Watching the swallow o'er the daisies flit;

Still shall your wandering limbs ere day is done
Make dawn desired by the sinking sun.

"And now, behold! in memory of all this
Take ye this girdle that shall waste and fade
As fadeth not your fairness and your bliss,
That when hereafter 'mid the blossoms laid
Ye talk of days and men now nothing made,
Ye may remember how the Theban man,
The son of Jove, came o'er the waters wan."

Their faces changed not aught for all they heard;
As though all things now fully told out were,
They gazed upon him without any word:
Ah! craving kindness, hope, or loving care,
Their fairness scarcely could have made more fair,
As with the apples folded in his fell
He went, to do more deeds for folk to tell.

Now as the girdle on the ground was cast
Those fellows turned and hurried toward the door,
And as across its broken leaves they passed
The old man saw they not, e'en as before;
But an unearthed blind mole bewildered sore
Was wandering there in fruitless, aimless wise,
That got small heed from their full-sated eyes.

Swift gat they to their anxious folk; nor had
More time than just to say, "Be of good cheer,
For in our own land may we yet be glad,"
When they beheld the guests a-drawing near;
And much bewildered the two fellows were
To see the old man, and must even deem
That they should see things stranger than a dream.

But when they were aboard the elder cried,
"Up sails, my masters, fair now is the wind;
Nor good it is too long here to abide,
Lest what ye may not loose your souls should bind."
And as he spake, the tall trees left behind
Stirred with the rising land-wind, and the crew,
Joyous thereat, the hawsers shipward drew.

Swift sped the ship, and glad at heart were all,
And the Strong Man was merry with the rest,
And from the elder's lips no word did fall
That did not seem to promise all the best;
Yet with a certain awe were men oppressed,
And felt as if their inmost hearts were bare,
And each man's secret babbled through the air.

Still oft the old man sat with them and told
Tales of past time, as on the outward way;
And now would they the face of him behold
And deem it changed; the years that on him lay
Seemed to grow nought, and no more wan and grey
He looked, but ever glorious, wise and strong,
As though no lapse of time for him were long.

At last, when six days through the kindly sea
Their keel had slipped, he said: "Come hearken now,
For so it is that things fare wondrously
E'en in these days; and I a tale can show
That, told by you unto your sons shall grow
A marvel of the days that are to come:
Take heed and tell it when ye reach your home.

"Yet living in the world a man there is
Men call the Theban King Amphitryon's son,
Although perchance a greater sire was his;
But certainly his lips have hung upon
Alcmena's breasts: great deeds this man hath won
Already, for his name is Hercules,
And e'en ye Asian folk have heard of these.

"Now ere the moon, this eve in his last wane,
Was born, this Hercules, the fated thrall
Of King Eurystheus, was straight bid to gain .
Gifts from a land whereon no foot doth fall
Of mortal man, beyond the misty wall
Of unknown waters; pensively he went
Along the sea on his hard life intent.

"And at the dawn he came into a bay
Where the sea, ebbed far down, left wastes of sand,
Walled from the green earth by great cliffs and grey;
Then he looked up, and wondering there did stand,
For strange things lay in slumber on the strand;
Strange counterparts of what the firm earth hath
Lay scattered all about his weary path:

"Sea-lions and sea-horses and sea-kine,
Sea-boars, sea-men strange-skinned, of wondrous hair;
And in their midst a man who seemed divine
For changeless eld, and round him women fair,
Clad in the sea-webs glassy green and clear,
With gems on head and girdle, limb and breast,
Such as earth knoweth not among her best.

"A moment at the fair and wondrous sight
He stared, then, since the heart in him was good,
He went about with careful steps and light

Till o'er the sleeping sea-god now he stood;
And if the white-foot maids had stirred his blood
As he passed by, now other thoughts had place
Within his heart when he beheld that face.

"For Nereus now he knew, who knows all things;
And to himself he said, 'If I prevail,
Better than by some god-wrought eagle-wings
Shall I be holpen;' then he cried out: 'Hail,
O Nereus! lord of shifting hill and dale!
Arise and wrestle; I am Hercules!
Not soon now shalt thou meet the ridgy seas.'

"And mightily he cast himself on him;
And Nereus cried out shrilly; and straightway
That sleeping crowd, fair maid with half-hid limb,
Strange man and green-haired beast, made no delay,
But glided down into the billows grey,
.And, by the lovely sea embraced, were gone,
While they two wrestled on the sea strand lone.

"Soon found the sea-god that his bodily might
Was nought in dealing with Jove's dear one there;
And soon he 'gan to use his magic sleight:
Into a lithe leopard, and a hugging bear
He turned him; then the smallest fowl of air
The straining arms of Hercules must hold,
And then a mud-born wriggling eel and cold.

"Then as the firm hands mastered this, forth brake
A sudden rush of waters all around,
Blinding and choking: then a thin green snake
With golden eyes; then o'er the shell-strewn ground
Forth stole a fly the least that may be found;
Then earth and heaven seemed wrapped in one huge flame,
But from the midst thereof a voice there came:

"'Kinsman and stout-heart, thou hast won the day,
Nor to my grief: what wouldst thou have of me?'
And therewith to an old man small and grey
Faded the roaring flame, who wearily
Sat down upon the sand and said, 'Let be!
I know thy tale; worthy of help thou art;
Come now, a short way hence will there depart

"'A ship of Tyre for the warm southern seas,
Come we a-board; according to my will
Her way shall be.' Then up rose Hercules,
Merry of face, though hot and panting still;
But the fair summer day his heart did fill
With all delight; and so forth went the twain,

And found those men desirous of all gain.

"Ah, for these gainful men—somewhat indeed
Their sails are rent, their bark beat; kin and friend
Are wearying for them; yet a friend in need
They yet shall gain, if at their journey's end,
Upon the last ness where the wild goats wend
To lick the salt-washed stones, a house they raise
Bedight with gold in kindly Nereus' praise."

Breathless they waited for these latest words,
That like the soft wind of the gathering night
Were grown to be: about the mast flew birds
Making their moan, hovering long-winged and white;
And now before their straining anxious sight
The old man faded out into the air,
And from his place flew forth a sea-mew fair.

Then to the Mighty Man, Alcmena's son,
With yearning hearts they turned till he should speak,
And he spake softly: "Nought ill have ye done
In helping me to find what I did seek:
The world made better by me knows if weak
My hand and heart are: but now, light the fire
Upon the prow and worship the grey sire."

So did they; and such gifts as there they had
Gave unto Nereus; yea, and sooth to say,
Amid the tumult of their hearts made glad,
Had honoured Hercules in e'en such way;
But he laughed out amid them, and said, "Nay,
Not yet the end is come; nor have I yet
Bowed down before vain longing and regret.

"It may be—who shall tell, when I go back
There whence I came, and looking down behold
The place that my once eager heart shall lack,
And all my dead desires a-lying cold,
But I may have the might then to enfold
The hopes of brave men in my heart?—but long
Life lies before first with its change and wrong."

So fair along the watery ways they sped
In happy wise, nor failed of their return;
Nor failed in ancient Tyre the ways to tread,
Teaching their tale to whomsoe'er would learn,
Nor failed at last the flesh of beasts to burn
In Nereus' house, turned toward the bright day's end
On the last ness, round which the wild goats wend.

He made an end, and gazed about the place,

With rest enow upon his ancient face,
And smiling; but to some the tale did seem
Like to the middle of some pleasant dream,
Which, waked from, leaves upon the troubled mind
A sense of something ill that lurked behind,
If morn had given due time to dream it out.

Yet as the women stirred, and went about
The board with flask and beaker, and the scent
Of their soft raiment 'mid the feasters went,
The hill-side sun of autumn-tide at least
Seemed to come back unto their winter feast;
Rest, half remembering time past, did they win,
And somewhat surely wrought the tale therein.

In late December shone the westering sun
Through frosty haze of the day nearly done,
Without the hall wherein our elders were:
Within, the firelight gleamed on raiment fair,
And heads far fairer; because youth and maid
Midwinter words of hope that day had said
Before the altars; and were come at last,
No worse for snowy footways over-past,
Or for the east wind upon cheek and brow,
Their fairness to the ancient folk to show;
And, dance and song being done, at end of day,
With ears pricked up, amid the furs they lay,
To have reward of tale for sound and sight
So given erewhile.

The flickering firelight,
And the late sun still streaming through the haze,
Made the hall meet enow for tale of days
So long past over: nigh the cheery flame
A wanderer sat, and a long sunbeam came
On to his knees, then to the hearth fell down.
There in the silence, with thin hands and brown
Folded together, and a dying smile
Upon his face, he sat a little while,
Then somewhat raised his bright eyes, and began
To name his people's best beloved man.


THE FOSTERING OF ASLAUG

ARGUMENT

**Aslaug, the daughter of Sigurd who slew the Dragon, and of Brynhild whom he loved, lost all her friends and kin, and was nourished amid great misery; yet in the end her fortune, her glory, and her beauty prevailed, and she came to mighty estate.**

A fair tale might I tell to you
Of Sigurd, who the dragon slew
Upon the murder-wasted heath,
And how love led him unto death,
Through strange wild ways of joy and pain;
Then such a story should ye gain,
If I could tell it all aright,
As well might win you some delight
From out the woefullest of days;
But now have I no heart to raise
That mighty sorrow laid asleep,
That love so sweet, so strong and deep,
That as ye hear the wonder told
In those few strenuous words of old,
The whole world seems to rend apart
When heart is torn away from heart.
But the world lives still, and to-day
The green Rhine wendeth on its way
Over the unseen golden curse
That drew its lords to worse and worse,
Till that last dawn in Atli's hall,
When the red flame flared over all,
Lighting the leaden, sunless sea.

Yet so much told of this must be,
That Sigurd, while his youth was bright
And unstained, 'midst the first delight
Of Brynhild's love—that him did gain
All joy, all woe, and very bane—
Begat on her a woman-child.
In hope she bore the maid, and smiled
When of its father's face she thought;
But when sad time the change had brought,
And she to Gunnar's house must go,
She, thinking how she might bestow
The memory of that lovely eve,
That morn o'er-sweet, the child did leave
With Heimir, her old foster-sire,
A mighty lord; then, with the fire
Of her old love still smouldering,
And brooding over many a thing,
She went unto her life and death.
Nought, as I said, the story saith
Of all the wrong and love that led
Her feet astray: together dead
They lie now on their funeral pile,
And now the little one doth smile
Upon the glittering war-array
Of the men come the sooth to say
To Heimir of that bitter end.

Silent he stared till these did wend
Into the hall to fire and board,
Then by the porch without a word
Long time he sat: then he arose
And drew his sword, and hard and close
Gazed on the thin-worn edge, and said:
"Smooth cheeks, sweet hands, and art thou dead?
O me thy glory! Woe is me!
I thought once more thine eyes to see—
Had I been young three years agone,
When thou a maiden burd-alone,
Hadst eighteen summers!"
As he spake,
He gat him swiftly to the brake
Of thorn-trees nigh his house: and some,
When calm once more he sat at home,
Deemed he had wept: but no word more
He spake thereof.
A few days wore,
And now alone he oft would be
Within his smithy; heedfully
He guarded it, that none came in;
Nor marvelled men; "For he doth win
Some work of craftsmanship," said they,
"And such before on many a day
Hath been his wont."
So it went on
That a long while he wrought alone;
But on the tenth day bore in there
Aslaug, the little maiden fair,
Three winters old; and then the thing
A little set folk marvelling;
Yet none the less in nought durst they
To watch him. So to end of day
Time drew, and still unto the hall
He came not, and a dread 'gan fall
Upon his household, lest some ill
The quiet of their lives should kill;
And so it fell that the next morn
They found them of their lord forlorn,
And Aslaug might they see no more;
Wide open was the smithy door,
The forge a-cold, and hammering tools
Lay on the floor, with woodwright's rules,
And chips and shavings of hard wood.
Moreover, when they deemed it good
To seek for him, nought might they do,
The tale says, for so dark it grew
Over all ways, that no man might
Know the green meads from water white.

So back they wended sorrowfully,
And still most like it seemed to be,
That Odin had called Heimir home;
And nothing strange it seemed to some
That with him the sweet youngling was,
Since Brynhild's love might bring to pass
E'en mightier things than this, they said,
And sure the little gold-curled head,
The pledge of all her earthly weal,
In Freyia's house she longed to feel.

Further the way was than they deemed
Unto that rest whereof they dreamed
Both to the greybeard and the child;
For now by trodden way and wild
Goes Heimir long: wide-faced is he,
Thin-cheeked, hooked-nosed, e'en as might be
An ancient erne; his hair falls down
From 'neath a wide slouched hat of brown,
And mingles white with his white beard;
A broad brown brand, most men have feared,
Hangs by his side, and at his back
Is slung a huge harp, that doth lack
All fairness certes, and so great
It is, that few might bear its weight;
Yea, Heimir even, somewhat slow
Beneath its burden walketh now,
And looketh round, and stayeth soon.

On a calm sunny afternoon,
Within a cleared space of a wood,
At last the huge old warrior stood
And peered about him doubtfully;
Who, when nought living he might see,
But mid the beech-boughs high aloft
A blue-winged jay, and squirrel soft,
And in the grass a watchful hare,
Unslung his harp and knelt down there
Beside it, and a little while
Handled the hollow with a smile
Of cunning, and behold, the thing
Opened, as by some secret spring,
And there within the hollow lay,
Clad in gold-fringed well-wrought array,
Aslaug, the golden-headed child,
Asleep and rosy; but she smiled
As Heimir's brown hand drew a-near,
And woke up free from any fear,
And stretched her hands out towards his face.
He sat him down in the green place,
With kind arms round the little one,

Till, fully waked now, to the sun
She turned, and babbling, 'gainst his breast
Her dimpled struggling hands she pressed:
His old lips touched those eyes of hers,
That Sigurd's hope and Brynhild's tears
Made sad e'en in her life's first spring;
Then sweet her chuckling laugh did ring,
As down amid the flowery grass
He set her, and beheld her pass
From flower to flower in utter glee;
Therewith he reached out thoughtfully,
And cast his arms around the harp,
That at the first most strange and sharp
Rang through the still day, and the child
Stopped, startled by that music wild:
But then a change carne o'er the strings,
As, tinkling sweet, of merry things
They seemed to tell, and to and fro
Danced Aslaug, till the tune did grow
Fuller and stronger, sweeter still,
And all the woodland place did fill
With sound, not merry now nor sad,
But sweet, heart-raising, as it had
The gathered voice of that fair day
Amidst its measured strains; her play
Amid the flowers grew slower now,
And sadder did the music grow,
And yet still sweeter: and with that,
Nigher to where the old man sat
Aslaug 'gan move, until at last
All sound from the strained strings there passed
As into each other's eyes they gazed;
Then, sighing, the young thing he raised,
And set her softly on his knee,
And laid her round cheek pitifully
Unto his own, and said:
"Indeed,
Of such as I shalt thou have need,
As swift the troubled days wear by,
And yet I know full certainly
My life on earth shall not be long:
And those who think to better wrong
By working wrong shall seek thee wide
To slay thee; yea, belike they ride
E'en now unto my once-loved home.
Well, to a void place shall they come,
And I for thee thus much have wrought
For thee and Brynhild—yea, and nought
I deem it still to turn my face
Each morn unto some unknown place
Like a poor churl—for, ah! who knows

Upon what wandering wind that blows
Drives Brynhild's spirit through the air;
And now by such road may I fare
That we may meet ere many days."

Again the youngling did he raise
Unto his face, for to the earth
Had she slipped down; her babbling mirth
Had mingled with his low deep speech;
But now, as she her hand did reach
Unto his beard, nor stinted more
Her babble, did a change come o'er
His face; for through the windless day
Afar a mighty horn did bray;
Then from beneath his cloak he drew
A golden phial, and set it to
Her ruddy lips in haste, and she
Gazed at him awhile fearfully,
As though she knew he was afraid;
But silently the child he laid
In the harp's hollow place, for now
Drowsy and drooping did she grow
'Neath the strong potion; hastily
He shut the harp, and raised it high
Upon his shoulder, set his sword
Ready to hand, and with no word
Stalked off along the forest glade;
But muttered presently:
"Afraid
Is a strange word for me to say;
But all is changed in a short day,
And full of death the world seems grown.
Mayhap I shall be left alone
When all are dead beside, to dream
Of happy life that once did seem
So stirring 'midst the folk I loved.
Ah! is there nought that may be moved
By strong desire? yea, nought that rules
The very Gods who thrust earth's fools,
This way and that as foolishly,
For aught I know thereof, as I
Deal with the chess when I am drunk?"

His head upon his breast was sunk
For a long space, and then again
He spake: "My life is on the wane;
Somewhat of this I yet may learn
Ere long; yet I am fain to earn
My rest by reaching Atli's land;
For surely 'neath his mighty hand
Safe from the Niblungs shall she be,

Safe from the forge of misery,
Grimhild the Wise-wife."
                    As a goad
That name was to him; on he strode
Still swifter, silent. But day wore
As fast between the tree-stems hoar
He went his ways; belike it was
That he scarce knew if he did pass
O'er rough or smooth, by dark or light,
Until at last the very night
Had closed round him as thinner grew
The wood that he was hurrying through;
And as he gained a grey hill's brow
He felt the sea-breeze meet him now,
And heard the low surf's measured beat
Upon the beach. He stayed his feet,
And through the dusky gathering dark
Peered round and saw what seemed a spark
Along the hill's ridge; thitherward
He turned, still warily on guard,
Until he came unto the door
Of some stead, lone belike and poor:
There knocking, was he bidden in,
And heedfully he raised the pin,
And entering stood with blinking gaze
Before a fire's unsteady blaze.

There sat a woman all alone
Whom some ten years would make a crone,
Yet would they little worsen her;
Her face was sorely pinched with care,
Sour and thin-lipped she was; of hue
E'en like a duck's foot; whitish blue
Her eyes were, seeming as they kept
Wide open even when she slept.
She rose up, and was no less great
Than a tall man, a thing of weight
Was the gaunt hand that held a torch
As Heimir, midmost of the porch,
Fixed his deep grey and solemn eyes
Upon that wretched wife's surprise.

"Well," said she, "what may be your will?
Little we have your sack to fill,
If on thieves' errand ye are come;
But since the goodman is from home
I know of none shall say you nay
If ye have will to bear away
The goodwife."
                As on a burned house
Grown cold, the moon shines dolorous

From out the rainy lift, so now
A laugh must crease her lip and brow.
"I am no thief, goodwife," he said,
"But ask wherein to lay my head
To-night."
"Well, goodman, sit," said she:
"Thine ugly box of minstrelsy
With thine attire befits not ill;
And both belike may match thy skill."

So by the fire he sat him down,
And she too sat, and coarse and brown
The thread was that her rock gave forth
As there she spun; of little worth
Was all the gear that hall did hold.
Now Heimir new-come from the cold
Had set his harp down by his side,
And, turning his grey eyes and wide
Away from hers, slouched down his hat
Yet farther o'er his brows, and sat
With hands outstretched unto the flame.
But had he noted how there came
A twinkle into her dead eyes,
He had been minded to arise,
Methinks; for better company
The wild-wood wolf had been than she.
Because, from out the hodden grey
That was the great man's poor array,
Once and again could she behold
How that the gleam of ruddy gold
Came forth: so therewith she arose,
And, wandering round the hall, drew close
Unto the great harp, and could see
Some fringe of golden bravery
Hanging therefrom.—And the man too,
In spite of patch and clouted shoe,
And unadorned sword, seemed indeed
Scarce less than a great king in need,
So wholly noble was his mien.
So, with these things thus thought and seen,
Within her mind grew fell intent
As to and fro the hall she went,
And from the ark at last did take
Meal forth for porridge and for cake,
And to the fire she turned, and 'gan
To look still closer on the man
As with the girdle and the pot
She busied her, and doubted not
That on his arm a gold ring was;
For presently, as she did pass,
Somewhat she brushed the cloak from him,

And saw the gold gleam nowise dim.
Then sure, if man might shape his fate,
Her greed impatient and dull hate
Within her eyes he might have seen,
And so this tale have never been.
But nought he heeded; far away
His thoughts were.

Therewith did she lay
The meal upon the board, and said,
"Meseems ye would be well apaid
Of meat and drink, and it is here,
Fair lord—though somewhat sorry cheer;
Fall to now."
Whining, with a grin
She watched, as one who sets a gin,
If at the name of lord at all
He started, but no speech did fall
From his old lips, and wearily
He gat to meat, and she stood by,
And poured the drink to him, and said:

"To such a husband am I wed
That ill is speech with him, when he
Comes home foredone with drudgery;
And though indeed I deem thee one
Who deeds of fame full oft hath done
And would not fear him, yet most ill
'Twould be the bliss of us to spill
In brawl with him, as might betide
If thou his coming shouldst abide.
Our barley barn is close hereby,
Wherein a weary man might lie
And be no worse at dawn of day."

"Well, goodwife," said he, "lead the way!
Worse lodging have I had than that,
Where the wolf howled unto the bat,
And red the woodland stream did run."

She started back, he seemed as one
Who might have come back from the dead,
To wreak upon her evil head
Her sour ill life, but nought the more
He heeded her; "Go on before,"
He said, "for I am in no case
To-night to meet an angry face
And hold my hand from my good sword."

So out she passed without a word,
Though when he took in careful wise

The heavy harp, with greedy eyes
And an ill scowl she gazed thereon,
Yet durst say nought. But soon they won
Unto the barn's door—he turned round,
And, gazing down the rugged ground,
Beheld the sea wide reaching, white
Beneath the new-risen moon, and bright
His face waxed for a little while,
And on the still night did he smile,
As into the dark place he went,
And saw no more of the grey bent,
Or sea, or sky, or morrow's sun.
Unless perchance when all is done,
And all the wrongs the Gods have wrought
Come utterly with them to nought,
New heavens and earth he shall behold,
And peaceful folk, and days of gold,
When Baldur is come back again
O'er an undying world to reign.

For when the carl came home that night,
In every ill wise that she might,
She egged him on their guest to slay
As sleeping in the barn he lay;
And, since the man was no ill mate
For her, and heedless evil fate
Had made him big and strong enow,
He plucked up heart to strike the blow,
Though but a coward thief he was.
So at the grey dawn did he pass
Unto the barn, and entered there;
But through its dusk therewith did hear
The sound of harp-strings tinkling: then,
As is the wont of such-like men,
Great fear of ghosts fell on his heart;
Yet, trembling sore, he thrust apart
The long stems of the barley-straw,
And, peering round about, he saw
Heimir asleep, his naked brand
Laid o'er his knees, but his right hand
Amid the harp-strings, whence there came
A mournful tinkling; and some name
His lips seemed muttering, and withal
A strange sound on his ears did fall
As of a young child murmuring low
The muffled sounds of passing woe.
Nought dreadful saw he; yet the hair
'Gan bristle on his head with fear,
And twice was he at point to turn
His bread by other craft to earn;
But in the end prevailed in him

His raging greed 'gainst glimmerings dim
Of awe and pity; which but wrought
In such wise in him that he thought
How good it were if all were done,
And day, and noise, and the bright sun
Were come again: he crept along,
Poising a spear, thick shafted, strong,
In his right hand; and ever fast
His heart beat as the floor he passed,
And o'er his shoulder gazed for fear
Once and again; he raised the spear,
As Heimir's hand the string still pressed,
And thrust it through his noble breast,
Then turned and fled, and heard behind
A sound as of a wildered wind,
Half moan, half sigh; then all was still.
But yet such fear his soul did fill
That he stayed not until he came
Into the hall, and cried the name
Of his wife, Grima, in high voice.

"Ah well," she said, "what needs this noise,
Can ye not see me here?—Well then?"

"Wife," said he, "of the sons of men
I deem him not, rather belike
Odin it was that I did strike."

She laughed an ill laugh. "Well," she said,
"What then, if only he be dead?"

"What if he only seemed to die?"
He said, "and when night draweth nigh
Shall come again grown twice as great,
And eat where yesternight he ate?
For certes, wife, that harp of his,
No earthly minstrelsy it is,
Since as in sleep the man was laid
Of its own self a tune it played;
Yea, yea, and in a man's voice cried;
Belike a troll therein doth bide."

"An ugly, ill-made minstrel's tool,"
She said; "thou blundering, faint-heart fool!
Some wind moaned through the barn belike,
And the man's hand the strings did strike."

And yet she shivered as she spake,
As though some fear her heart did take,
And neither durst to draw anigh
The barn until the sun was high,

Then in they went together, and saw
The old man lying in the straw,
Scarce otherwise than if asleep,
Though in his heart the spear lay deep,
And round about the floor was red.
Then Grima went, and from the dead
Stripped off the gold ring, while the man
Stood still apart; then she began
To touch the harp, but in no wise
Might open it to reach the prize.
Wherefore she bade her husband bring
Edge-tools to split the cursed thing.
He brought them trembling, and the twain
Fell to, and soon their end did gain;
But shrank back trembling to see there
The youngling, her grey eyes and clear
Wide open, fearless; but the wife
Knew too much of her own sour life
To fear the other world o'ermuch,
And soon began to pull and touch
The golden raiment of the may;
And at the last took heart to say:

"Be comforted! we shall not die;
For no work is this certainly
Wrought in the country never seen.
But raiment of a Hunnish queen—
Gold seest thou, goodman! gems seest thou!—
No ill work hast thou wrought I trow.
But, for the maiden, we must give
Victuals to her that she may live;
For though to-day she is indeed
But one more mouth for us to feed,
Yet as she waxeth shall she do
Right many a thing to help us two;
Yea, whatso hardest work there is,
That shall be hers—no life of bliss
Like sewing gold mid bower-mays;
She shall be strong, too, as the days
Increase on her."
Then said the man:
"Get speech from her, for sure she can
Tell somewhat of her life and state."
But whatso he or his vile mate
Might do, no word at all she spake
Either for threat or promise sake;
Until at last they deemed that she
Was tongue-tied: so now presently
Unto the homestead was she brought,
And her array all golden-wrought
Stripped from her, and in rags of grey

Clad was she. But from light of day
The carl hid Heimir dead, and all
Into dull sodden life did fall.


SO with the twain abode the may,
Waxing in beauty day by day,
But ever as one tongue-tied was,
What thing soever came to pass;
And needs the hag must call her Crow:
"A name," she said, "full good enow
For thee—my mother bore it erst."
So lived the child that she was nursed
On little meat and plenteous blows;
Yet nowise would she weep, but close
Would set her teeth thereat, and go
About what work she had to do,
And ever wrought most sturdily;
Until at last she grew to be
More than a child. And now the place
That once had borne so dull a face
Grew well-nigh bright to look upon,
And whatso thing might shine there shone;
Yea, all but her who brought about
That change therein—for, past all doubt,
Years bettered in nowise our hag,
And ever she said that any rag
Was good enough to clothe the Crow.
And still her hate did grow and grow
As Aslaug grew to womanhood;
Oft would she sit in murderous mood
Long hours, with hand anigh a knife,
As Aslaug slept, all hate at strife
With greed within her; yet withal
Something like fear of her did fall
Upon her heart, and heavy weighed
That awful beauty, that oft stayed
Her hand from closing on the hilt,
E'en more than thought of good things spilt.
Hard words and blows this scarce might stay,
For like the minutes of the day,
Not looked for, noted not when gone,
Were all such things unto the crone,
And, smitten or unsmitten, still
The Crow was swift to work her will.

In spring-tide of her seventeenth year,
On the hill-side the house anear

Went Aslaug, following up her goats:
On such a day as when Love floats
Through the soft air unseen, to touch
Our hearts with longings overmuch
Unshapen into hopes, to make
All things seem fairer for the sake
Of that which cometh, who doth bear
Who knows how much of grief and fear
In his fair arms. So Aslaug went,
On vague and unnamed thoughts intent,
That seemed to her full sweet enow,
And ever greater hope did grow,
And sweet seemed life to her and good,
Small reason why: into the wood
She turned, and wandered slim and fair
'Twixt the dark tree-boles: strange and rare
The sight was of her golden head,
So good, uncoifed, unchapleted,
Above her sordid dark array,
That over her fair body lay
As dark clouds on a lilied hill.
The wild things well might gaze their fill,
As through the wind-flowers brushed her feet,
As her lips smiled when those did meet
The lush-cold blue-bells, or were set
Light on the pale dog-violet
Late April bears: the red-throat jay
Screamed not for nought, as on her way
She went, light-laughing at some thought;
If the dove moaned 'twas not for nought,
Since she was gone too soon from him,
And e'en the sight he had was dim
For the thick budding twigs. At last
Into an open space she passed,
Nigh filled with a wide, shallow lake,
Amidmost which the fowl did take
Their pastime; o'er the firmer grass,
'Twixt rushy ooze, swift did she pass,
Until upon a bank of sand
Close to the water did she stand,
And gazed down in that windless place
Upon the image of her face,
And as she gazed laughed musically
Once and again; nor heeded she
Her straying flock: her voice, that none
Had heard since Heimir was undone
Within that wretched stead, began
Such speech as well had made a man
Forget his land and kin to make
Those sweet lips tremble for his sake:

"Spring bringeth love," she said, "to all."
She sighed as those sweet sounds did fall
From her unkissed lips: "Ah," said she,
"How came that sweet word unto me,
Among such wretched folk who dwell,
Folk who still seem to carry hell
About with them?—That ancient man
They slew, with whom my life began,
I deem he must have taught me that,
And how the steel-clad maiden sat
Asleep within the ring of flame,
Asleep, and waiting till Love came,
Who was my father: many a dream
I dream thereof, till it doth seem
That they will fetch me hence one day.
Somewhere I deem life must be gay,
The flowers are wrought not for the sake
Of those two murderers."
While she spake
Her hands were busy with her gown,
And at the end it slipped adown
And left her naked there and white
In the unshadowed noontide light.
Like Freyia in her house of gold,
A while her limbs did she behold
Clear mirrored in the lake beneath;
Then slowly, with a shuddering breath,
Stepped in the water cold, and played
Amid the ripple that she made,
And spoke again aloud, as though
The lone place of her heart might know:
"Soothly," she said, "if I knew fear,
Scarcely should I be sporting here,
But blinder surely has the crone
In those last months of winter grown,
Nor knows if I be foul or sweet,
Or sharp stripes might I chance to meet,
As heretofore it hath been seen
When I have dared to make me clean
Amid their foulness: loathes her heart
That one she hates should have a part
In the world's joy.—Well, time wears by,
I was not made for misery.
Surely if dimly do mine eyes
Behold no sordid tale arise,
No ill life drawing near—who knows
But I am kept for greater woes,
Godlike despair that makes not base,
Though like a stone may grow the face
Because of it, yea, and the heart
A hard-wrought treasure set apart

For the world's glory?"
Therewith she
Made for the smooth bank leisurely,
And, naked as she was, did pass
Unto the warm and flowery grass
All unashamed, and fearing not
For aught that should draw nigh the spot:
And soothly had some hunter been
Near by and all her beauty seen,
He would have deemed he saw a fay
And hastened trembling on his way.
But when full joyance she had had
Of sun and flowers, her limbs she clad
In no long time, forsooth, and then
Called back her wandering flock again
With one strange dumb cry, e'en as though
Their hearts and minds she needs must know,
For hurrying back with many a bleat
They huddled round about her feet.
And back she went unto the stead,
Strange visions pressing round her head,
So light of heart and limb, that though
She went with measured steps and slow,
Each yard seemed but a dance to her.

So now the thick wood did she clear,
And o'er the bent beheld the sea,
And stood amazed there suddenly,
For a long ship, with shield-hung rail,
And fair-stained flapping raven-sail,
And golden dragon-stem, there lay
On balanced oars amidst the bay,
Slow heaving with the unrippled swell.
With a strange hope she might not tell
Her eyes ran down the strand, and there
Lay beached a ship's boat painted fair,
And on the shingle by her side
Three blue-clad axemen did abide
Their fellows, sent belike ashore
To gather victuals for their store.

She looked not long; with heart that beat
More quickly and with hurrying feet
Unto the homestead did she pass,
And when anigh the door she was
She heard men's voices deep and rough;
Then the shrill crone, who said, "Enough
Of work I once had done for you,
But now my days left are but few
And I am weak; I prithee wait,
Already now the noon is late,

My daughter, Crow, shall soon be here."
"Nay," said a shipman, "have no fear,
Goodwife, a speedy death to get,
Thou art a sturdy carline yet:
Howbeit we well may wait a while."

Thereat Aslaug, with a strange smile,
Fresh from that water in the wood,
Pushed back the crazy door, and stood
Upon the threshold silently;
Bareheaded and barefoot was she,
And scarce her rags held each to each,
Yet did the shipmen stay their speech
And open-mouthed upon her stare,
As with bright eyes and face flushed fair
She stood; one gleaming lock of gold,
Strayed from her fair head's plaited fold,
Fell far below her girdlestead,
And round about her shapely head
A garland of dog-violet
And wind-flowers meetly had she set:
They deemed it little scathe indeed
That her coarse homespun ragged weed
Fell off from her round arms and lithe
Laid on the door-post, that a withe
Of willows was her only belt;
And each as he gazed at her felt
As some gift had been given him.

At last one grumbled, "Nowise dim
It is to see, goodwife, that this
No branch of thy great kinship is."

Grima was glaring on the may,
And scarce for rage found words to say;
"Yea, soothly is she of our kin:
Sixty-five winters changeth skin.
And whatsoever she may be,
Though she is dumb as a dead tree,
She worketh ever double-tide.
So, masters, ope your mealsacks wide
And fall to work; enow of wood
There is, I trow."
And there she stood,
Shaking all o'er, and when the may
Brushed past her going on her way,
From off the board a knife she caught,
And well-nigh had it in her thought
To end it all. Small heed the men
Would take of her, forsooth; and when
They turned their baking-work to speed,

And Aslaug fell the meal to knead,
He was the happiest of them all
Unto whose portion it did fall
To take the loaves from out her hand;
And gaping often would he stand,
And ever he deemed that he could feel
A trembling all along the peel
Whenas she touched it—sooth to say,
Such bread as there was baked that day
Was never seen: such as it was
The work was done, and they did pass
Down toward the ship, and as they went
A dull place seemed the thymy bent,
Gilded by sunset; the fair ship,
That soft in the long swell did dip
Her golden dragon, seemed nought worth,
And they themselves, all void of mirth,
Stammering and blundering in their speech,
Still looking back, seemed each to each
Ill-shapen, ugly, rough and base
As might be found in any place.

Well, saith the tale, and when the bread
Was broken, just as light as lead
Men found the same, as sweet as gall,
Half baked and sodden; one and all
Men gave it to the devil; at last
Unto their lord the story passed,
Who called for them, and bade them say
Why they had wrought in such a way;
They grinned and stammered, till said one:
"We did just e'en as must be done
When men are caught; had it been thou
A-cold had been the oven now."

"Ye deal in riddles," said the lord,
"Enough brine is there overboard
To fill you full if even so
Ye needs must have it."
"We did go,"
The man said, "to a house, and found
That lack of all things did abound;
A yellow-faced and blear-eyed crone
Was in the sooty hall alone;
But as we talked with her, and she
Spake to us ill and craftily,
A wondrous scent was wafted o'er
The space about the open door,
And all the birds drew near to sing,
And summer pushed on into spring,
Until there stood before our eyes

A damsel clad in wretched guise,
Yet surely of the gods I deem,
So fair she was;—well then this dream
Of Freyia on midsummer night,
This breathing love, this once-seen sight,
Flitted amidst us kneading meal,
And from us all the wits did steal;
Hadst thou been wise?"

"Well," said the lord,
"This seemeth but an idle word;
Yet since ye all are in one tale
Somewhat to you it may avail—
Speak out! my lady that is dead—
Thora, the chief of goodlihead—
Came this one nigh to her at all?"

One answer from their mouths did fall,
That she was fairest ever seen.
"If two such marvellous things have been
Wrought by the gods, then have they wrought
Exceeding well," the lord said; "nought
Will serve me now but to have sight
Of her, and hear the fresh delight
Of her sweet voice."
"Nay, nay," one cried,
"The carline called the maid tongue-tied
E'en from her birth."
But thoughtfully
The lord spake: "Then belike shall be
Some wonder in the thing. Lo now,
Since I, by reason of my vow
Made on the cup at Yule, no more
May set foot upon any shore
Till I in Micklegarth have been,
And somewhat there of arms have seen,
Go ye at earliest morn and say
That I would see her ere the day
Is quite gone by; here shall she come
And go as if her father's home
The good ship were, and I indeed
Her very brother. Odin speed
The matter in some better wise,
Unless your words be nought but lies!"

So the next morn she had the word
To come unto their king and lord;
She answered not, but made as though
Their meaning she did fully know,
And gave assent: the crone was there,
And still askance at her did glare,

And mid her hatred grew afeard
Of what might come, but spoke no word;
And ye may well believe indeed
That those men gave her little heed,
But stared at Aslaug as she stood
Beside the greasy, blackened wood
Of the hall's uprights, fairer grown
Than yesterday, soft 'neath her gown
Her fair breast heaving, her wide eyes
Mid dreams of far-off things grown wise,
The rock dropped down in her left hand;
There mazed awhile the men did stand,
Then gat them back. And so the sun
Waxed hot and waned, and, day nigh done,
Gleamed on the ship's side as she lay
Close in at deepest of the bay,
Her bridge gold-hung on either hand
Cast out upon the hard white sand;
While o'er the bulwarks many a man
Gazed forth; and the great lord began
To fret and fume, till on the brow
Of the low cliff they saw her now,
Who stood a moment to behold
The ship's sun-litten flashing gold;
Then slowly 'gan to get her down
A steep path in the sea-cliff brown,
Till on a sudden did she meet
The slant sun cast about its feet,
And flashed as in a golden cloud;
Since scarcely her poor raiment showed
Beneath the glory of her hair,
Whose last lock touched her ankles bare.

For so it was that as she went
Unto this meeting, all intent
Upon the time that was to be,
While yet just hidden from the sea,
She stayed her feet a little while,
And, gazing on her raiment vile,
Flushed red, and muttered,—
"Who can tell
But I may love this great lord well?
An evil thing then should it be
If he cast loathing eyes on me
This first time for my vile attire."

Then, while her cheek still burned like fire,
She set hand to her hair of gold
Until its many ripples rolled
All over her, and no great queen
Was e'er more gloriously beseen;

And thus she went upon her way.

Now when the crew beheld the may
Set foot upon the sand there rose
A mighty shout from midst of those
Rough seafarers; only the lord
Stood silent gazing overboard
With great eyes, till the bridge she gained,
And still the colour waxed and waned
Within his face; but when her foot
First pressed the plank, to his heart's root
Sweet pain there pierced, for her great eyes
Were fixed on his in earnest wise,
E'en as her thoughts were all of him;
And somewhat now all things waxed dim,
As unto her he stretched his hand,
And felt hers; and the twain did stand
Hearkening each other's eager breath.
But she was changed, for pale as death
She was now as she heard his voice.

"Full well may we this eve rejoice,
Fair maid, that thou hast come to us;
That this grey shore and dolorous
Holds greater beauty than the earth
Mid fairer days may bring to birth,
And that I hold it now. But come
Unto the wind-blown woven home,
Where I have dwelt alone awhile,
And with thy speech the hours beguile."

For nothing he remembered
Of what his men unto him said,
That she was dumb. Not once she turned
Her eyes from his; the low sun burned
Within her waving hair, as she
Unto the poop went silently
Beside him, and with faltering feet,
Because this hour seemed over sweet,
And still his right hand held her hand.

But when at last the twain did stand
Beneath the gold-hung tilt alone,
He said, "Thou seemest such an one
As who could love; thou lookst on me
As though thou hopedst love might be
Betwixt us—thou art pale, my sweet,
Good were it if our lips should meet."

Then mouth to mouth long time they stood,
And when they sundered the red blood

Burnt in her cheek, and tenderly
Trembled her lips, and drew anigh
His lips again: but speech did break
Swiftly from out them, and she spake:
"May it be so, fair man, that thou
Art even no less happy now
Than I am."
With a joyous cry
He caught her to him hastily;
And mid that kiss the sun went down,
And colder was the dark world grown.
Once more they parted; "Ah, my love,"
He said, "I knew not aught could move
My heart to such joy as thy speech."

She made as if she fain would reach
Her lips to his once more; but ere
They touched, as smitten by new fear,
She drew aback and said: "Alas!
It darkens, and I needs must pass
Back to the land, to be more sad
Than if this joy I ne'er had had.
And thou—thou shalt be sorry too,
And pity me that it is so."

"To-morrow morn comes back the day,"
He said, "If we should part, sweet may:
Yet why should I be left forlorn
Betwixt this even and the morn?"

His hand had swept aback her hair,
And on her shoulder, gleaming bare
From midst her rags, was trembling now;
But she drew back, and o'er her brow
Gathered a troubled thoughtful frown,
And on the bench she sat her down
And spake: "Nay, it were wise to bide
Awhile. Behold, the world is wide,
Yet have we found each other here,
And each to other seems more dear
Than all the world else.—Yet a king
Thou art, and I am such a thing,
By some half-dreamed-of chance cast forth
To live a life of little worth,
A lonely life—and it may be
That thou shouldst weary soon of me
If I abode here now—and I,
How know I? All unhappily
My life has gone; scarce a kind word
Except in dreams my ears have heard
But those thy lovely lips have said:

It might be when all things were weighed
That I too light of soul should prove
To hold for ever this great love."

Down at her feet therewith he knelt,
And round her his strong arms she felt
Drawing her to him, as he said:
"These are strange words for thee, O maid;
Are those sweet loving lips grown cold
So soon? Yet art thou in my hold,
And certainly my heart is hot.
What help against me hast thou got?"

Each unto each their cheeks were laid,
As in a trembling voice she said:
"No help, because so dear to me
Thou art, and mighty as may be;
Thou hast seen much, art wiser far
Than I am; yet strange thoughts there are
In my mind now—some half-told tale
Stirs in me, if I might avail
To tell it."
Suddenly she rose,
And thrust him from her; "Ah, too close!
Too close now, and too far apart
To-morrow!—and a barren heart,
And days that ever fall to worse,
And blind lives struggling with a curse
They cannot grasp! Look on my face,
Because I deem me of a race
That knoweth such a tale too well.
Yet if there be such tale to tell
Of us twain, let it e'en be so,
Rather than we should fail to know
This love—ah me, my love forbear!
No pain for thee and me I fear;
Yet strive we e'en for more than this!
Thou who hast given me my first bliss
To-day, forgive me, that in turn
I see the pain within thee burn,
And may not help—because mine eyes
The Gods make clear. I am grown wise
With gain of love, and hope of days
That many a coming age shall praise."

Awhile he gazed on her, and shook
With passion, and his cloak's hem took
With both hands as to rend it down;
Yet from his brow soon cleared the frown:
He said: "Yea, such an one thou art,
As needs alone must fill my heart

If I be like my father's kin,
And have a hope great deeds to win;
And surely nought shall hinder me
From living a great life with thee—
Say now what thou wouldst have me do."

"Some deed of fame thou goest to,"
She said, "for surely thou art great;
Go on thy way then, and if fate
So shapen is, that thou mayst come
Once more unto this lonely home,
There shalt thou find me, who will live
Through whatso days that fate may give,
Till on some happy coming day
Thine oars again make white the bay."

"If that might be remembered now,"
He said, "last Yule I made a vow
In some far land to win me fame.
Come nigher, sweet, and hear my name
Before thou goest; that if so be
Death take me and my love from thee,
Thou mayst then think of who I was,
Nor let all memory of me pass
When thou to some great king art wed:
Then shalt thou say, 'Ragnar is dead,
Who was the son of Sigurd Ring,
Among the Danes a mighty king.
He might have had me by his side,'
Then shalt thou say, 'that hour he died;
But my heart failed and not his heart.'"

"Nay, make it not too hard to part,"
She said, when once again their lips
Had sundered; "as gold-bearing ships
Foundered amidmost of the sea,
So shall the loves of most men be,
And leave no trace behind. God wot
This heart of mine shall hate thee not
Whatso befall; but rather bless
Thee and this hour of happiness;
And if this tide shall come again
After hard longing and great pain,
How sweet, how sweet! O love, farewell,
Lest other tale there be to tell:
Yet heed this now lest afterward
It seem to thee a thing too hard
To keep thy faith to such as me;
I am belike what thou dost see,
A goatherd girl, a peasant maid,
Of a poor wretched crone afraid

From dawn to dusk; despite of dreams
In morning tides, and misty gleams
Of wondrous stories, deem me such
As I have said, nor overmuch
Cast thou thy love upon my heart
If even such a man thou art
As needs must wed a great man's child."

He stepped aback from her and smiled,
And, stooping 'neath the lamp, drew forth
From a great chest a thing of worth—
A silken sark wrought wondrously
In some far land across the sea.
"One thing this is of many such
That I were fain thy skin should touch,"
He said, "If thou wouldst have it so."
But his voice faltered and sank low,
As though her great heart he 'gan fear.
She reached her fine strong hand anear
The farfetched thing; then smiling said:
"Strange that such fair things can be made
By men who die; and like it is
Thou think'st me worthy of all bliss;
But our rough hills and smoky house
Befit not aught so glorious,
E'en if thou come again to me;
And if not, greater grief to see
The gifts of dead love!—what say I,
Our crone should wear these certainly
If I but brought them unto land."

He flushed red, and his strong right hand
Fell to his sword-hilt. "Nay," she said,
"All that is nought if rightly weighed;
Hope and desire shall pass the days
If thou come back."
Grave was her face
And tremulous: he sighed; "Then take
This last gift only for my sake."
And once again their lips did touch
And cling together. "O many such,"
She said, "if the time did not fail,
And my heart too: of what avail
Against the hand of fate to strive?
Let me begin my life to live,
As it must be a weary space."

The moon smote full upon her face,
As on a trembling sea, as now
From the lamp-litten gold tilt low
She stepped into the fresher air,

He with her. Slow the twain did fare
Amidst the wondering men, till they
Had reached the bridge; then swift away
She turned, and passed the gold-hung rail,
And o'er the sands the moon made pale
Went gleaming, all alone: and he
Watched till her light feet steadily
Stepped up upon the dark cliff's brow:
But no one time she turned her now,
But vanished from him into night.
So there he watched till changing light
Brought the beginning of the tide
Of longing that he needs must bide;
Then he cried out for oars and sail,
And ere the morning star did fail
No more those cliffs his bird beheld,
As 'neath the wind the broad sail swelled.

But for the maiden, back she went
Unto the stead, and her intent
She changed in nought: no word she spake
What wrath soe'er on her might break
From the fell crone, on whom withal
Still heavier did that strange awe fall;
As well might be, for from the may
Had girlish lightness passed away
Into a sweet grave majesty,
That scarce elsewhere the world might see.

So wore the spring, and summer came,
And went, and all the woods did flame
With autumn, as in that old tide
When slowly by the mirk hill-side
Went Heimir to his unseen death:
Then came the first frost's windless breath,
The steaming sea, the world all white,
And glittering morn and silent night,
As when the little one first felt
The world a-cold; and still she dwelt
Unchanged since that first spark of love
Wrought the great change, that so did move
Her heart to perfect loveliness.
Nor overmuch did the days press
Upon her with the weary waste
Of short life, that too quick doth haste
When joy is gained: if any thought
Thereof unto her heart was brought,
Rather it was, "Ah, overlong
For brooding over change and wrong
When that shall come! Good gain to me
My love's eyes one more time to see,

To feel once more his lips' delight,
And die with the short summer night,
Not shamed nor sorry! But if I
Must bear the weight of misery
In the after days, yet even then
May I not leave to unborn men
A savour of sweet things, a tale
That midst all woes shall yet prevail
To make the world seem something worth?"

So passed the winter of the North,
And once again was come the spring;
Then whiles would she go loitering
Slow-footed, and with hanging head,
Through budding brake, o'er flowery mead,
With blood that throbbed full quickly now
If o'er the flowers her feet were slow,
And bonds about her seemed to be.
Yet wore the spring past lingeringly
Till on a morn of latter May,
When her soft sleep had passed away,
Nought but the bright-billed sweet-throat bird
Within the thorn at first she heard;
But, even as her heart did meet
The first wave of desire o'ersweet,
The winding of a mighty horn
Adown the breeze of May was borne,
And throbbing hope on her did fall:
Yet from her bed she leapt withal,
And clad herself, and went about
Her work, as though with ne'er a doubt
That this day e'en such like should be
As was the last; and so while she
Quickened the fire and laid the board,
Mid the crone's angry, querulous word
Of surly wonder, the goodman,
With axe on shoulder, swiftly ran
Adown the slope; but presently
Came breathless back:
"Ah, here they be!
Come back again for something worse,"
Said he. "This dumb maid is some curse
Laid on us."
"Well," the goodwife said,
"Who be they?" "They who baked their bread
Within this house last spring," said he.
"Oft did I marvel then why she,
This witch-maid, went unto the strand
That eve."
"Nay, maybe comes to hand
Some luck," the crone said. "Hold thy peace,"

He said. "What goodhap or increase
From that ill night shall ever come?
Rather I deem that now come home
Those fifteen years of murder: lo,
The worst of all we soon shall know,
I hear their voices."
Silently,
If somewhat pale, Aslaug passed by
From fire to board, as though she heard
And noted nothing of that word,
Whate'er it was: yet now, indeed,
The clink of sword on iron weed,
And voices of the seafarers,
Came clear enow unto her ears;
Nor was it long or e'er the door
Was darkened, as one stood before
The light and cried:
"Hail to this house,
If here still dwells the glorious
Fair maiden, that across the seas
We come for!"
Aslaug on her knees
Knelt by the brightening fire and dropped
The meal into the pot, nor stopped
For all their words, but with her hand
Screened her fair face. Then up did stand
The goodman, quaking:
"Well," he said,
"Good be my meed! for we have fed
This dumb maid all for kindness' sake."

"No need," he said, "long words to make,
And little heed we thy lies now,
But if she doom thee to the bough.
All hail, our Lady and our Queen!"

For she, arisen, with glorious mien
Was drawing near the board, and bare
The porridge-bowl and such-like gear
Past where the men stood; tremblingly
The leader of them drew anigh,
And would have taken them, but she
Swerved from his strong hand daintily,
Smiled on him and passed by, and when
They were set down turned back again
And spoke, and well then might rejoice
That dusky place to hear her voice
For the first time:
"I doubt me not,
O seafarers, but ye have got
A message from that goodly lord

Who spake last year a pleasant word,
Hard to believe for a poor maid."

Trembled the twain at what she said
Less than the unexpected sound,
For death seemed in the air around.
But the man spake: "E'en thus he saith,
That he, who heretofore feared death
In no-wise, feared this morn to come
And seek thee out in thy poor home,
Lest he should find thee dead or gone;
For scarce he deemed so sweet a one
Could be for him: 'But if she live,'
He said, 'and still her love can give
To me, let her make no delay,
For fear we see no other day
Wherein to love.'"
She said: "Come, then!
It shames me not that of all men
I love him best. But have ye there
Somewhat these twain might reckon dear?
Their life is ill enow to live
But that withal they needs must strive
With griping want when I am gone."

He answered, "O thou goodly one,
Here have we many a dear-bought thing,
Because our master bade us bring
All queenly gear for thee, and deems
That thou, so clad as well beseems
That lovely body, wouldst aboard;
But all we have is at thy word
To keep or spend."
"Nay, friends," she said,
"If thy lord loves my goodlihead,
Fain would I bear alone to him
What wealth I have of face or limb,
For him to deck when all is his,
So full enow shall even this
That I am dight with be for me;
But since indeed of his bounty
He giveth unto me to give—
Take ye this gold, ye twain, and live
E'en as ye may—small need to bless
Or curse your sordid churlishness,
Because methinks, without fresh curse,
Each day that comes shall still be worse
Than the past day, and worst of all
Your ending day on you shall fall.
Yet, if it may be, fare ye well,
Since in your house I came to dwell

A certain time of my life-days."

E'en as she spake, her glorious face
Shone the last time on that abode,
And her light feet the daisies trod
Outside the threshold. But the twain
Stood 'mazed above the bounteous gain
Of rings and gems and money bright,
And a long while, for mere affright
And wonder, durst not handle it.

But while the butterfly did flit
White round about the feet of her,
Above the little May-flowers fair,
She went adown the hill with these,
Until the low wash of the seas
They heard, and murmuring of the men
Who manned the long-ships; quickly then
They showed above the grey bent's brow,
And all the folk beheld them now
'Twixt oar and gunwale that abode,
And to the sky their shout rose loud.
But when upon the beach she came,
A bright thing in the sun did flame
'Twixt sun and ship-side, and the sea
Foamed, as one waded eagerly
Unto the smooth and sea-beat sand,
And for one moment did she stand
Breathless, with beating heart, and then
To right and left drew back the men;
She heard a voice she deemed well known,
Long waited through dull hours bygone,
And round her mighty arms were cast:
But when her trembling red lips passed
From out the heaven of that dear kiss,
And eyes met eyes, she saw in his
Fresh pride, fresh hope, fresh love, and saw
The long sweet days still onward draw,
Themselves still going hand in hand,
As now they went adown the strand.

Next morn, when they awoke to see
Each other's hands draw lovingly
Each unto each, awhile they lay
Silent, as though night passed away
They grudged full sore: till the King said
Unto the happy golden head
That lay upon his breast, "What thought
By those few hours of dark was brought
Unto thy heart, my love? Did dreams
Make strange thy loving sleep with gleams

Of changing days that yet may be?"

She answered, but still dreamily:
"In sleep a little while ago
O'er a star-litten world of snow
I fared, till suddenly nearby
A swirling fire blazed up on high;
Thereto I went, and without scathe
Passed through the flame, as one doth bathe
Within a summer stream, and there
I saw a golden palace fair
Ringed round about with roaring flame.
Unto an open door I came,
And entered a great hall thereby,
And saw where 'neath a canopy
A King and Queen there sat, more fair
Than the world knoweth otherwhere:
And much methought my heart smiled then
Upon that goodliest of all men,
That sweetest of all womankind.
Then one methought a horn did wind
Without, and the King turned and spake:

"'Wherewith do the hall pillars shake,
O Queen, O love?'
She moved her head,
And in a voice like music said:
'This is the fame of Ragnar's life,
The breath of all the glorious strife
Wherewith his days shall wear.'
Then he:
'What is the shadow that I see
Adown the hall?'
Then said the Queen:
'Our daughter surely hadst thou seen
If thine eyes saw as clear as mine:
Well worth she is our love divine,
And unto Ragnar is she wed,
The best man since that thou wert dead,
My King, my love, mine own, mine own!'

"Then the twain kissed upon the throne,
And the dream passed and sleep passed too."

Therewith the King her body drew
Nearer to him, if it might be,
And spake: "A strange dream came to me.
Upon a waste at dawn I went
And wandered over vale and bent,
And ever was it dawn of day,
And still upon all sides there lay

The bones of men, and war-gear turned
To shards and rust; then far off burned
A fire, and thither quick I passed.
And when I came to it at last
Dreadful it seemed, impassable;
But I, fain of that land to tell
What things soever might be known,
Went round about, and up and down,
And gat no passing by the same;
Until, methought, just where the flame
Burned highest, through the midst I saw
A man and woman toward me draw,
Even as through a flowery wood:
So came they unto where I stood,
And glad at heart therewith I grew,
For such fair folk as were the two
Ne'er had I seen; then the man cried:

"'Hail to thee, Ragnar! well betide
This dawn of day. Stretch forth thine hand.'

"E'en as he bade me did I stand,
Abiding what should hap, but he
Turned to the woman lovingly,
And from her bosom's fresh delight
Drew forth a blooming lily white,
And set it in mine hand, and then
Both through the flame went back again.

"Then afterwards in earth I set
This lily, and with soft regret
Watched for its fading; but withal
Great light upon the world did fall,
And fair the sun rose o'er the earth,
And blithe I grew and full of mirth:
And no more on a waste I was,
But in a green world, where the grass
White lily-blooms well-nigh did hide;
O'er hill and valley far and wide
They waved in the warm wind; the sun
Seemed shining upon everyone,
As though it loved it: and with that
I woke, and up in bed I sat
And saw thee waking, O my sweet!"

With that last word their lips did meet,
And even the fresh May morning bright
Was noted not in their delight.

Let be—as ancient stories tell
Full knowledge upon Ragnar fell

In lapse of time, that this was she
Begot in the felicity
Swift-fleeting of the wondrous twain,
Who afterwards through change and pain
Must live apart to meet in death.

But, would ye know what the tale saith,
In the old Danish tongue is writ
Full many a word concerning it,
The days through which these lovers passed,
Till death made end of all at last.
But so great Ragnar's glory seemed
To Northern folk, that many deemed
That for his death, when song arose
From that Northumbrian adder-close,
England no due atonement paid
Till Harald Godwinson was laid
Beside his fallen banner, cold
Upon the blood-soaked Sussex mould,
And o'er the wrack of Senlac field
Full-fed the grey-nebbed raven wheeled.

In the dim place that the sun knew no more
He rose up when his tale was fully o'er,
And 'gan to pace the long hall to and fro
With old eyes looking downward, e'en as though
None else were there: at last with upraised face
He walked back swiftly to his fire-lit place,
And sat him down, and turned to the young folk
Smiling perforce; then from their lips outbroke
The murmuring speech his moody looks had stilled,
And with a sweet sound was the hall fulfilled;
E'en like the noise that from the thin wood's side
Swims through the dawning day at April-tide
Across the speckled eggs, when from the brown
Soft feathers glittering eyes are looking down
Over the dewy meads, too fresh and fair
For aught but lovely feet to wander there.

Drag on, long night of winter, in whose heart,
Nurse of regret, the dead spring yet has part!
Drag on, O night of dreams! O night of fears!
Fed by the summers of the bygone years!


JANUARY

From this dull rainy undersky and low,
This murky ending of a leaden day,
That never knew the sun, this half-thawed snow,

These tossing black boughs faint against the grey
Of gathering night, thou turnest, dear, away
Silent, but with thy scarce-seen kindly smile
Sent through the dusk my longing to beguile.

There, the lights gleam, and all is dark without!
And in the sudden change our eyes meet dazed—
O look, love, look again! the veil of doubt
Just for one flash, past counting, then was raised!
O eyes of heaven, as clear thy sweet soul blazed
On mine a moment! O come back again
Strange rest and dear amid the long dull pain!

Nay, nay, gone by! though there she sitteth still,
With wide grey eyes so frank and fathomless
Be patient, heart, thy days they yet shall fill
With utter rest—Yea, now thy pain they bless,
And feed thy last hope of the world's redress—
O unseen hurrying rack! O wailing wind!
What rest and where go ye this night to find?

The year has changed its name since that last tale;
Yet nought the prisoned spring doth that avail.
Deep buried under snow the country lies;
Made dim by whirling flakes the rook still flies
South-west before the wind; noon is as still
As midnight on the southward-looking hill,
Whose slopes have heard so many words and loud
Since on the vine the woolly buds first showed.
The raven hanging o'er the farmstead gate,
While for another death his eye doth wait,
Hears but the muffled sound of crowded byre
And winds' moan round the wall. Up in the spire
The watcher set high o'er the half-hid town
Hearkens the sound of chiming bells fall down
Below him; and so dull and dead they seem
That he might well-nigh be amidst a dream
Wherein folk hear and hear not.

Such a tide,
With all work gone from the hushed world outside,
Still finds our old folk living, and they sit
Watching the snow-flakes by the window flit
Midmost the time 'twixt noon and dusk; till now
One of the elders clears his knitted brow,
And says:
"Well, hearken of a man who first
In every place seemed doomed to be accursed;
To tell about his ill hap lies on me;
Before the winter is quite o'er, maybe
Some other mouth of his good hap may tell;

But no third tale there is, of what befell
His fated life, when he had won his place;
And that perchance is not so ill a case
For him and us; for we may rise up, glad
At all the rest and triumph that he had
Before he died; while he, forgetting clean
The sorrow and the joy his eyes had seen,
Lies quiet and well famed—and serves to-day
To wear a space of winter-tide away."


BELLEROPHON AT ARGOS

ARGUMENT

**Hipponus, son of Glaucus King of Corinth, unwittingly slew his brother Beller, and, fleeing from his country, came to Prœtus King of Argos, who purified him of his guilt; and thereafter was he called Bellerophon. He dwelt long with Prœtus, well loved by him, and receiving many good things at his hands; but at last he lost the King's favour by the guile of the Queen Sthenobœa, and was sent to Jobates King of Lycia, her father, with a covert message of evil.**

Prœtus, the King of Argos, on a day
In tangled forests drave the boar to bay,
And had good hap, for ere the noon was o'er
He set his foot upon the third huge boar
His steel that day had reached; then, fain of rest,
The greensward 'neath the spreading oak-trees pressed,
And, king-like, feasted with his folk around.
Nor lacked he for sweet music's measured sound,
For when somewhat were men's desires appeased
Of meat and drink, their weary limbs well eased,
There 'gan an ancient hunter and his son
To tell of glorious deeds in old days done
Within the wood; but as Lyæus' gift,
And measured words from common life did lift
The thoughts of men, and noble each man seemed
Unto his fellow, from afar there gleamed
Sun-litten arms, and 'twixt the singer's word
The slow tramp of a great horse soon they heard,
And from a glade that pierced the thicket through
In sight at last a mounted man there drew.
Then the dogs growled, and midst their weapons' clang
Unto their feet the outmost hunters sprang,
Handling their spears; but still King Prœtus lay,
Till nigh the circle that lone man made stay,
And with wild eyes gazed down upon the throng.
Wearied he seemed, and his black war-horse strong
On many a mile had left both sweat and blood,
And panting now with drooping head he stood,
Forgetting all the eager joys of speed;

And tattered was his rider's lordly weed,
His broken sheath now held a sword no more,
With rust his armour bright was spotted o'er,
Unkempt and matted was the yellow hair
That crowned his head, nor was there helmet there;
His face, that should have been as fair and bright
And ruddy as a maid's, was deadly white,
And drawn and haggard; and his grey eyes stared,
As though of something he were sore afeard
That other folk saw not at all. But now
A hunter cried out, "Nay, and who art thou?
What God or man pursues thee? bide and speak;
Nor yet shalt thou for nought the King's rest break."
A scared look did the man behind him fling,
Then said, "Stand close around me: to your King,
When I may see him, will I tell the tale;
Unless indeed, meanwhile, my life should fail."

With that, as one who hath but little might,
From off his wearied steed did he alight.
They led him to the King, who 'gainst a tree
Stood upright now, the new-come man to see;
Who brought unto him would not meet his eyes,
But stood and stared distraught in dreamy wise;
Till cheerily the King of Argos said,
"Cast somewhat off; O friend, thy drearyhead;
Sit thee and eat and drink, and be my guest;
I will not harm thee though thou be unblest;
Let Gods or men take vengeance as they can,
Nor ask my help, who dwell a peaceful man
'Twixt white-walled Argos and the rustling trees."
The man turned round, as asking what were these,
The words he said; then, casting here and there
A troubled look, as if not safe he were
From some dread thing that followed even yet,
He sat him down, and like a starved man ate:
Yet did he tremble as he took the food,
And in the cup he gazed, as though the blood
Of man it held, and not the blood of earth,
The stirrer up to kindly words and mirth.
But when his hunger now was satisfied,
Casting his hair aback the King he eyed,
And in a choked and husky voice he said:
"Now can ye see, O folk, I am not dead;
But tell me, King, how shall I name thee here,
Since he in whose heart lieth any prayer,
To nameless Gods will let no warm words flow?"
"To Prœtus pray for what thou wouldest now,"
The King said; "by the soil of Argos pray:
To no light matter will I say thee nay,
For my heart giveth to thee: name thy name,

And say whereby these evils on thee came."

With changing eyes now gazed the outcast man
On Prœtus' cheery face, and colour ran
O'er his wan visage. "Thou art kind," he said;
"But kinder eyes I knew, that on the dead
Must look for ever now; and joy is gone:
Best hadst thou cast forth such a luckless one;
For what I love I slay, and what I hate
I strive to save from out the hands of Fate.
Listen and let me babble: I have seen
Since that hour was, nought but the long leaves green,
The tree-trunks, and the scared things of the wood."
Then silently awhile he seemed to brood
O'er what had been, but even as the King
Opened his lips to mind him of the thing
That he should tell, from his bent head there came
Slow words, as if from one confessing shame,
While nigher to his mouth King Prœtus drew.

"Hipponoüs men have called me, ere I knew
The hate of Gods and fear of men; my life
Went past at Corinth free from baneful strife,
For there my father ruled from sea to sea,
Glaucus the Great: and fair Eurymede,
My mother, bare another son to him,
Like unto me in mind and face and limb,
Whom men called Beller; and most true it is
That I with him dwelt long in love and bliss,
However long ago that seems to be.
What plans we laid for joyous victory!
What lovely lands untilled we thought to win,
And be together even as Gods therein,
Bringing the monsters of the world to nought!
How eagerly from elders news we sought
Of lands that lay anigh the ocean-stream!
And yet withal what folly then did seem
Their cold words and their weary hopeless eyes,
When this alone of all things then seemed wise,
To know how sweet life was, how dear the earth,
And only fluttering hope stayed present mirth—
Ah, how I babble! What a thing man is,
Who, falling unto misery out of bliss,
Thinks that new wisdom but the sole thing then
That binds the many ways of toiling men!

"In one fair chamber did we sleep a-night,
I and my brother—there, 'twixt light and light,
Three nights together did I dream a dream,
Where lying on my bed I still did seem
E'en as I was indeed, when a cold hand

Was laid upon me, and a shape did stand
By my bed-head, a woman clad in grey,
Like to the lingering time 'twixt night and day,
And veiled her face was, and her tall gaunt form.
She drew me from my peaceful bed and warm,
And led me, shuddering, bare-foot, o'er the floor,
Until, with beating heart, I stood before
My brother's bed, and knew what I should do;
For from beneath her shadowy robe she drew
A well-steeled feathered dart, and that must I,
Casting all will aside, clutch mightily,
And, still unable with her will to strive,
E'en as her veiled hand pointed, madly drive
Into the heart of mine own mother's son,
Striving to scream as that ill deed was done.

"No cry came forth, but even with the stroke,
With sick and fainting heart, I nigh awoke.
And when the dream again o'er me was cast,
Chamber, and all I knew, away had passed,
Nor saw I more the ghost: alone I stood
In a strange land, anigh an oaken wood
High on a hill; and far below my feet
The white walls of a glorious town did meet
A yellow strand and ship-beset green sea;
And all methought was as a toy for me,
For I was king thereof and great enow.

"But as I stood upon that hill's green brow,
Rejoicing much, yet yearning much indeed
For something past that still my heart must need,
Once more was all changed; by the windy sea
Did men hold games with great solemnity
In honour of some hero past away,
Whose body dead upon a huge pile lay
Waiting the torch, and people far and wide
About the strand a name I knew not cried,
Lamenting him who once had been their king;
But when I saw the face of the dead thing
Over whose head so many a cry was thrown
On to the wind, I knew it for mine own.

"Cold pangs shot through me then, sleep's bonds I broke;
Shuddering with terror in my bed I woke,
And when thought came again, a weight of fear
Lay on my heart and still grew heavier
But when the next night and the third night came,
And still in sleep my visions were the same,
No longer in mine own heart could I hold
The story of that marvel quite untold,
For fear possessed me: good at first it seemed

That I should tell the dream so strangely dreamed
Unto my brother; then I feared that he
Might for that tale look with changed eyes on me
As deeming that some secret hope had wrought
Within my false heart, and that pageant brought
Before mine eyes; or he might flee the land
To save our house from some accursed hand;
And either way that dream seemed hard to tell
That yet, untold, made for my soul a hell.

"But of a certain elder now I thought,
Who much of lore to both of us had taught
And loved us well; Diana's priest was he,
And in the wild woods served her faithfully,
Dwelling with few folk in her woodland shrine.
That from the hillside such a man sees shine
As goes from Corinth unto Sicyon.
"And now amid these thoughts was night nigh done,
And the dawn glimmered; I grew hot to go
To that old priest these troublous things to show;
So from my bed I rose up silently,
And with all haste I did my weed on me,
And went unto the door; but as I passed
The fair porch through, I saw how 'gainst the last
Brass-adorned pillar lay a feathered dart;
And therewith came new fear into my heart,
For as the dart that I in dreams had seen
So was it fashioned, and with feathers green
And scarlet was the hinder end bedight,
And round the shaft were bands of silver white.
Then scarcely did I know if still I dreamed,
Yet, looking at the shaft, withal it seemed
Good unto me to take it in my hand,
That the old man the more might understand
How real my dream had been in very deed,
And give me counsel better to my need.
"With that I caught it up, and went my way,
And almost ere the sun had made it day
Was I within the woods, and hastening on,
Afire until the old man's house was won,
And like a man who walks in sleep I went,
Nor noted aught amid my strong intent.
"But when I reached the little forest fane
I found my labour had but been in vain;
For there the priest's folk told me he had gone
The eve before to Corinth, all alone,
And on some weighty matter, as they deemed;
For measurelessly troubled still he seemed.
His trouble troubled me, because I thought
That unto him sure knowledge had been brought
Of some great danger hanging over me,

And that he thither went my face to see,
While I was seeking him; and therewithal
Great fear and heaviness on me did fall;
And all the life I once had thought so sweet
Now seemed a troublous thing and hard to meet.
"So cityward again I set my face,
And through the woodland glades I rode apace,
And halfway betwixt dawn and noon had I
Unto the wood's edge once more come anigh;
And now upon the wind I seemed to hear
The sound of mingled voices drawing near;
Whereon I stayed to hearken and cried out,
But feeble was the sound from my parched throat;
And listening afterward I heard not now
Those sounds, and timorous did my faint heart grow,
And tales of woodfolk my vexed mind did take.
But just as I the well-wrought reins would shake,
Grown nigher did I hear those sounds again,
And drew aback the hand that held the rein,
And even therewith stalked forth into the way
From out the thicket a huge wolf and grey,
And stood with yellow eyes that glared on me;
And I stared too; my folly made me see
No wolf, but some dread deity, in him;
But trembling as I was in every limb,
E'en as his growling smote upon my heart,
Tighter my fingers clutched the dreadful dart,
I made a shift in stirrups up to stand,
And hurled the quivering shaft from out my hand;
Then fire seemed all around me, and a pang
Crushed down my heart as from the thicket rang
A dreadful cry: clear saw I, even as he
Who meets the Father's visage suddenly;
No wolf was there; but o'er the herbage ran
With staggering steps a pale and bleeding man:
His left hand on the shaft, whose banded wood
Over the barbs within his bosom stood,
His right hand raised against me, as he fell
Close to my horse-hoofs; and I knew full well
That this my brother's last farewell should be,
And thus his face henceforward should I see.

"What else? it matters not; the priest I saw,
And armed men from the thicket toward me draw,
With scared eyes fixed on mine; I drew my sword,
And sat there, waiting for a dreadful word,
Bidding the rush of many men on me;
But they began to draw round silently,
And ere the circle yet was fully made,
I, who at first might even thus have stayed
For death and curses, felt the love of life

Stir up my heart again to hope and strife;
Yea, even withal I saw in one bright gleam
The latter ending of my dreaded dream.
So, crying out, strongly my horse I spurred,
And as he, rearing up, dashed forth, I heard
Clatter of arms and cries, a spear flew o'er
My bended head, a well-aimed arrow tore
My helm therefrom; yet then a cry there came:
'Take him alive, nor bring a double shame
Upon the great house!' Even therewith I drave
Against a mighty man as wave meets wave;
Back flew my right arm, and my sword was gone,
Whirled off as from a sling the wave-worn stone,
And my horse reeled, but he before me lay
Rolled over, horse and man, and in my way
Was no one now, as I spurred madly on:
And so in no long time the race I won,
For nobly was I mounted; and I deem
That to the most of those men did it seem
No evil thing that I should 'scape away.

"O King, I think this happed but yesterday,
And now already do I deem that I
Did no good deed in seeking not to die,
For I am weary, and the Gods made me
A luckless man among all folk to be—
I care not if their purpose I undo,
Since now I doubt not that the thing is so—
And yet am I so made, that, having life,
Must I, though ever worsted in the strife,
Cling to it still too much to gain the rest
Which yet I know of all things is the best.
Then slay me, King! to now, I pray for this,
And no least portion of thy hoarded bliss;
Slay me, and let the oak-boughs say their say
Over my bones through the wild winter day!
Slay me, for I am fain thereto to go,
Where no talk is of either bliss or woe."

"Nay," said the King, "didst thou not eat and drink
When hunger drave thee e'ennow? yea, and shrink
When my men's spears were pointed at thy breast?
Be patient; thou indeed shalt gain thy rest,
But many a thing has got to come ere then:
For all things die, and thou midst other men
Shalt scarce remember thou hast had a friend.
At worst before thou comest to the end
Joy shalt thou have, and sorrow: wherefore come;
With me thou well mayst have no hapless home.
Dread not the Gods; ere long time has gone by
Thy soul from all guilt will we purify,

And sure no heavy curse shall lie on thee.
Nay, did their anger cause this thing to be?
Perchance in heaven they smile upon thy gain—
—Lo, for a little while a burning pain,
Then yearning unfulfilled a little space,
Then tender memories of a well-loved face
In quiet hours, and then—forgetfulness—
How hadst thou rather borne, still less and less
To love what thou hadst loved, till it became
A thing to be forgotten, a great shame
To think thou shouldst have wasted life thereon?
Come then—thou spakest of a kingdom won
Thy dream foretold, and shall not this be too,
E'en as the dreadful deed thou cam'st to do?
To horse! and unto Argos let us wend,
Begin thy life afresh with me for friend.
Wide is the world, nor yet for many a day
Will every evil thing be cleared away
That bringeth scathe to men within its girth;
Surely a man like thee can win the mirth
That cometh of the conquering of such things;
For not in vain art thou the seed of kings
Unless thy face belie thee—nay, no more:
Why speak I vain words to a heart still sore
With sudden death of happiness? yet come
And ride with us unto our lovely home."

Hipponoüs to the King's word answered nought,
But sat there brooding o'er his dreary thought,
Nor seemed to hear; and when the Argive men
Brought up to him his battle-steed again,
Scarce witting of the company or place,
He mounted, and with set and weary face
Rode as they bade him at the King's left hand:
Nor did the sight of the fair well-tilled land,
When that they gained from out the tangled wood,
Do aught in dealing with his mournful mood;
Nor Argos' walls as from the fields they rose,
Such good things with their mightiness to close
From chance of hurt; scarce saw he the fair gate,
Dainty to look on, yet so huge of weight;
Nor did the streets' well-ordered houses draw
His eyes to look at them; unmoved he saw
The south-land merchants' dusky glittering train;
About the fountain the slim maids in vain
Drew sleek arms from the water, or turned round
With shaded eyes at the great horn's hoarse sound.
The sight of the King's house, deemed of all men
A wonder mid the houses kings had then,
Drew from him but a troubled frown, as though
Men's toilsome folly he began to know;

The carven Gods within the banquet-hall,
The storied hangings that bedight the wall,
Made his heart sick to think of labour vain,
Telling once more the oft-told tale of pain.
Cold in the damsel's hand his strong hand lay,
When to the steaming bath she led the way;
And when another damsel brought for him
Raiment wherein the Tyrian dye showed dim
Amid the gold lines of the broideries,
Her face downcast because she might not please,
He heeded not. When to the hall he passed,
And by the high seat he was set at last,
Then Prœtus, smiling from his mild eyes, laid
A hand upon his combed-out hair and said:

"Surely for no good luck this golden hair
Has come to Argos, and this visage fair,
To make us, who were well enow before,
Seem to our maids like churls at the hall-door,
Prying about when men to war are gone
And girls and children sit therein alone."

But nought Hipponoüs heeded the King's say,
But, turning, roughly put his hand away,
And frowning muttered, and still further drew,
As a man touched amid his dream might do.

In sooth he dreamed, and dreary was his dream;
A bitter thing the world to him did seem;
The void of life to come he peopled now
With folk of scornful eyes and brazen brow;
And one by one he told the tale of days
Wherein an envious mock was the world's praise;
Where good deeds brought ill fame, and truth was not,
Hate was remembered, love was soon forgot;
No face was good for long to look upon,
And nought was worthy when it once was won;
And narrow, helpless, friendless was the way,
That led unto the last most hopeless day
Of hopeless days, in tangled, troubled wise.
So thought he, till the tears were in his eyes
Since he was young yet, for hope lying dead.

But on his fixed eyes and his weary head
The happy King of Argos gazed awhile,
Till from his eye faded the scornful smile
That lingered on his lips; and now he turned,
As one who long ago that task had learned,
And unto the great men about him spoke,
And was a merry king of merry folk.

So passed the feast and all men drew to sleep,
And e'en Hipponoüs his soul might steep
In sweet forgetfulness a little while;
And somewhat did the fresh young day beguile
His treasured sorrow when he woke next morn,
And somewhat less he felt himself forlorn:
Nor did the King forget him, but straight sent
Unto the priests, and told them his intent
That this his guest should there be purified,
Since he with honour in his house should bide.

So was Jove's house made ready for that thing,
And thither amid songs and harp-playing,
White-robed and barefoot, was Hipponoüs brought;
Who, bough in hand, for peace the God besought.
Noiseless the white bulls fell beneath the stroke
Of the gold-girdled, well-taught temple folk:
Up to the roof arose the incense-cloud;
The chanted prayer of men, now low now loud,
Thrilled through the brazen leaves of the great door;
Thick lay the scattered herbs upon the floor,
And in the midst at last the hero stood,
Freed of the guilt of shedding kindred blood.
And then the chief priest cried, "Bellerophon,
With this new hapless name that thou hast won,
Go forth, go free, be happy once again,
But no more called Hipponoüs of men."

Then forth Bellerophon passed wearily,
Although so many prayers had set him free;
Yet somewhat was he ready to forget,
And turn unto the days that might be yet.

But when before King Prœtus' throne he came,
The King called out on him by his new name;
"O fair Bellerophon, like me, be wise,
And set things good to win before thine eyes,
Lands, and renown, and riches, and a life
That knows from day to day so much of strife
As makes men happy, since the age of gold
Is past, if e'er it was, as a tale told."

"O King," he said, "thou sittest in full day,
Thou strivest to put thoughts of night away;
My life has not yet left the morning-tide,
And I, who find the world that seemed so wide,
Now narrowed to a little troublous space
Where help is not, astonied turn my face
Unto the coming hours, nor know at all
What thing of joy or hope to me will fall.
Be patient, King; perchance within a while

No marfeast I may be, but learn to smile
Even as thou, who lovest life so much.
Who knows but grief may vanish at a touch,
As joy does? and a long way off is death:
Some folk seem glad even to draw their breath."

"Yea," said the King, "thou hast it, for indeed
I fain would live, like most men—but what need
Unto a fevered man to talk of wine?
Thy heart shall love life when it grows like mine.
But come thou hence, and I will show to thee
What things of price the Gods have given to me.
Not good it is to harp on the frayed string;
And thou, so seeing many a lovely thing,
Mayst hide thy weary pain a little space."

And therewith did King Prœtus from that place
Draw forth Bellerophon, and so when he
In his attire was now clad royally,
From out the precinct to his palace fair
Did the King bring him; and he showed him there
His stables, where the war-steeds stood arow
Over the dusty grain: then did they go
To armouries, where sword and spear and shield
Hung bloodless, ready for the fated field:
The treasury showed he, where things richly wrought
Together into such a place were brought,
That he who stole the oxen of a God,
For all his godlike cunning scarce had trod
Untaken on its floor—withal he showed
The chamber where the broidered raiment glowed,
Where the spice lay, and scented unguents fit
To touch Queen Venus' skin and brighten it;
The ivory chairs and beds of ivory
He showed him, and he bid his tired eyes see
The stories wrought on brazen doors, the flowers
And things uncouth carved on the wood of bowers;
The painted walls that told things old and new.
Things come to pass, and things that onward drew.

But all the while Bellerophon's grave face
And soon-passed smile seemed unmeet for that place,
And ever Prœtus felt a pang of fear,
As if it told of times a-drawing near,
When all the wealth and beauty that was his
Should not avail to buy one hour of bliss.
And sometimes when he watched his wandering eyes
And heard his stammering speech, would there arise
Within his heart a feeling like to hate,
Mingled with scorn of one so crushed by fate:
For ever must the rich man hate the poor.

Now at the last they stood before a door
Adorned with silver, wrought of precious wood;
Then Prœtus laughed, and said, "O guest, thy mood
Is hard to deal with; never any leech
Has striven as I thy sickness' heart to reach;
And I grow weary and must get me aid."
Therewith upon the lock his hand he laid
And pushed the door aback, and then the twain
The daintiest of all passages did gain,
And as betwixt its walls they passed along
Nearer they drew unto the measured song
Of sweet-voiced women; and the King spake then:
"Drive fire out with fire, say all wise men;
Here mayst thou set thine eyes on such an one,
That thou no more wilt think of days agone,
But days to come; for here indeed my spouse
Watches the damsels in the weaving-house,
Or in the pleasance sits above their play;
And certes here upon no long-passed day,
Unless my eyes were bleared with coming eld,
Fair sights for such as thou have I beheld."
Across the exile's brow a frown there came,
As though his sorrow of such things thought shame,
Yet mayhap his eye brightened as he heard
The song grow louder and the hall they neared;
But the King smiled, and swiftlier led him on,
Until unto the door thereof they won.

Now noble was that hall and fair enow,
Betwixt whose slim veined pillars set arow,
And marble lattice wrought like flowering trees,
Showed the green freshness of the summer seas,
Made cheery by the sun and many a ship,
Whose black bows smoothly through the waves did slip.
In bowls whereon old stories pictured were
The bright rose-laurels trembled in the air,
That from the sea stole through the lattices,
And round them hummed a few bewildered bees.
Midmost the pavement wrought by toil of years,
A tree was set, gold-leaved like that which bears
Unto the maids of Hesperus strange fruit;
A many-coloured serpent from the root
Curled upward round the stem, and, reaching o'er
A four-square silver laver, did outpour
Bright glittering water from his throat of brass;
And at each corner of the basin was
A brazen hart who seemed at point to drink;
And these the craftsman had not made to shrink
Though in the midst Diana's feet pressed down
The forest greensward, and her girded gown
Cleared from the brambles fell about her thigh,

And eager showed her terrible bright eye.
But 'twixt the pillars and that marvellous thing
Were scattered those they had e'en now heard sing;
Their song had sunk now, and a murmuring voice,
But mingled with the clicking loom's sharp noise
And splashing of the fountain, where a maid
With one hand lightly on a brass deer laid,
One clasped about her own foot, knelt to watch
Her brazen jar the tinkling water catch;
Withal the wool-comb's sound within the fleece
Began and grew, and slowly did decrease,
And then began as still it gat new food;
And by the loom an ancient woman stood
And grumbled o'er the web; and on the floor
Ten spindles twisted ever; from the store
Raised on high pillars at the gable end.
Adown a steep stair did a maiden wend,
Who in the wide folds of her gathered gown
Fresh yarn bright-dyed unto the loom bare down.

But on the downy cushions of a throne,
Above all this sat the fair Queen alone,
Who heeded not the work, nor noted aught;
Nor showed indeed that there was any thought
Within her heaving breast; but though she moved
No whit the limbs a God might well have loved,
Although her mouth was as of one who lies
In peaceful sleep; though over her deep eyes
No shadow came to trouble her white brow,
Yet might you deem no rest was on her now;
Rather too weary seemed she e'en to sigh
For foolish life that joyless passed her by.
So thus the King Bellerophon led in
Just as the old song did again begin
From the slim maids, that by the loom's side spun;
But ere it had full sway, the nighest one
Unto the door stopped singing suddenly,
And pressed her neighbour's arm, that she might see
What new folk were come in; and therewithal
An angry glance from the Queen's eyes did fall
Upon the maid; so that Bellerophon
A cruel visage had to look upon,
When first he saw the Queen raised high above
The ordered tresses of that close of love.
But when the women knew the King indeed
They did him reverence, and with lowly heed
Made way for him, while a girl here and there
Made haste to hide what labour had made bare
Of limb or breast; and the King smiled through all,
And now and then a wandering glance let fall
Upon some fairest face; and so at last

Through the sweet band unto the Queen they passed,
Who rose and waited them by her fair throne
With eyes wherefrom all care once more had gone
Of life and what it brought: then the King said—
"O Sthenobœa, hither have I led
A man, who, from a happy life down-hurled,
Looks with sick eyes upon this happy world;
Not knowing how to stay here or depart:
Thou know'st and I know how the wounded heart
Forgetteth pain and groweth whole again,
Yet is the pain that passes no less pain.
"But since this man is noble even as we,
And help begets help, and withal to me
Worthy he seems to be a great king's friend,
Now help me to begin to make an end
Of his so heavy mood; for though indeed
This daintiness may nowise help his need,
Yet may kind words avail to make him kind
Unto himself; kind eyes may make him blind
Unto the ugly, tangled whirl of life;
Or in some measured image of real strife
He may forget the things that he has lost,
Nor think of how he needs must yet be tost
Like other men from wave to wave of fate."

Gravely she set herself the end to wait
Of the King's speech; and what of scorn might be
Within her heart changed nowise outwardly
Her eyes that looked with scorn on everything;
And yet withal while still the cheery King
Let his tale flow, unto the exile's place
She glanced with scornful wonder at his face
At first, because she deemed it soft and kind;
Yet was he fair, and she—she needs must find
Something that drew her to his wide grey eyes;
And presently as with some great surprise
Her heart 'gan beat, and she must strive in vain
To crush within it a sweet rising pain,
She deemed to be that pity that she knew
As the last folly wise folk turn unto.
For pain was wont to rouse her rage, and she
Was like those beasts that slaughter cruelly
Their wounded fellows—truth she knew not of,
And fain had killed folk babbling over love;
Justice she thought of as a thing that might
Balk some desire of hers, before the night
Of death should end it all: nor hope she knew,
Nor what fear was, how ill soe'er life grew.
This wisdom had she more than most of folk,
That through the painted cloud of lies she broke
To gain what brought her pleasure for awhile,

However men might call it nought and vile;
Nor was she one to make a piteous groan
O'er bitter pain amid her pleasure grown.

But she was one of those wrought by the gods
To be to foolish men as sharpest rods
To scourge their folly; wrought so daintily
That scarcely could a man her body see
Without awaking strife 'twixt good and ill
Within him; and her sweet, soft voice would fill
Men's hearts with strange desires, and her great eyes,
Truthful to show her to the cold and wise
E'en as she was, would make some cast aside
Whatever wisdom in their breasts might hide,
And still despite what long ill days might prove,
They called her languid hate the soul of love.

But now that fire that to her eyes arose
She cast aback awhile to lie all close
About her heart; her full lips trembled not,
And from her cheek faded the crimson spot
That erst increased thereon.
"O Prince," she said,
"Strive to get back again thy goodlihead;
Life flitteth fast, and while it still abides,
Our folly many a good thing from us hides,
That else would pierce our hearts with its delight
Unto the quick, in all the Gods' despite."

He gazed upon her wondering, for again
That new-born hope, that sweet and bitter pain,
Flushed her smooth cheek, and glittered in her eyes,
And wrought within her lips; yet was she wise,
And gazing on his pale and wondering face,
In his frank eyes she did not fail to trace
A trouble like unto a growing hate,
That, yet unknown to him, her love did wait;
Then once more did she smother up that flame,
Calm grew she, from her lips a false voice came.

"Yea, and bethink thee, mayst thou not be born
To raise the crushed and succour the forlorn,
And in the place of sorrow to set mirth,
Gaining a great name through the wondering earth?
Now surely has my lord the King done well
To bring thee here thy tale to me to tell;
Come, then, for nearby such a bower there is
As most men deem to be a place of bliss;
There, when thy tale is o'er that I am fain
To hearken, may sweet music ease thy pain
Amidst our feast; or of these maids shall one

Read of some piteous thing the Gods have done
To us poor folk upon the earth that dwell.
Yea, and the reader will I choose so well,
That such an one herself shall seem to be
As she of whom the tale tells piteously.
And thou shalt hear when all is past and o'er,
And with its sorrow still thine heart is sore,
The Lydian flutes come nigher and more nigh,
Till glittering raiment cometh presently,
And thou behold'st the dance of the slim girls,
Wavering and strange as the leaf-wreath that whirls
Down in the marble court we walk in here
Mid sad October, when the rain draws near:
So delicate therewith, that when all sound
Of sobbing flute has left the air around,
And, panting, lean the dancers against wall
And well-wrought pillar, you hear nought at all
But their deep breathing, so are all men stilled,
So full their hearts with all that beauty filled."

Coldly and falsely was her speech begun,
But she waxed warm ere all the tale was done;
Nay, something soft was in her voice at last,
As round his soul her net she strove to cast
Almost despite herself.
Unmoved he stood,
But that some thought did cross his weary mood
That made him knit his brow, and therewith came
A flush across his face as if of shame
Because of that new thought; but when an end
Her speech had, then he spake:
"What love or friend
Can do me good? God-hated shall I be,
And bring to no man aught but misery;
And thou, O royal man, and thou, O Queen,
Who heretofore in bliss and mirth have been,
Hearken my words, and on your heads be all
The trouble that from me shall surely fall
If I abide with you.: yet doubt it not
That this your love shall never be forgot
Wherewith ye strive to win a helpless man,
And ever will I labour as I can
To make my ill forebodings come to nought."

But midst these things, pleased by some hidden thought,
The King smiled, turning curious eyes on them,
And smoothing down his raiment's golden hem
As one who hearkens music; then said he,
"Wilt thou give word for our festivity,
O Sthenobœa? But come thou, O guest,
And by the great sea we will take our rest,

Speaking few words."
So from her golden throne
She passed to do what things must needs be done,
And with firm feet amid her maids she went
On this new tyrannous sweetness all intent;
So did it work in her, that scarcely she
Might bear the world now, as she turned to see
The stranger and the King a-going down
By marble stairs unto the foreshores brown.
So slipped the morn away, and when the sun
His downward course some three hours had begun,
Summoned by sound of horns they took their way
Unto a bower that looking westward lay,
Yet was by trellised roses shaded so
That little of the hot sun did it know
But what the lime-trees' honey-sweet scent told,
And their wide wind-stirred leaves, turned into gold
Against the bright rays of the afternoon.

So to that chamber came the fair Queen soon,
Well harbingered by flutes; nor had she spared
To veil her limbs in raiment that had fared
O'er many a sea, before it had the hap
The Lycian's smooth skin in its folds to lap.
But as she entered there in queenly guise,
With firm and haughty step, and careless eyes
Over the half-hid beauty of her breast,
One moment on the exile did they rest,
And softened to a meek, imploring gaze—
One moment only; as with great amaze
His eyes beheld her, doubtful what was there,
All had gone thence, but the proud empty stare
That she was wont to turn on everything.
Withal she sat her down beside the King,
And the feast passed with much of such delight
As makes to happy men the world seem bright,
But from the hapless draws but hate and scorn,
Because the Gods both happy and forlorn
Have set in one world, each to each to be
A vain rebuke, a bitter memory.
Yet the Queen held her word, and when that they
Had heard the music sing adown the day,
After the dancing women had but left
Sweet honeyed scents behind, or roses, reft
By their own hands from head or middle small,
Then came with hurried steps into the hall
The reader and her scroll; sweet-eyed was she,
And timid as some loving memory
Midst the world's clamour: clad in gown of wool
She sat herself adown upon a stool
Anigh the proud feet of the Lycian Queen,

And straight, as if no soul she there had seen,
With slender hand put back her golden hair,
And 'gan to read from off the parchment fair.
In a low voice, and trembling at the first,
She read a tale of lovers' lives accurst
By cruel Gods and careless foolish men:
Like dainty music was her voice, and when
From out her heart she sighed, as she must read
Of folk unholpen in their utmost need,
Still must the stranger turn kind eyes on her.
At last awhile she paused, as she drew near
The bitter end of spilt and wasted bliss,
And death unblessed at last by any kiss;
Her voice failed, and adown her book did sink,
And midst them all awhile she seemed to think
Of the past days herself; but still so much
Her beauty and the tale their hearts did touch,
Folk held their breath till she began again,
And something 'twixt a pleasure and a pain
It was when all the sweet tale was read o'er
And her voice quivered through the air no more.
Then round the maiden's neck King Prœtus cast
A golden chain, and from the hall she passed,
And yet confused and shamefaced; for the Queen,
Who at the first the Prince's eyes had seen
Upon the maid, and then would look no more,
But kept her eyes fixed on the marble floor
As listening to the tale; her head now raised,
And with cold scorn upon the maiden gazed
As she bent down the golden gift to take;
And meanwhile, for her tender beauty's sake,
Over the exile's face a pleased smile came.

But she departed to the bliss or shame
Life had for her, and all folk left the bower;
For now was come the summer night's mid-hour:
The great high moon that lit the rippling sea
'Twixt the thin linden-trees shone doubtfully
Upon the dim grey garden; the sea-breeze
Stooped down on the pleached alleys; the tall trees
Over the long roofs moved their whispering leaves,
Nor woke the dusky swifts beneath the eaves.

Now from that fair night wore the time away,
Until with lapse of many a quiet day,
And stirring times withal, Bellerophon
To love of life and hope of joy was won.
Still grave and wise he was beyond his years,
No eager man among his joyous peers
To snatch at pleasure; careful not to cheat
His soul with vain desires all over sweet;

A wary walker on the road of life;
E'en as a man who in a garden, rife
With flowers, has gone unarmed, and found that there
Are evil things amid the blossoms fair,
And paid with wounds for folly: yet when he
Is whole once more, since there he needs must be,
And has no will its sweets to cast aside,
Well armed he walks there ware of beasts that hide
Beneath the shade of those vine-trellises,
Amid the grey stems of the apple-trees.

Yet at his heart, about the root of it
Strange thoughts there lay, which at sweet times would flit
Before his eyes, as things grown palpable;
Strange hopes that made the weltering world seem well
While he abode there: therefore was he kind
To man and maid, and all men's hearts did bind
With bonds of love, for mid the struggling folk,
The forgers and the bearers of the yoke,
Weary with wronging and with wrongs, he seemed
As one on whom a light from heaven had beamed,
That changed him to a god yet being alive.
But midst all folk there did King Prœtus give
Great gifts to him; great trust in him he had,
And ever by his sight was he made glad:
For well did all things prosper in his hand,
Nor was there such another in the land
For strength or goodliness.

Now so it was,
That he on matters of the King would pass
About the country here and there, nor dwell
At Argos much, and that thing pleased him well;
For while all else grew better, ye shall know
That greater in his heart the fear did grow
That sprung up therein on that summer eve;
And though sometimes the Queen would make believe
To heed him nought—yea, or depart maybe
At whiles, when he the King would come to see—
Yet was this but at whiles; the next day came,
And scarce would she hold parley with her shame.
One noon of the late autumn, when the sun
Brightened the parting year, so nearly done,
With rays as hot as early June might shed,
Dawn past an hour, upon the tulip-bed,
In the great pleasance, 'neath a wall of yew,
Walked the Corinthian, pondering what to do
In some great matter late given unto him.
So clad he was, that both on breast and limb
Steel glittered, though his head as yet was bare;
But in his face was just so much of care

As seemed to show he had got that to do
He feared but little well to carry through,
But which must have his heed a little while:
And still in going would he stop and smile,
And seem to cast the shreds of thought away
In honour of the bright fresh autumn day
And all the pleasure of the lovely place.
But at the last, turning about his face
Unto the sunny garden's other side,
He saw where, down a grassy path and wide,
The Queen came, with her head bent down to earth,
As though mid thoughts she were that slew her mirth;
Slowly she went, with two maids following her,
Who in their delicate slim hands did bear,
The one a cithern and some verse-book old,
The other a white osier maund, to hold
Some of such flowers as still in fear and doubt
Against the sickness of the year held out.
But as they went, nigh to the Prince they drew,
And soon the maidens' eyes his beauty knew,
And one at other glanced, smiling and glad,
For soft love of him in their hearts they had;
Yet nought they said, nor did the Queen turn round,
But kept her eyes still bent upon the ground.
So in their walk they came to where there stood
A thin-leaved apple-tree, where, red as blood,
Yellow as gold, a little fruit hung yet,
The last rays of the fainting sun to get;
And a tall clump of autumn flowers, cold-grey,
Beneath it, mocked the promise of the day,
And to them clung a hapless bee or twain,
A butterfly spread languid wings in vain
Unto the sun, that scarce could heat her now.
There the Queen stayed awhile her footsteps slow,
And to the flowers wandered her slender hand;
But with her eyes cast down she still did stand,
And pondered.

Full of melody and peace
About her was the lingering year's decease;
Strange spicy scents there were that yet were sweet,
Green was the grass about her gold-shod feet,
And had no memory of the dawn's white rime;
Loud was the birds' song in that windless time,
Strange the sharp crying of the missel-thrush
Within the close heart of the hawthorn-bush,
Strange the far-off rooks' sweet tumultuous voice
That in the high elms e'en now must rejoice
And know not why—peace e'en if end of peace.
The while her burning heart did never cease
To give words to such longings, as she knew

To swift destruction all her glory drew.
"Ah! mine, mine, mine!" she thought, "ah! mine a while!
Ah! mine a little day, if all be vile
The coming years can bring unto my heart!
Ah! mine this eve, if we to-morn must part!
Mine, that a sweet hour I may know at last
How soon soever all delight is passed!
Ah! mine, mine, mine, if for a little while!"

So stood she, that her parted lips did smile
As if of one that memories make half sad,
Her breast heaved, as no stronger wish she had
Than for some careless lover, lightly won,
And soon forgot, to lay his lips thereon;
The flower-stem that her finger-tips did hold
Was crushed not, and within her shoe of gold
Lightly her foot was laid upon the grass;
No tremors through her dainty limbs did pass,
And healthy life alone did paint her cheek:
For if indeed at first she had felt weak,
Ere well she knew what she was bent upon,
Now at the last, when every doubt was gone,
She would not show the net unto the prey
Until she deemed that in her toils he lay.

She raised her eyes at last with a light sigh,
Despite herself, a flush passed suddenly
Over her face, and then all pale she grew;
For now withal Bellerophon she knew,
Though at that very point of time the sun
Along his upraised steel-clad arm had run,
And made an earthly sun that dazzled her.
Yet cast she back her trembling hope and fear
Into her heart, and as before she went
Slowly, with head a little downward bent,
But when she had gone on a few yards space,
Once more unto the Prince she raised her face;
Then stopped again, and turning round, she said,
From lips wherein all passion now seemed dead:
"Damsels, go home again; thou, Mysian, go
Unto the little treasury thou dost know
Anigh my bower, and taking this gold key,
Draw forth that ancient prophet's book for me
Which shows the stars: for that I fain would show
To Prince Bellerophon, who bides me now
Ere he goes forth to bring the island folk
Once more beneath King Prœtus' equal yoke.
And thou, Leucippe, bide our coming there,
And bid our folk set forth a feast as fair
As may be done; for we within a while
May need thy cithern dull thoughts to beguile."

E'en as they turned she passed on carelessly
Toward the Prince, nor looked aback to see
That they were gone; but he indeed had heard
Through the calm air her clearly-spoken word,
And saw the maidens go, and felt as one
Who bideth, when the herald's speech is done,
The word that bids the grinded spears fall down.
But she, with slim hand folded in her gown,
Went o'er the dewy grass to where he stood,
And in despite the fire within her blood
Was calm, and smiled on him, till nigh he thought
That surely all his fear was vain and nought.
He bowed before her as she drew anear,
But she held out her right hand, and in clear
Sweet tones she cried, "O fair Bellerophon,
Would that the victory were already won,
And thou wert back again at this thy home
We have made glad for thee: behold! I come
To say farewell—yet come a little way—
For something else indeed I had to say."

And still she held his hand, but yet durst not
Clasp as she would the treasure she had got.
Then to a place together did they pass,
Where yew-trees hemmed around a plot of grass,
And kept it scarce touched by the faint sun's rays
A place well made for burning summer days,
But cheerless now. There on a marble seat
She bade him sit; while she with restless feet
Paced to and fro, while from the yew-twigs close,
With his scared cry the creeping blackbird rose.
But he, with eyes cast down upon the ground,
Deemed that his battle easier would be found
Than this.

And so at last she stayed by him
And cried: "The cup is full unto the brim;
For now thou goest where thou mayst be slain:
I speak then—and, alas! I speak in vain—
Thy cold eyes tell me so—How shall I move
Thy flinty heart my curse has made me love?
For what have other women done, when they
Were fair as I, and love before them lay?
Was not a look enough for them, a word
Low murmured, midst the hum of men scarce heard?
What have I left undone that they have done?
What askest thou of me, O heart of stone?"

Choked by her passion here awhile she stayed,
And he from off the bench sprang up dismayed,

And turned on her to speak; but she withal
Before him on her knees made haste to fall,
And cried out loud and shrilly: "Nay, nay, nay—
Say not the word thou art about to say;
Let me depart, and things be still as now;
So that my dreams sweet images may show,
As they have done—that waking I may think,
'If he, my love, from looks of love did shrink,
That was because I had not prayed him then
To be my love alone of living men;
Because he did not know that I, a Queen,
Who hitherto but loveless life have seen,
Could kneel to him, and pray upon my knees
To give me my first pleasure, my first peace'
Thou knewest not—nay, nay, thou know'st not now—
Thou with the angry eyes and bended brow!—
Surely I talk my mother-tongue no more,
Therefore thou knowest not that I implore
Thy pity, that I give myself to thee,
Thy love, thy slave, thy castaway to be-
Hear'st thou? thy castaway! when in a while
Thou growest weary of my loving smile!
Oh, take me, madman! In a year or twain
I will not thwart thee if thou lov'st again,
Nor eye thee sourly when thou growest cold;
Or art thou not the man that men call bold,
And fear'st thou? Then what better time than this
For we twain to begin our life of bliss?
Thy keel awaits thee, and to thee alone,
Not to the wretched dastard on the throne,
Thy men will hearken—Nay, thou shalt not speak,
My feeble reed of hope thou shalt not break!—
Let me be gone, thou knowest not of love,
Thou semblance of a man that nought can move!
It O wise, wise man, I give thee good farewell:
Gather fresh wisdom, thinking of my hell."

She sprang up to her feet and turned away
Trembling, and no word to her could he say
For grief and pity; and the Queen did go
A little way with doubtful steps and slow,
Then turned about, and once again did stand
Before his troubled face, hand laid in hand,
And sobbing now as if her heart would break;
But when from his grieved soul he fain would speak,
Again from midst her tears she cried, "No, no
Do I not know what thou wouldst bid me do?
And yet forgive me!—thou art wise and good.
Surely some evil thing has turned my blood,
That even now I wished that thing to slay
That I of all things only till this day

Have loved. Ah, surely thou wilt not be slain!
Come back, and I will tell thee once again
How much I love thee, and will not forget
To say such things as might have moved thee yet,
Could I have told thee now, couldst thou have seen
These lips that love thee as they might have been.
Farewell, I durst not pray thee for one kiss!"

Nearer she drew to him as she spake this,
Yet, when she ended, turned about again,
And still, as hoping all was not in vain,
Lingered a little while, and then at last,
With raging heart, swiftly therefrom she passed.

But, she clean vanished now, Bellerophon
Went slowly toward the palace, all alone,
And pondering on these things: and shamed he felt,
E'en as a just man who in sleep has dealt
Unjustly; nor had all her prayers and tears
Moved love in him, but rather stirred his fears,
For ever was he wise among wise men;
And though he doubted not her longing, when
She turned and spake soft words, he knew that she
So spake midst hope of what things yet might be,
And yet had left another kind of word,
Whereby a friendless man might well be feared;
Lonely he felt thereat, as one accurst,
With whom all best things still must turn to worst,
And e'en sweet love curdle to bitter hate.
Yet was he one not lightly crushed by fate,
And when at last he had his helmet on,
And heard the folk cry out 'Bellerophon,'
As toward the ship he passed, kind the world seemed,
Nor love so far away indeed he deemed
When he some gentle maiden's kind grey eyes
Fixed on his own he did at whiles surprise,
Or when his godlike eyes, on some maid turned
More fair than most, set fire to thoughts that burned
On breast and brow of her. So forth he passed,
And reached the border of the sea at last,
And there took ship, and hence is gone a space.

But for the Queen, when she had left that place,
About the pleasance paths did she go still,
So 'wildered in her mind because her will
Might not be done, that at the first she knew
No more what place she might be passing through
Than one who walks in sleep. Yet hope and sham
Twain help, at last unto her spirit came;
Yea, her bright gown, soiled with the autumn grass,
Told her the tale of what had come to pass,

And to her heart came hatred of the spot
Where she had kneeled to one who loved her not,
And even therewith his image did she see
As he had been; then cried she furiously:
"Ah, fool! ah, traitor! must I love thee then,
When in the world there are so many men
My smile would drive to madness?—for I know
What things they are that men desire so,
And which of all these bear I not with me?
Hast thou not heart and eyes to feel and see?
Then shalt thou die, then shalt thou die, at least,
Nor sit without me at life's glorious feast,
While I fall ever unto worse and worse—
Ah me! I rave!—what folly now to curse
That which I love, because its loveliness
Alone has brought me unto this distress!
I know not right nor wrong, but yet through all
Know that the Gods a just man him would call;
Nay, and I knew it, when I saw him first,
And in my heart sprang up that glorious thirst—
And should he, not being base, yield suddenly,
And as the basest man, not loving me,
Take all I gave him, and cast all his life
Into a tangled and dishonoured strife?
Nay, it could never be—but now, indeed,
Somewhat with pity of me his heart may bleed,
Since he is good; and he shall think of me,
And day by day and night by night shall see
The image of that woman on her knees,
Whom men here liken to the goddesses.
And certainly shall he come back again:
Nor shall my next speech to him be so vain."

She smiled, and toward the house made swiftly on
In triumph, even as though the game were won:
For, now his face was gone, she, blind with love,
Deemed but his honour she had got to move
From its high place, before his heart should fall
A prey unto her; e'en as when the wall
By many a stroke of stones is battered down,
And all may work their will upon the town.

Now of Bellerophon must it be said
That, what by wisdom, what by hardihead,
His task was done, and great praise gained thereby;
So he at last, midst shouts and minstrelsy,
In the first days of spring, passed up once more
Unto the palace from the thronging shore.
Him Prœtus met half-way, and, in the face
Of all the people, in a straight embrace
Held him awhile, and called him his dear son,

Praising the Gods for all that he had done;
Then hand in hand did they go up the street,
And on their heads folk cast the spring-flowers sweet,
And bands of maids met them with joyous song
And gracious pageants as they went along:
And all this for the brave Corinthian's sake—
Such joy did his return in all hearts make.

But though the man, once from his home driven forth,
Was so much loved and held of so much worth,
And though he throve thereby, and seemed to be
Scarcely a man but some divinity
To people's eyes, yet in his soul no less
There lingered still a little heaviness,
And therefrom hardly could he cast away
The memory of that sunny autumn day
And of the fear it brought; and one more fear
He had besides, and as they drew anear
The palace, therewith somewhat faltering,
He needs must turn a while, and of the King
Ask how the Lycian fared: the King laughed low,
And said:
               "Nay, surely she is well enow,
As her wont is to be, for, sooth to say,
She for herself is ever wont to pray,
And heedeth nothing other grief and wrong:
And be thou sure, my son, that such live long
And lead sweet lives; but those who ever think
How he and she may fare, and still must shrink
From sweeping any foe from out the way,
These—living other people's lives, I say,
Besides their own, and most of them forlorn—
May hap to find their lives of comfort shorn
And short enow—let pass, for as to me,
I weep for others' troubles certainly,
But for mine own would weep a little more,
And so I jog on somehow to the shore
Whence I shall not return—Thou laughest—well,
I deem I was not made for heaven or hell,
But simply for the earth; but thou, O son,
I deem of heaven, and all hearts hast thou won—
Yea, and this morn the Queen is merrier,
Because she knoweth that thou art anear."

The Prince smiled at his words and gladder felt,
Yet somewhat of his old fear by him dwelt
And shamed him midst his honour. But withal,
With shouts and music, entered they the hall,
And there great feast was made; but ere the night
Had 'gun to put an end to men's delight,
A maid came up the hall with hurrying feet,

And there in lowly wise the King did greet,
And bid him know that Sthenobœa had will
The joyance of that high-tide to fulfil,
And Prince Bellerophon to welcome home;
And even as she spoke the Queen was come
Unto the door, and through the hall she passed,
And round about her ever looks she cast,
As though her maidens, howsoever fair
And lovesome unto common eyes they were,
Were fashioned in another wise than she,
They made for time, she for eternity;
So 'twixt the awed and wondering folk she moved,
Hapless and proud, glorious and unbeloved,
And hating all folk but her love alone:
And he a shadow seemed, one moment shown
Unto her longing eyes, then snatched away
Ere yet her heart could win one glorious day.
Cruel and happy was she deemed of men—
Cruel she was, but though tormented then
By love, still happier than she ere had been.
Now when she saw the Prince, with such-like mien
She greeted him but as a Queen might greet
Her husband's friend fresh from a glorious feat;
Frank-seeming were her words, and in her face
No sign of all that storm the Prince could trace
That had swept over her—and yet therefore
Amidst his joy he did but fear her more.

So time slipped by, and still was she the same,
Till he 'gan deem she had forgot the shame
Of having shameful gifts cast back to her,
That scorned love was a burden light to bear.
Yea, and the moody ways that once she had
Seemed changing into life all frank and glad;
She saw him oft now, and alone at whiles;
But still, despite her kind words and her smiles,
No word of love fell from her any more.
But when the lush green spring was now passed o'er,
And the green lily-buds were growing white,
A feast they held for pastime and delight
Within the odorous pleasance on a tide,
And down the hours the feast in joy did glide.
Venus they worshipped there, her image shone
Above the folk from thoughts of hard life won;
About her went the girls in ordered bands,
And scattered flowers from out their slender hands,
And with their eager voices, sweet but shrill,
Betwixt the o'erladen trees the air did fill;
Or, careless what their dainty limbs might meet,
Ungirded and unshod, with hurrying feet,
Mocked cold Diana's race betwixt the trees,

Where the long grass and sorrel kissed their knees,
About the borders of the neighbouring field;
Or in the garden were content to yield
Unto the sun, and by the fountain-side,
Panting, love's growing languor would abide.
Surely the Goddess in the warm wind breathed,
Surely her fingers wrought the flowers that wreathed
The painted trellises—some added grace
Her spirit gave to every limb and face,
Some added scent to raiment long laid hid
Beneath the stained chest's carven cypress lid;
Fairer the girdle round the warm side clung,
Fairer the dainty folds beneath it hung,
Fairer the gold upon the bosom lay
Than was their wont ere that bewildering day,
When fear and shame, twin rulers of the earth,
Sat hoodwinked in the maze of short-lived mirth.
Songs cleft the air, and little words therein
Were clean changed now, and told of honeyed sin,
And passionate words seemed fire, and words, that had.
Grave meaning once, were changed, and only bade
The listeners' hearts to thoughts they could not name.
Shame changed to strong desire, desire seemed shame,
And trembled; and such words the lover heard
As in the middle of the night afeard
He once was wont alone to whisper low
Unto himself, for fear the day should know
What his love really was; the longing eyes
That unabashed were wont to make arise
The blush of shame to bosom and grave brow,
Beholding all their fill, were downcast now;
The eager heart shrank back, the cold was moved,
Wooed was the wooer, the lover was beloved.

But yet indeed from wise Bellerophon
Right little by Queen Venus' wiles was won:
Joyous he was, but nowise would forget
That long and changing might his life be yet,
Nor deemed he had to do with such things now,
So let all pass, e'en as a painted show.
But the Queen hoped belike, and many a prayer
That morn had made to Venus' image fair;
And as the day wore, hushed she grew at whiles
And pale; and sick and scornful were her smiles,
Nor knew her heart what words her lips might say.

So through its changing hours went by the day,
And when at last they sang the sun a-down,
And, singing, watched the moon rise, and the town
Was babbling through the clear eve, saddened now,
And faint and weary went, with footsteps slow,

The lover and beloved, to e'en such rest
As they might win; and soon the daisies, pressed
By oft-kissed dainty feet and panting side,
Now with the dew were growing satisfied,
And sick blind passion now no more might spoil
The place made beautiful by patient toil
Of many a man. And now Bellerophon
Slept light and sweetly as the night wore on,
Nor dreamed about the morrow; but the Queen
Rose from her bed, and, like a sin unseen,
Stole from the house, and, barefoot as she was,
Through the dark belt of whispering trees did pass
That girt the fair feast's pleasant place around:
And when she came unto that spot of ground
Whereas she deemed Bellerophon had lain,
Then low adown she lay, and as for pain
She moaned, and on the dew she laid her cheek,
Then raised her head, and cried:
"Now may I speak,
Now may I speak, since none can hear me now
But thou, O Love, thou of the bitter bow.
Didst thou not see, O Citheræa's son,
Thine image, that men call Bellerophon?
Thine image, with the heart of stone, the eyes
Of fire, those forgers of all miseries?
And shall I bear thy burden all alone,
In silent places making my low moan?
Nay, but once more I try it—help thou me,
Or on the earth a strange deed shalt thou see.
Lo, now! thou knowest what my will has been:
Day after day his fair face have I seen
And made no sign—thus had I won him soon.
But thou, the dreadful sun, the cruel moon,
The scents, the flowers, the half-veiled nakedness
Of wanton girls, my heart did so oppress,
That now the chain is broken—Didst thou see
How when he turned his cruel face on me
He laughed?—he laughed, nor would behold my heart—
He laughed, to think at last he had a part
In joyous life without me: here, e'en here,
He drank, rejoicing much, still drawing near,
As the fool thought, to riches and renown.
And such an one wilt thou not cast adown
When thou rememberest how he came to me
With wan worn cheek?—Ah, sweet he was to see!
I loved him then—how can I love him now,
So changed, so changed?
"But thou—what doest thou?
Hast thou forgotten how thy temples stand,
Made rich with gifts, in many a luckless land?
Hast thou forgotten what strange rites are done

To gain thy goodwill underneath the sun?
Thou art asleep, then! Wake!—the world will end
Because thou sleepest—e'en now doth it wend
Unto the sickening end of all delights;
Black, black the days are, dull grey are the nights,
No more the night hides shame, no more the day
Unto the rose-strewn chamber lights the way;
And folk begin to curse thee, 'Love is gone,
Grey shall the earth be, filled with rocks alone,
Because the generations shall die out;
Grey shall the earth be, lonely, wrapped about
With cloudy memories of the moans of men.'
Thus, thus they curse. Shall I not curse thee then,
Thou who tormentest me and leav'st me lone,
Nor thinkest once of all that thou hast done?—
Spare me! What cruel God taught men to speak,
To cast forth words that for all good are weak
And strong for all undoing?—thou know'st this,
O lovely one! take not all hope of bliss
Away from me, because my eager prayer
Grows like unto a curse. O great and fair,
Hearken a little, for to-morn must I
Speak once again of love to him, or die;
Hast thou no dream to send him, such as thou
Hast shown to me so many a time or now?
Wilt thou not make him weep without a cause,
As I have done, as sleep her dark veil draws
From off his head? or his awaking meet
With lovely images, so soft and sweet
That they, forgotten quite, yet leave behind
Great yearning for bright eyes and touches kind.
Alas, alas! wilt thou not change mine eyes,
Or else blind his, the cold, the over-wise?
O Love, he knows my heart, and what it is—
No fool he is to cast away his bliss
On such as me: nay, rather he will take
Some grey-eyed girl to love him for his sake,
Not for her own—he knows me, and therefore
I, grovelling here where he has lain, the more
Must burn for him—he knows me; and thou, too,
Better than I, knowest what I shall do.
O Love, thou knowest all, yet since I live
A little joyance hope to me doth give;
Wilt thou not grant me now some sign, O Love;
Wilt thou not redden this dark sky, or move
Those stark hard walls, or make the spotted thrush
Cry as in morn through this dark scented hush?"

She ceased, and leaned back, kneeling, and all spent
And panting, with her trembling fingers rent
The linen from her breast, and, with shut eyes,

Waited awhile as for some great surprise,
But yet heard nothing stranger or more loud
Than the leaves' rustle; a long bank of cloud
Lay in the south, low down, and scarcely seen
'Gainst the grey sky, and when at last the Queen
Opened her eyes, she started eagerly,
Although the strangest thing her eyes could see
Was but the summer lightning playing there;
Then she put back her over-hanging hair,
And in a hard and grating voice she said:
"O Sthenobœa, art thou then afraid
Of a god's presence?—did a god e'er come
To help a good and just man when his home
Was turned to hell? I was but praying here
Unto myself, who to myself am dear
Alone of all things, mine own self to aid.
And therewithal I needs must grow afraid
E'en of myself—O wretch, unholpen still,
To-morrow early thou shalt surely fill
The measure of thy woe—and then—and then—
Alas for me! What cruellest man of men
Had made me this, and left me even thus?"

Unto the sky wild eyes and piteous
She turned, and gat unto her feet once more,
And, led by use, came back unto the door
Whence she went out, and with no stealthy tread,
Careless of all things, gat her to her bed,
And there at last, in grief and care's despite,
Slept till the world had long forgotten night.

Bellerophon arose the morrow morn
Unlike the man that once had been forlorn;
Bright-eyed and merry was he, and such fear
As yet clung round him did but make joy dear,
And more in hope he was, and knew not why,
Than any day that yet had passed him by.
Now ere the freshness of the morn had died,
Restless with happiness, he thought to ride
Unto a ship, that in a little bay
Anigh to Phlius, bound for outlands, lay,
Unto whose Phrygian master had the King
Given commands to buy him many a thing,
And soon he sailed, since fair was grown the wind.
But as Bellerophon in such a mind
Passed slow along the marble cloister-wall,
He heard a voice his name behind him call,
And turning, saw the Thracian maiden fair,
Leucippe, coming swiftly toward him there,
Who when she reached him stayed, and drawing breath
As one who rests, said, "Sir, my mistress saith

That she awhile is fain to speak with thee
Before thou goest down unto the sea;
And in her bower for thee doth she abide."
He gave her some light word, and side by side
The twain passed toward the bower, he all the while
Noting the Thracian with a well-pleased smile;
For his fear slept, or he felt strong enow
Things good and ill unto his will to bow.
Yet was the gentle Thracian pale that day,
And still she seemed as she some word would say
Unto him, that her lips durst not to frame;
And when unto the Queen's bower-door they came,
And he passed there, and it was shut on him,
She lingered still, and through her body slim
A tremor ran, her pale face waxed all red,
And her lips moved as though some word they said
She durst not utter loud; then she looked down
Upon her bare feet and her slave's wool gown,
And to her daily task straight took her way.

Now on his throne King Prœtus judged that day,
And heard things dull, things strange, but when at last
The summer noon now by an hour had passed,
He went to meat, and thought to see thereat
Bellerophon's frank face, who ever sat
At his right hand; but empty was his place.
And when the King, who fain had seen his face,
Asked whither he was gone, a certain man
Said: "King, I saw the brave Corinthian,
Two hours agone, pass through the outer door,
And in his face there seemed a trouble sore,
So that I needs must ask him what was wrong;
But staring at me as he went along,
Silent he passed, as if he heard me not;
Afoot he was, nor weapon had he got."
The King's face clouded, but the meal being done
In his fair chariot did he get him gone
Unto the haven, where the Phrygian ship
Was waiting his last word her ropes to slip;
Restless he was, and wished that night were come.
But ere he left the fair porch of his home,
Unto the Queen a messenger he sent,
And bade her know whereunto now he went,
And prayed her go with him; but presently
Back came the messenger, and said that she
Was ill at ease and in her bower would bide,
For scarcely she upon that day might ride.
So at that word of hers the Argive King
Went on his way, but somewhat muttering,
For heavy thoughts were gathering round his heart;
But when he came where, ready to depart,

The ship lay, with the bright-eyed master there
Some talk he had, who said the wind was fair
And all things ready; then the King said, "Friend,
To-morrow's noon I deem will make an end
Of this thy lingering; I will send to thee
A messenger to tell the certainty
Of my last wishes, who shall bring thee gold
And this same ring that now thou dost behold
Upon my finger, for a token sure
Farewell, and may thy good days long endure."

He turned, but backward sent his eyes awhile,
Sighing, though on his lips there was a smile;
The half-raised sail that clung unto the mast,
The tinkling ripple 'gainst the black side cast,
The thin blue smoke that from the poop arose,
The northland dog that midst of ropes did doze,
The barefoot shipmen's eyes upon him bent,
Curious and half-defiant, as they went
About their work—all these things raised in him
Desire for roving—stirred up thoughts that, dim
At this time, clear at that, still oft he had,
That there his life was not so overglad;
And as toward Argos now he rode along
By the grey sea, the shipmen's broken song
Smote on his ear and with the low surf's fall
Mingled, and seemed to him perchance to call
To freedom and a life not lived in vain.

But even so his palace did he gain,
And the dull listless day slipped into night,
And smothering troublous thoughts e'en as he might,
Did he betake himself to bed, and there
Lay half-asleep beneath the tester fair,
Waiting until the low-voiced flutes gave sign
That thither drew the Lycian's feet divine—
For so the wont was, that she still was led
Unto her chamber as a bride new-wed.

Of that sweet sound nought heard the King at all,
But straightway into a short sleep did fall,
Then woke as one who knoweth certainly
That all the hours he now shall hear pass by,
Nor sleep until the sun is up again.
So, waking, did he hear a cry of pain
Within the chamber, and thereat adrad
He turned him round, and saw the Queen, so clad
That on her was her raiment richly wrought,
Yet in such case as though hard fate had brought
Some bane of Kings into the royal place,
And with that far-removed and dainty grace

The rough hands of some outland foe had dealt;
For dragged athwart her was the jewelled belt,
Rent and disordered the Phœnician gown,
The linen from her shoulders dragged adown,
Her arms and glorious bosom made half-bare,
And furthermore such shameful signs were there,
As though not long past hands had there been laid
Heavier than touches of the tiring-maid.

So swiftly through the place from end to end
She paced, but yet stopped now and then to send
Low bitter moans forth on the scented air;
And through the King's heart shot a bitter fear,
Nor could he move—he had believed her cold,
And wise to draw herself from pleasure's hold
When it began to sting the heart—but now
What shameful thing would these last minutes show?

Now as she went a look askance she cast
Upon the King, and turning at the last,
With strange eyes drew anigh the royal bed,
And, with clasped hands, before him stood, and said:
"Thou wakest, then? thou wonderest at this sight?
I have a tale to tell to thee this night
I cannot utter, unless words are taught
Unto my lips to draw forth all my thought
Thou wonderest at my words? Then ask, then ask!
The sooner will be done my heavy task."

Upright in bed the King sat, pale with doubt
And gathering fear; his right hand he stretched out
To take the Queen's hand, but aback she drew,
Shuddering; and half he deemed the truth he knew,
As o'er her pale face and her bosom came
Beneath his gaze a flush as if of shame:
"Wilt thou not speak, and make an end?" she cried.
Then he spake slowly, "Why dost thou abide
Without my bed to-night? why dost thou groan,
Whom I ere now no love-sick girl have known?"

She covered up her face at that last word;
The thick folds of her linen gown were stirred
As her limbs writhed beneath them—nought she said,
As though the word was not remembered
She had to say; and, loth the worst to hear,
The King awhile was tongue-tied by his fear.

At last the words came: "Thou bad'st ask of thee
Why thou to-night my playmate wouldst not be—
What hast thou done? Speak quickly of the thing!"

She drew her hands away, and cried, "O King,
Art thou awake yet, that this shameful guise
Seems nothing strange unto thy drowsy eyes,
Wilt thou not ask why this and this is torn?
Why this is bruised? Lo, since the long-passed morn
Thus have I sat, that thou e'en this might see,
And ask what madness there has been in me.
Thus have I sat, and cursed the God who made
The day so long, the night so long delayed.
"Ask! thou art happy that the Lycian sod
Unwearied oft my virgin feet have trod
From dawn to dusk; that in the Lycian wood
Before wild things untrembling I have stood;
That this right arm so oft the javelin threw—
These fingers rather the grey bowstring knew
Than the gold needle: even so, indeed,
Of more than woman's strength had I had need
If with a real man I had striven to-day;
But he who would have shamed thee went his way
Like a scourged woman—thou wilt spare him, then—
Lay down thy sword!—that is for manly men."

For while she spake, and in her eyes did burn
The fires of hate, the King's face had waxed stern,
And ere her bitter speech was fully o'er,
He had arisen, and from off the floor
Had gat his proven sword into his hand,
And eager by the trembling Queen did stand,
And cried, "Nay, hold! for surely I know well
What tale it is thy lips to-night would tell;
Therefore my sword befits me, the tried friend
That many a troublous thing has brought to end.
Yet fear not, for another friend have I
To help me deal with this new villany,
Even the godlike man Bellerophon;
So with one word thy heavy task is done.
O Sthenobœa, speak the name of him
Who wrought this deed, then let that name wax dim
Within thy mind till it is dead and past;
For, certes, yesterday he saw the last
Of setting suns his doomed eyes shall behold."

Pale as a corpse she waxed, and stony cold
Amidst these words; silent awhile she was
After the last word from the King did pass,
But in a low voice at the last she said:
"Yea, for this deed of his must he be dead?
And must he be at peace, because he strove
To take from me honour, and peace, and love?
Must a great King do thus? or hast thou not
Some lightless place in mighty Argos got

Where nought can hap to break the memory
Of what he hoped in other days might be;
For great he has been, and of noble birth
As any man who dwelleth on the earth.
Thou hast forgotten that the dead shall rest,
Whate'er they wrought on earth of worst or best."

But the King gazed upon her gloomily,
And said, "Nay, nay;—the man shall surely die—
His hope die with him, is it not enow?
But no such mind I bear in me as thou,
Who speakest not as a great Queen should speak,
But rather as a girl made mad and weak
By hope delayed and love cast back again,
Who knoweth not her words are words and vain.
Content thee, thou art loved and honoured still—
Speak forth the name of him who wrought the ill,
For I am fain to meet Bellerophon,
So that we twain may do what must be done."

He spake, but mid the tumult of her mind
She heard him not, and deaf she was and blind
To all without, nor knew she if her feet
The marble cold or red-hot iron did meet.
She moved not and she felt not, but a sound
Came from her lips, and smote the air around
With slow hard words:
"Ah! thou hast named him then
Twice in this hour alone of earthly men;
That same Bellerophon, that all folk love,
In manly wise this morn against me strove!"

Ah, how the world was changed, as she went by
The King, bewildered with new misery—
Ah, and how little time it was agone
When all that deed of hers was not yet done,
When yet she might have died for him, and made
A little love her lonely tomb to shade
Spring up within his heart—when hope there was
Of many a thing that yet might come to pass—
And now, and now—those spoken words must be
A part of her, an unwrought misery
That would not let her rest till all was o'er,
Nay, nay, no rest upon the shadowy shore.

Slowly she left the chamber, none the less
With measured steps her feet the floor did press
As a Queen's should, nor fainted she at all,
But straight unto the door 'twixt wall and wall
She went, and still perchance had forced a smile
Had she met any one; and all the while

Set in such torment as men cannot name,
If she did think, wondered that still the same
Were all things round her as they had been erst—
That the house fell not—that the feet accurst
To carry her yet left no sign in blood
Of where the wretchedest on earth had stood—
That round about her still her raiment clung—
That no great sudden pain her body stung,
No inward flame her false white limbs would burn,
Or into horror all her beauty turn—
That still the gentle sounds of night were there
As she had known them: the light summer air
Within the thick-leaved trees, as she passed by
Some open window, and the nightbird's cry
From far; the gnat's thin pipe about her head,
The wheeling moth delaying to be dead
Within the taper's flame—yea, certainly
Shall things about her as they have been be,
And even that a torment now has grown.
Yet must she reap the grain that she has sown;
No thought of turning back was in her heart,
No more in those past days can she have part;
Nay, when her glimmering bower she came unto,
She muttered through the dusk, "As I would do
So have I done—so would I do again."

Lo, thus in unimaginable pain
Leave we her now, and to the King turn back;
Who stood there overwhelmed by sudden lack
Of what he leaned on—with his life left bare
Of a great pleasure that was growing there.
A storm of rage swept through his heart, to think
That he of such a cup as this must drink;
For if he doubted aught, this was his doubt,
That all the tale was not told fully out—
That for Bellerophon the Queen's great scorn
And loathing was a thing but newly born—
That bitter hate was but a lover's hate,
Which even yet beneath the hand of fate
Might turn to hottest love. He groaned thereat,
And staggering back, upon the bed he sat;
His bright sword from his hand had fallen down
When that last dreadful word at him was thrown,
And now, with head sunk 'twixt his hands, he sought
Some outlet from the weary girth of thought
That hemmed him in.
                      "And must I slay him then,
Him whom I loved above all earthly men?
Behold, if now I slept here, and next morn,
Ere the day's memory should be fully born
From out of sleep, men came and said to me,

'Sire, the Corinthian draweth nigh to thee,'
My first thought would be joy that he had come.
And yet I am a King, nor shall my home
Become a brothel before all men's eyes.
He who drinks deadly poison surely dies,
And he hath drunk, and must abide the end.
Yet hath the image of him been my friend—
What shall I do? Not lightly can I bear
The voice of men about these things to hear;
'He trusted him, he thought himself right wise
To look into men's souls through lips and eyes—
Behold the end!—' Yea, and most certainly
I will not bear once more his face to see;
Nor in the land where he was purified
Shall grass or marble by his blood be dyed,
Since he must go—green grew a bough of spring
Amidst the barren death of many a thing;
Not barren it, since poison fruits it bore—
Behold now, I, who loved my life of yore,
Begin to weary that I e'er was born;
But let it pass—rather let good men mourn;
Great men, the earth's salt, wear their lives away
In weeping for the ne'er-returning day:
For surely all is good enough for me.
"And yet alas! what truth there seemed in thee—
What can I do? Might he not die in war?
Nay, but at peace through him my borders are.
He shall not die here—the deep sea were good
To hide the story of his untamed blood—
Or, further—O thou fool, that so must make
My life so dull, e'en for a woman's sake!
There in that land, then, shall thy bones have rest
Beneath the sod her worshipped feet have pressed.
In Lycia shalt thou die; her father's hand
Shall draw the sword, or his lips give command
To make an end of thee—So shall it be,
And that swift Phrygian ready now for sea
Shall bear thee hence—Would I had known thee not;
A new pain hast thou been—a heavy lot
My life in early morn to me shall seem,
When I have dreamed that all was but a dream,
And waked to truth again and lonely life.
"Let be; now must I forge the hidden knife
Against thee, and I would the thing were done.
Thou mayst not die so; thou art such an one
As the Gods love, whatever thou mayst do,
Perchance they pay small heed to false or true
In such as we are. But the lamps burn low,
The night wears, grey the eastern sky doth grow;
I must forget thee; fellow, fare thee well,
Who might have turned my feet from lonely hell!"

So saying, slowly, as a man who needs
Must do a deed that woe and evil breeds,
He rose, and took his writing tools to him.
And ere the day had made the tapers dim,
Two letters with his own hand had he made,
And open was the first one, and it said
'These words:
Unto the wise Bellerophon—
To Lycia the Gods call thee, O my son;
So when thou hast this letter in thine hand,
Abide no longer in the Argive land
Than if thou fleddest some avenging man,
But make good speed to that swift Phrygian
Who for the southlands saileth this same day.
Take thou this gold for furtherance and stay,
And this for his reward who rules the heel,
And for a token show him this my seal.
This casket to the Lycian king bear forth,
That hath in it a thing of greatest worth;
And let no hand be laid on it but thine
Till in Jobates' hands its gold doth shine.
Then bid him mind how that he had of me
When last I saw his face the fellow key
To that which in mine hands doth open it—

Awhile the King had stayed when this was writ,
And on the gathering greyness of the morn
Long fixed his eyes, unseeing and forlorn,
Then o'er the tablets moved his hand again.

Mayst thou do well among these outland men.
Perchance my face thou never more shalt see,
Perchance but little more remains to thee
Of thy loved life—thou wert not one to cry
Curses on all because life passeth by.
If woe befalls thee there, think none the less
That I erewhile have wrought thee happiness;
Farewell! and ask thou not to see me first:
Life worsens here, and ere it reach the worst,
Unto the Jove that may be would I speak
To help my people, wandering blind and weak.

Another letter by the King's side lay,
But closed and sealed; so in the twilight grey
Now did he rise, and summoned presently
A slumbering chamberlain that was thereby,
And bade him toward the treasury lead, and take
Two leathern bags for that same errand's sake;
So forth the twain went to that golden place;
But when they were therein, a mournful face

Still the King seemed to see, e'en as it was
When he from room to room with him did pass
Who now had wronged him; then the gold waxed dim,
For bitter pain his vexed heart wrought for him,
And filled with unused tears his hard wise eyes.
But choking back the thronging memories,
He laid the letter that he erst did hold
Within a casket wrought of steel and gold,
Which straight he locked; then bade his fellow fill
The bags he bore from a great golden hill,
Then to his room, made cold with morn, returned;
And since for change and some swift deed he yearned,
He bade his chamberlain bring hunter's weed,
And saddle him straightway his fleetest steed:
"And see," said he, "before the Prince arise
Ye show this letter to his waking eyes,
And give into his hands these things ye see;
And make good speed, the time grows short for me."
So spake he, and there grew on him a thought
That thither might Bellerophon be brought
Ere he could get him gone; and therewithal
At last the low sun topped the garden-wall,
And o'er the dewy turf long shadows threw;
Then, being new clad, the porch he hurried to,
And paced betwixt its pillars feverishly,
Until he heard the horse-boys' cheery cry
And the sharp clatter of the well-shod feet;
Then he ran out, the joyous steed to meet,
And mounted, and rode forth, he scarce knew where,
Until the town was passed, and 'twixt the fair
Green corn-fields of the June-tide he drew rein,
To ponder on his life, so spoiled and vain.

But when Bellerophon awoke that morn,
Weary he felt, as though he long had borne
Some heavy load, and his perplexed heart
Must chide the life wherein he had a part.
But ere he gat him down to meet the day
With its new troubles, 'thwart his weary way
Was come that chamberlain, who bade him read,
And say what other thing he yet might need.
He read, and knit his anxious brows in thought,
For in his mind great doubt that letter brought
If yet he were in friendship with the King;
And therewith came a dark imagining
Of unseen dangers, and great anger grew
Within his soul, as if the worst were true
Of all he thought might be; and in his mind
It was, that going, he might leave behind
A bitter word to pay for broken troth:
And still the King's man saw that he was wroth,

And watched him curiously, till he had read
The letter thrice, but nought to him he said.
At last he spake, "Sir, even as the King
Now bids me, will I make no tarrying;
And as I carne to Argos, even so,
Unfriended, bearing nothing, will I go;
And few farewells are best to-day, I deem,
For like a banished man I would not seem
Among these folk that love me: get we gone,
And tell the King his full will shall be done."

So forth they ride, and ever as the way
Lengthened behind them, and the summer day
Grew hotter on the lovely teeming earth,
The fresh soft air and sounds and sights of mirth
Wrought on Bellerophon, until it seemed
That things might not be e'en as he had deemed
At first. "What thoughts are mine; have I not had
Gifts from his hands—hath he not made me glad
When I was sorry? Therefore will I take
What chance there lies herein for honour's sake.
Nay, more, and may not friendship lie herein?—
May he not drive me forth from shame and sin
And evil fate? Well, howsoe'er it is,
But little evil do I see in this:
Yea, I may see his face again once more,
And crowned with honour come back to this shore,
For now I fear nought—if he thinks to see
Some evil thing that nowise is in me,
Another day the truth of all will show.
Let pass, again from out the place I go
Wherein the sport of fortune I have tried;
If it has failed me, yet the world is wide
And I am young. Now go I forth alone
To do what in my life must needs be done,
And in my own hands lies my fate, I think,
And I shall mix the cup that I must drink:
So be it; thus the world is merrier,
And I shall be a better man than here."

Amid these thoughts, unto the ship he came,
And higher yet sprang up the new-stirred flame
Of great desires when first he saw the sea
Leap up against her black sides lovingly,
And heard the sails flap, and the voice of folk,
Who at the sight of him in shouts outbroke,
Since they withal were eager to be gone.
And now were all things done that should be done;
The money rendered up, the King's seal shown,
Unto the master all his will made known,
And on the deck stood the Corinthian.

As up the mast clattering the great rings ran,
And back the hawser to the ship was cast,
The helmsman took the tiller, and at last
The head swung round, trimly the great sail drew,
The broad bows pierced the land of fishes through,
Unheard the red wine fell from out the cup
Into the noisy sea; and then rose up
The cloud of incense-smoke a little way,
But driven from the prow, with the white spray
It mingled, and a little dimmed the crowd
Of white-head braves; then rose the sea-song loud,
While on the stern still stood Bellerophon,
Bidding farewell to what of life was gone,
Pensive, but smiling somewhat to behold
The lengthening wake, and field, and hill, and wold,
And white-walled Argos growing small astern,
That he the pleasure of the gods might learn.

But when the King's man, with a doubtful smile,
Had watched the parting sails a little while,
He turned about, revolving many things
Within his mind, of the weak hearts of kings,
Because the Prince's glory seemed grown dim,
And nowise grand this parting seemed to him;
"For day-long leave-taking there should have been,"
He grumbled, "and fair tables well beseen
Should have been spread the gilded ship anigh,
And many a perfect beast been slain thereby
Unto the gods—Had this Bellerophon
Too great fame for the King of Argos won?
I will be lowly, for no little bliss
I have in Argos, a good place it is—
Or else what thing has happed?"
Howe'er it was,
Slowly again to Argos did he pass,
And here and there he spake upon that day
Of how Bellerophon had gone away,
Perchance as one who would no more return;
And sore hearts were there, who thereat must yearn
To see the face that let a weak hope live;
And folk still doomed with many things to strive,
Who found him helpful—few indeed were there
Who did not pray that well he still might fare
Whereso he was, and few forgot him quite
For many a day and many a changing night.
But Sthenobœa, when she knew that morn
That she was not alone of love forlorn,
But of the thing too that fed love in her,
Yet coldly at the first her lot did bear
In outward seeming: in no other wise
She sat among her maids than when his eyes

Had first met hers. "No babble shall there be
In this fool's land concerning him and me.
Gone is he,—let him die and be forgot:
Cold is my heart that yesterday was hot,
Quenched is the fervent flame of yesterday;
Past is the time when I had cast away,
If he had bidden me, name, and fame, and all:
Now in this dulls world e'en let things befall
As they are fated; I am stirred no more
By any hap—hope, hate, and love are o'er."
So spake she in the morn, when, still a Queen,
She sat among her folk as she had been,
Dreaded, unloved; yet as the day wore on
She felt as though it never would be done.
And now she took to wandering restlessly,
And set her face to go unto the sea,
But soon turned back, and through the palace ranged,
And thought she thought not of him, and yet changed
Her face began to grow; and if she spoke,
As one untroubled, aught unto her folk,
Her speech grew wild and broken ere its end;
And as about the place she still did wend,
More than its wonted chill her presence threw
On those who of her coming footsteps knew—
Yea, as she passed by some, she even thought
A look like pity to their eyes was brought,
And then, amidst her craving agony,
Must she grow red with wrath that such could be.

Now came the night, and she must cast aside
All semblance of her coldness and her pride,
And find the weary night was longer yet
Than was the day, and harder to forget
The thoughts that came therewith. How can I tell
In any words the torment of that hell,
That she for her own soul had fashioned so,
That from it never any path did go
To lands of rest, no window was therein,
Through which there shone a hope of happier sin;
But close the fiery walls about her glared,
And on one dreadful picture still she stared,
Intent on that desire, that dreadful love,
The dullness of her savage heart that clove
With wasting fire, a bane to her, and all
Who in the net of her vain life might fall.

The next day wore, and thereto followed night,
And changed through dark and dusk and dawn to light;
And when at last high-risen was the sun,
The women came to do what should be done
In the Queen's chamber: water for the bath

They brought, and dainties such as Venus hath;
Gold combs, embroidered cloths, pearl-threaded strings,
Such unguents as the hidden river brings
Through strange-wrought caverns down into a sea
Where seldom any keel of man may be;
Fine Indian webs, the work of many a year,
And incense that the bleeding tree doth bear
Lone in the desert;—yea, and fear withal
Of what new thing upon that day might fall
From her they served, for on the day now dead
Wild words, strange threatenings had her writhed lips said.
But when within the chamber door they were,
A new hope grew within them, a new fear,
For empty 'neath the golden canopy
The bed lay, and when one maid drew anigh,
She saw that all untouched the linen was
As for that night; so when it came to pass
That in no chamber of that house of gold
Might any one the Lycian's face behold,
Nor any sign of her, then therewithal
To others of the household did they call,
And asked if they had tidings of the Queen;
And when they found that she had not been seen
Since at the end of day to bed she passed,
Within their troubled minds the thing they cast,
And thus remembered that at whiles of late
She had been wont the rising sun to wait
Within the close below her bower; so then
They called together others, maids and men,
And passed with troubled eyes adown the stair;
And coming to the postern-door that there
Led out into the pleasance, that they found
Still open, and thereby upon the ground,
And on a jagged bough of creeping vine,
Gold threads they saw, and silken broidery fine,
That well they knew torn from the Lycian's gown;
Therewith with hasty feet were trodden down
The beds of summer flowers that lay between
The outer wicket of that garden green
And the bower-door—feet that had heeded nought
By what wild ways they to their end were brought;
Then by the gate where the faint sweetbriar-rose
Grew thick about the edges of the close,
Had one pushed through their boughs in such a way
That fragments of a dainty thin array
Yet fluttered on the thorns in the light breeze,
Nor might they doubt who once had carried these.
But when the pleasance-gate they had passed through,
At first within the lingering strip of dew
Beneath the wall, footprints they well could see;
But as the shadow failed them presently,

And little could the close-cropped summer grass
Tell them of feet that might have chanced to pass
Thereby before the dawn, their steps they stayed,
And this and that thing there betwixt them weighed
With many words; then splitting up their band,
Some took the way unto the well-tilled land,
Some seaward went, and some must turn their feet
Unto the wood: yet did not any meet
A further sign; and though some turned again
To tell the tale at once, yet all in vain
Did horsemen scour the country far and wide,
And vainly was the sleuth-hounds' mettle tried—
Gone was the Lycian, and in such a guise
That silence seemed the best word for the wise.
But many a babbling tongue in Argos was,
Who for no gold had let such matters pass;
And some there were who, mindful of her face
As down the street she passed in queenly grace,
Said that some god had seen her even as they,
And with no will that longer she should stay
Midst dying men, had taken her to his home—
"And we are left behind," they said; but some,
Who had been nigher to her, said that she,
Smitten by some benign divinity
Who loved the world and lovely Argos well,
Had fled with changed heart far from man to dwell—
Yea, and might be a goddess even yet.
But other folk, well ready to forget
Her bitter soul, and well content to bear
The changed life that she erst had filled with care,
Smiled, and said yea to better and to worse,
But inly thought that many a heart-felt curse
Her careless ears had heard upon the earth
Had not returned to where it had its birth.

The Gods are kind, and hope to men they give
That they their little span on earth may live,
Nor yet faint utterly; the Gods are kind,
And will not suffer men all things to find
They search for, nor the depth of all to know
They fain would learn: and it was even so
With Sthenobœa; for a fisher old
That day a tale unto his carline told,
E'en such as this:
"When I last night had laid
The boat up 'neath the high cliff, and had made
All things about it trim, and left thee here,
Even as thou knowest, I set out to bear
Those mullets unto Argos. Nought befell
At first whereof is any need to tell,
But when the night had now grown very old,

And, as my wont is, I was waxing bold,
And thinking of the bright returning day,
That drives the sprites of wood and wave away,
As the path leads, I entered the beech-wood
Which, close to where the ancient palace stood,
Clothes the cliff's edge; I entered warily,
Yet thought no evil thing therein to see.
Scarce lighter than dark night it was therein,
Though swift without the day on night did win.
So I went on, I say, and had no fear,
So nigh to day; but getting midmost, where
Thinner it grows and lighter, toward the sea,
I stayed my whistling, for it seemed to me
The wind moaned louder than it should have done,
Because of wind without was well-nigh none.
When I stood still it ended, and again,
E'en as I moved, I seemed to hear it plain.
Trembling, I stopped once more, and heard indeed
A sound as though one moaned in bitter need,
Clearer than was the moaning of the surf,
Now muffled by a rising bank of turf
On the cliff's edge; fear-stricken, yet in doubt,
Through the grey glimmer now I peered about,
And turned unto the sea: then my heart sank,
For by the tree the nighest to that bank
A white thing stood, like, as I now could see,
The daughters of us sons of misery,
Though such I deemed her not—and yet had I
No will or power to turn about and fly;
And now it moaned and moaned, and seemed to writhe
Against the tree its body long and lithe.
Long gazed I, while still colourless and grey,
But swift enow, drew on the dawn of day;
But as I trembled there, at last I heard
How in a low voice it gave forth this word:

"What say'st thou?—'Live on still—I loved thee not
The while I lived; my bane from thee I got:
And canst thou think that I shall love thee, then,
Where no will is, or power to sons of men?'
I know not, thou mayst hate me, yet I come
That I may look on thee in that new home
My hands built for thee: if the priests speak truth,
What heart thou hast may yet be stirred by ruth,
When thy changed eyes behold the traitorous Queen
Tormented for the vile thing she has been—
If, as the books say, e'en such ways they have
As we on this explored side of the grave.
Yea, thou mayst pity then mine agony,
When no more evil I can do to thee.
Here on the earth I could not weep enow,

Or show thee all my misery here, and thou
Must ever look upon me as a Queen,
Thy mistress and thy fear. Couldst thou have seen
My weary ways upon this long, long night—
Couldst thou behold the coming day's new sight,
When round this tree the folk come gathering
To see the wife and daughter of a King,
Slain by her own hand, and in such a wise—
O thou I hoped for once, might not thine eyes
Have softened had they seen me shivering here,
Alone, unholpen, sick with my first fear,
Beat down by coming shame, and mocked by these
Gay fluttering rags of dainty braveries
That decked my state; by gold, and pearl, and gem,
Over my wretched breast, set in the hem
This night has torn, and o'er my bleeding feet;
Mocked by this glittering girdle, nowise meet
To do the hangman's office?—Couldst thou see
That even so I needs must think of thee—
Whom I have slain, whose eyes I have made blind,
Whose feet I stayed that me they might not find,
That I might not be helped of any one?

"The day was dawning when her words were done,
And to her waist I saw her set her hand,
And take the girdle thence, and therewith stand
With arms that moved above her head a space
Within the tree; and still she had her face
Turned from me, and I stirred not, minding me
Of tales of treacherous women of the sea,
The bane of men; but now her arms down fell,
And low she spake, yet could I hear her well:

"Thou bitter noose, that thus shalt end my days,
Rather than blame, shalt thou have thanks and praise
From all men: I have loved one man alone,
And unto him the worst deed have I done
Of all the ill deeds I have done on earth.
—I curse men not, although midst mocks and mirth,
They say, Rejoice, for Sthenobœa is dead.'

"I started forward as that word she said,
And she beheld me—face to face we met
In the grey light, nor shall I e'er forget
Those dreadful eyes, for such indeed I deem
A goddess high up in the heavens might seem
If she should learn that all was changed, to bring
Death on her head as on an earthly thing.
Alas! I have beheld men die ere now,
But eld or sickness sore their hearts did bow
With feebleness to bear what might betide,

Or else mid hope of name and fame they died,
And the world left them unawares; but she,
Full of hot blood and life yet, I could see
Was red-lipped as an image, and still had
Such smooth, soft cheeks as made beholders glad:
In many a feast and solemn sacrifice;
But yet such dreadful hate was in her eyes,
Such loathing of the ways of Gods and men,
Such gathered-up despair, that truly then
I shook so that my hands might hold no more
The staff and half-filled basket that I bore.

"But in a moment slowly she turned round,
And toward the rising swarded space of ground
Betwixt the beech-trees and the sea she went;
And I, although I knew well her intent,
Yet could not stir. There on the brink she stood;
A cool sea-wind now swept into the wood,
And drave her raiment round her; I could see,
E'en in the dawn, that jewelled broidery
Gleam in the torn folds of the glittering hem;
And now she raised her arms, I saw on them
Jewels again—Then sightless did I stand,
For such a cry I heard, as though a hand
Of fire upon her wasted heart was laid,
And to and fro, I deem, a space she swayed
Her slender body; then I moved at last,
And hurried toward the sheer cliff's edge full fast,
But ere I reached the green brink, was she gone;
And, hanging o'er the rugged edge alone,
With trembling hands, far down did I behold
A white thing meet the dark grey waves and cold;
For overhanging is that foreland high,
And little sand beneath its feet doth lie
At lowest of the tide, and on that morn
Against the scarped rock was the white surf borne.

"Ah, long I looked before I turned away.
No friend, indeed, was lost to me that day—
I knew her not but by the people's voice,
And they 'twas like hereat would e'en rejoice;
Yet o'er my heart a yearning passion swept,
And there where she had stood I lay and wept,
Worn as I am by care and toil and eld.

"But when I rose again, then I beheld
The girdle to the rough bough hanging yet,
And this I loosed and in my hand did get,
And lingered for a while; then went my way,
Nor thought at first if it were night or day,
So much I pondered on the tale so wrought,

What God to nothing such a life had brought.
"But when unto the city gate I came,
I found the thronging people all aflame
With many rumours, and this one they knew
Among all other guesses to be true,
That of the Queen nought knew her wonted place;
But unto me who still beheld that face
There in the beech-wood, idle and base enow
Seemed all that clamour carried to and fro—
Curses and mocks, and foolish laughter loud,
And gaping wonder of the empty crowd;
So in great haste I got my errand done,
And sold my wares e'en unto such an one
As first remembered he must eat to-day,
What king or queen soe'er had passed away.
Thus I returned, bringing the belt with me—
Behold it!—And what way seems best to thee
To take herein?—Poor are we: these bright stones
Would make us happier than the highest ones;
Yet danger hangs thereby, nor have I yet
My living from dead corpses had to get;
Nay, scarcely can I deem this Queen will be
At rest for long beneath the unquiet sea.
How say'st thou, shall I go unto the King,
And tell him every word about the thing
E'en as I know it?"
"Nay, nay, nay," she said,
"Certes but little do I fear the dead,
Yet think thou not to call the girdle thine;
With a man's death doth every gem here shine—
Our deaths the first: but do thou bide at home,
And let the King hear what may even come
To a King's ears; meddle thou not, nor make
With any such; still shall the brass pot break
The earthen pot—a lord is thanked for what
A poor man often has in prison sat.
But down the beach run thou thy shallop straight,
And from the net take off the heaviest weight,
And do this belt about it; and then go
And in the deepest of the green bay sow
This seed and fruit of love and wrath and crime,
And let this tale be dealt with by great time;
But 'twixt the sea and the green southering hill
We will abide, peaceful if toilsome still."

So was it done, and e'en as in her heart
Was hidden from all eyes her traitrous part,
So the sea hid her heart from all but those,
Who, having passed through all eld's dreamy doze,
Died with their tale untold.

Time passed away,
And dimmer grew her name day after day;
And the fair place, where erst her eyes had chilled
Sweet laughter into silence, now was filled
By folk who, midst of fair life slipping by,
No longer had her deeds in memory;
There where she once had dwelt mid hate and praise,
No smile, no shudder now her name could raise.


THE night had fallen or ere the tale was done,
And on the hall-floor now the pale moon shone
In fitful gleams, for the snow fell no more,
But ragged clouds still streamed the pale sky o'er:
A while they sat, and seemed to hear the sea
Beat 'gainst the ice-glazed cliffs unceasingly,
Though nought belike that noise was but the wind
Caught in some corner, half blocked-up and blind
With the white drift:—just so the mournfulness
Of the tale told out did their hearts oppress
With seeming sorrow, for a glorious life
Twisted awry and crushed dead in the strife
Long ages past; while yet more like it was
That with the old tale o'er their souls did pass
Shades of their own dead hopes, and buried pain
By measured words drawn from its grave again,
Though no more deemed a strange unheard-of thing
Made but for them; as when their hearts did cling
To those dead hopes of things impossible,
While their tale's ending yet was left to tell.

Still the hard frost griped all things bitterly,
And who of folk might now say when or why
The earth should change and spring come back again.
Spring clean forgotten, as amidst his pain
Some hapless lover's chance unmeaning kiss
Given unto lips that never shall be his
In time long passed, ere bitter knowledge came,
And cherished love was grown a wrong and shame.
Yet mid the dead swoon of the earth, the days
'Gan lengthen now, and on the hard-beat ways
No more the snow drave down; and, spite of all,
The goodman's thoughts must needs begin to fall
Upon the seed hid in the dying year,
And he must busy him about his gear;
And in the city, at the high noon, when
The faint sun glimmered, sat the ancient men,
With young folk gathered round about once more,

Who heeded not the east wind's smothered roar,
Since unto most of them for mere delight
Were most things made, the dull days and the bright;
And change was life to them, and death a tale
Little believed, that chiefly did avail
To quicken love and make a story sweet.

Now the old Swabian's glittering eyes did meet
A maiden's glance, who reddened at his gaze,
Whereon a pleasant smile came o'er his face,
As from his pouch a yellow book he drew
And spake:
"Of many things the wise man knew,
The man who wrote this; many words he made
Of haps that still perchance for great are weighed
There in the East: how kings were born and died,
And how men lied to them, and how they lied,
And how they joyed in doing good and ill:
Now mid the great things that his book do fill,
Here is a tale, told, saith he, by a crone
At some grand feast forgotten long agone,
Which may perchance scarce be of much less worth
Than tales of deeds that reddened the green earth—
Fools' deeds of men, who well may be to you
As good as nameless, since ye never knew
The ways of those midst whom they lived erewhile,
And what their hearts deemed good, or nought, and vile."

THE RING GIVEN TO VENUS

ARGUMENT

**There was a man in a certain great city who on his wedding- day unwittingly gave his spousal-ring to the Goddess Venus, and for this cause trouble came upon him, till in the end he got his ring back again.**

The story of this chronicle
Doth of an ancient city tell,
Well built upon a goodly shore;
The wide lands stretched behind it bore
Great wealth of oil and wine and wheat;
The great sea carried to its feet
The dainty things of many lands;
There the hid miners' toiling hands
Dragged up to light the dull blue lead,
And silver white, and copper red,
And dreadful iron; many a time
The sieves swung to the women's rhyme
O'er gravelly streams that carried down

The golden sand from caves unknown;
Dark basalt o'er the sea's beat stood,
And porphyry cliffs as red as blood;
From the white marble quarries' edge
Down to the sweeping river's sedge,
Sheep bore the web that was to be;
The purple lay beneath the sea,
The madder waved in the light wind,
The woad-stalks did the peasant bind
That were to better his worn hood;
And ever, amid all things good,
Least of all things this lucky land
Lacked for the craftsman's cunning hand.

So richer grew that city still
Through many a year of good and ill,
And when the white beasts drew the car
That bore their banner to the war,
From out the brazen gates enwrought
With many a dreamer's steadfast thought,
An hundred thousand men poured out
To shake the scared earth with their shout.

Now little will your wonder be
That mid so great prosperity
Enough there was of ill and sin;
That many folk who dwelt therein
Lived evil lives from day to day,
Nor put their worst desires away.
But as in otherwise indeed
Of God's good pardon had they need,
And were herein as other folk,
So must they bear this added yoke,
That rife was wicked sorcery there;
And why I know not; if it were
Wrought by a lingering memory
Of how that land was wont to be
A dwelling-place, a great stronghold
Unto the cozening gods of old.
It might be so; but add thereto
That of all men life's sweets they knew,
That death to them was wholly bad,
So that perchance a hope they had
That yet another power there was
Than His who brought that death to pass.

Howe'er that may be, this I know,
That in that land men's lives were so
That they in trouble still must turn
Unholy things and strange to learn:
Had this man mid the infidel

A lost son, folk might buy and sell;
Did that one fear to pass his life
With unrewarded love at strife;
Or had he a long-missing keel;
Or was he with the commonweal
In deadly strife; or perchance laid
Abed, by fever long downweighed;
Or were his riches well-nigh done;—
Love, strife, or sickness, all was one,
This seemed the last resource to them,
To catch out at the strange-wrought hem
Of the dark gown that hid away
The highest ill from light of day.
Yea, though the word unspoken was,
And though each day the holy mass
At many an altar gold-arrayed
From out the painted book was said,
And though they doubted nought at all
Of how the day of days must fall
At last upon the earth, and range
All things aright that once seemed strange;
Yet Evil seemed so great a thing
That 'neath its dusk o'ershadowing wing
They needs must cower down; now at least
While half a god and half a beast
Man seemed; some parley must they hold
With God's foe, nor be overbold
Before the threatening of a hand
Whose might they did not understand,
Though oftentimes they felt it sore:
And through this faithlessness, the more
Ill things had power there, as I deem,
Till some men's lives were like a dream,
Where nought in order can be set,
And nought worth thence the soul may get,
Or weigh one thing for what it is;
Yea, at the best mid woe and bliss,
Some dreamlike day would come to most.

Now this great city still made boast
That, mid her merchant's, men there were
Who e'en from kings the bell might bear
For wealth and honour: and I think
That no men richer wines might drink,
Were better housed, or braver clad,
Or more of all the world's joy had
Than their rich men; that no king's door
Could show forth greater crowds of poor,
Who lacked for bread and all things good,
Than in that land a merchant's could—
Yea, rich indeed 'mongst all were they.

Now on a certain summer day
One of their fairest palaces,
A paradise midst whispering trees,
Beyond its wont was bright and fair;
Great feast did men get ready there,
Because its young lord, lately come
Back from the eastlands to his home,
That day should wed a lovely maid;
He, for that tide too long delayed,
A lading of great rarities
Had brought to dazzle those sweet eyes;
So had you wandered through the house
From hall to chamber amorous,
While in the minster church hard by,
Mid incense smoke and psalmody,
The gold-clad priest made one of twain,
So wandering had you tried in vain
To light on an uncomely thing;
Such dyes as stain the parrot's wing,
The May-flowers or the evening sky,
Made bright the silken tapestry;
And threaded pearls therein were wrought,
And emeralds from far eastlands brought
To deck the shapes of knight and king;—
His maybe who of old did sing
God's praises 'twixt the shield and spear,
Or his the Trojan folk did fear.
Or from the silken mimicry
Of fair Cassandra might you see
Oileus the red ruby tear,
As he her snowy breast made bare;
Since woe itself must there be sweet
For such a place to be made meet.

If such things hid the marble walls,
What wonder that the swift footfalls
Were dulled upon the marble floor
By silken webs from some far shore,
Whereon were pictured images
Of other beasts and other trees
And other birds than these men knew;
That from the vaulted ceilings' blue
Stars shone like Danaë's coming shower,
Or that some deftly painted bower
Thence mocked the roses of that day?
Full many a life had passed away,
And many a once young hand grown old,
Dealing with silk and gems and gold,
Through weary days and anxious nights,
That went to fashion those delights,

Which added now small bliss indeed
To those who pleasure had to meed
Upon a day when all were glad:
Yet when the Church all dues had had,
And the street, filled with minstrelsy,
Gave token of the twain anigh;
When through the hall-doors, open wide,
Streamed in the damsels of the bride;
When the tall brown-cheeked bridegroom came
Flushed with hot love and pride and shame,
And by the hand his love led on,
Who midst that glorious company shone
Like some piece of the pale moonlight
Cut off from quietness and night,—
Then all these dainty things in sooth
Seemed meet for such an hour of youth;
And vain were words such joy to stay;
And deathless seemed that little day,
And as a fitful hapless dream
The past and future well might seem.

What need to tell how sea and earth
Had been run through to make more mirth,
For folk already overglad—
What cunning pageants there they had;
What old tales acted o'er again,
Where grief and death glad folk did feign,
Who deemed their own joy still would bide;
What old songs sung wherein did hide
Meet meanings for that lovesome day;
What singing of the bridal lay
By a fair, soft-voiced trembling maid,
Like to the Goddess well arrayed,
Who, dreaded once, was grown to be
A pageant-maker's imagery?
Why make long words of that sweet band
Who scattered flowers from slender hand,
And brought the garlands forth? How tell
What music on the feasters fell,
So sweet and solemn, that from mirth
O'erstrained well-nigh must tears have birth?
Nay, let all pass, and deem indeed
That every joyance was their meed
Wherewith men cheat themselves to think
That they of endless joy may drink;
That every sense in turn must bear
Of o'er-sweet pleasure its full share,
Till for awhile the very best
They next might gain seemed utter rest,
And of some freshness were they fain.
So then the garden did they gain,

And wandered there by twos and threes
Amidst the flowers, or 'neath the trees,
Sat, keeping troublous thoughts at bay.
So fared they through the earlier day;
But when the sun did now decline,
And men grew graver for the wine
That erst such noble tales had told;
And maids no more were free and bold,
But reddened at the words half-said,
While round about the rebecks played;
Then needs must the feastmasters strive
Too pensive thoughts away to drive,
And make the sun go down with mirth
At least upon that spot of earth;
So did the minstrel men come in,
And tale-tellers the lay begin,
And men by fabled woes were stirred,
Or smiling their own follies heard
Told of some other; and withal
Here did the dice on table fall,
Here stout in arms the chess-king stood;
There young men stirred their sluggish blood
With clattering sword and buckler play,
There others on the daisies lay
Above the moat, and watched their quill
Make circles in the water still,
Or laughed to see the damsel hold
Her dainty skirt enwrought with gold
Back from the flapping tench's tail,
Or to his close-set dusky mail
With gentle force brought laughingly
The shrinking finger-tip anigh.

Midst these abode a little knot
Of youths and maidens, on a spot
Fenced by a cloister of delight,
Well wrought of marble green and white;
Wherein upon a wall of gold
Of Tristram was the story told,
Well done by cunning hands that knew
What form to man and beast was due;
Midmost, upon a space of green,
Half shaded from the summer sheen,
Half with the afternoon sun thrown
Upon its daisies glittering strewn,
Was gathered that fair company
Wherewith the bridegroom chanced to be,
Who through the cloister door must gaze
From time to time 'thwart the sun's blaze
On to a shaded space of grass
Whereon his new-wed maiden was,

Hearkening in seeming to a song
That told of some past love and wrong;
But as he strained his ear to catch
Across the wind some louder snatch
Of the sweet tune, new-coming folk
The sweet sight hid, the music broke;
Of these one maiden trimly girt
Bore in her gleaming upheld skirt
Fair silken balls sewed round with gold;
Which when the others did behold
Men cast their mantles unto earth,
And maids within their raiments' girth
Drew up their gown-skirts, loosening here
Some button on their bosoms clear
Or slender wrists, there making tight
The laces round their ankles light;
For folk were wont within that land
To cast the ball from hand to hand,
Dancing meanwhile full orderly;
So now the bridegroom with a sigh,
Struggling with love's quick-gathering yoke,
Turned round unto that joyous folk,
And gat him ready for the play.

Lovely to look on was the sway
Of the slim maidens 'neath the ball
As they swung back to note its fall
With dainty balanced feet; and fair
The bright outflowing golden hair,
As swiftly, yet in measured wise
One maid ran forth to gain the prize;
Eyes glittered and young cheeks glowed bright,
And gold-shod foot, round limb and light,
Gleamed from beneath the girded gown
That, unrebuked, untouched, was thrown
Hither and thither by the breeze;
Shrill, laughter smote the thick-leaved trees,
Familiar names clear voices cried,
Sweet sound rose up as sweet sound died,
And still the circle spread and spread,
As folk to all that goodlihead
Kept thronging in, till they must stay
A little while the eager play,
And now, for very breathlessness,
With rest the trodden daisies bless.
So now against the wall some leaned,
Some from amidst the daisies gleaned
The yellow trefoil, and the blue
Faint speedwell in the shade that grew;
Some panting sat and clasped their knees
With faces turned unto the breeze,

And midst them the new-corners stood,
With hair smooth yet and unstirred blood.

Laurence, the bridegroom, as the game
Unto this tide of resting came,
Turned idle eyes about, and met
An image in the grey wall set,
A thing he knew from early days:
There in a gilded carven place
Queen Venus' semblance stood, more fair
Than women whom that day did bear,
And yet a marvel for the life
Wherewith its brazen limbs were rife.
Not in that country was she wrought,
Or in those days; she had been brought
From a fair city far away,
Ruined e'en then for many a day;
Full many a tale had there been told
Of him who once that Queen did mould,
And all of these were strange to hear,
And dreadful some, and full of fear.
And now as Laurence gazed upon
That beauty, in the old days won
He knew not from what pain and toil,
Vague fear new-risen-up seemed to spoil
The summer joy; her loveliness
That hearts, long dead now, once did bless,
Grown dangerous, 'gan to lead his mind
On through a troublous maze and blind
Of unnamed thoughts, and silently,
With knitted brow, he drew anigh,
And midst the babbling close did gaze
Into the marvel of her face:
Till, with a sudden start, at last
His straying thoughts he seemed to cast
Aside, and laughed aloud, and said:

"O cold and brazen goodlihead,
How lookest thou on those that live?
Thou who, tales say, wert wont to strive
On earth, in heaven, and 'neath the earth,
To wrap all in thy net of mirth,
And drag them down to misery
Past telling—and didst thou know why?—
And what has God done with thee then,
That thou art perished from midst men
E'en as the things thou didst destroy,
Thy Paris and thy town of Troy,
And many a man and maid and town?
How is thy glory fallen adown,
That I, even I, must sigh for thee!"

So spake he, as the minstrelsy
Struck up once more a joyous strain,
And called them to the play again;
And therewithal he looked about,
In answer to the merry shout
That called on him by name to turn.
But even therewith the sun did burn
Upon his new-gained spousal-ring—
A wondrous work, a priceless thing,
Whereon, 'neath mulberries white and red,
And green leaves, lay fair Thisbe dead
By her dead love; the low sun's blaze
It caught now, and he fell to gaze
Thereon, and said at last:
"Perchance
The ball might break it in the dance,
And that an ugly omen were;
Nay, one to ward it well is here.
Thou, Goddess, that heardst Thisbe's vow,
From blind eyes gaze upon her now
Till I return mine own to claim;
And as thou mayst, bear thou the shame
Of being the handmaid to my love;
Full sure I am thou wilt not move."

Know that this image there did stand
With arm put forth and open hand,
As erst on Ida triumphing;
And now did Laurence set the ring
On the fourth finger fair and straight,
And laughing, "Thou mayst bear the weight,"
Turned back again unto the play.

To him slow passed the time away;
But when at last in purple shade
'Twixt wall and wall the grass was laid,
And he grew gladder therewithal,
Then weariness on folk 'gan fall;
The fifes left off their dancing tune,
And sang of lovers fain of June,
And thence that company 'gan go
By twos and threes with footsteps slow,
Pensive at end of mirthful day;
But from them Laurence turned away
Unto the carven dame, to take
The ring he wore for true-love's sake;—
Daylight it was, though broad and red
The sun was grown, and shadows led
Eastward with long lines o'er the grass—
Daylight, but what had come to pass?

Nearby those voices still he heard
In laugh and talk and careless word;
Upon his cheek the wind blew cold;
His own fair house he did behold
Changed nowise; from the little close
The scent of trodden grass arose—
How could it be a dream?—Yet there
She stood, the moveless image fair,
The little-noticed, oft-seen thing,
With hand fast closed upon his ring.

At first, in agony and haste,
A frantic minute did he waste
In pulling at the brazen hand,
That was as firm as rocks that stand
The day-long beating of the sea;
Then did he reel back dizzily,
And gaze at sky and earth and trees
Once more, as asking words from these
To ravel out his tale for him.
But now as they were waxing dim
Before his eyes, he heard his name
Called out, and therewith fear of shame
Brought back his heart and made him man.
Unto his fellows, pale and wan,
He turned, who, when they saw him so,
What thing might ail him fain would know,
For wild and strange he looked indeed;
Then stammered he, "Nay, nought I need
But wine, in sooth: John, mind'st thou not
How on the steaming shore and hot
Of Serendib a sting I gat
From some unseen worm, as we sat
Feasting one eve? Well, the black folk
E'en saved my life from that ill stroke,
By leech-craft; yet they told me then
I oft should feel that wound again,
Till I had fifty years or more:
This is a memory of that shore;
A thing to be right soon forgot."
And to himself, "If this is not
An empty dream, a cutting file
My ring therefrom shall soon beguile,
When, at the ending of the day,
These wearying guests have gone away."

Now unto supper all folk turned,
And 'neath the torches red gold burned,
And the best pageants of the day
Swept through the hall and said their say,

Departing e'en as men's lives go:
But though to Laurence slow and slow
Those hours must needs seem, none the less
He gave himself to mirthfulness,
At least in seeming; till at last
All guests from out the palace passed.
And now the short soft summer night
Was left at peace for their delight;
But Laurence, muffled up and hid,
Shrinking, betwixt his servants slid,
For now he had a little space
To come unto that mystic place,
Where still his ring he thought to see.
A file and chisel now had he,
And weighty hammer; yet withal
As he drew toward the cloister-wall,
Well-nigh he called himself a fool,
To go with cloak and blacksmith's tool,
And lay hard blows upon a dream;
For now in sooth he nigh must deem
His eyes had mocked him; reaching soon
That cloister by the broad high moon
He hurried through the door, and heard
All round the sound of June's brown bird
Above the voices of the night;
Trembling, he sprang into the light
Through the black arches of the place,
And stealing on stood face to face
With the old smiling image there,
And lowered to her fingers fair
His troubled, wild, and shrinking eyes,
And stretched his hand out to the prize:
His eyes, his hand, were there in vain.

Once more, as sure of coming gain,
As erst in Ida she did stand,
So stood she now; her open hand,
That late he saw closed round the ring,
Empty and bare of anything:
Gaping awhile he stood, for fear
Now made him think a voice to hear,
And see her change soon, and depart
From out her midst; but gathering heart,
He muttered, "Yet, what have I seen?
Should it not even thus have been,
If the closed hand was but a dream?
Of some guest worser must I deem;
Go, fool; thine own love waiteth thee."
Therewith he went, yet fearfully
Looked o'er his shoulder on the way,
And terror on his heart still lay.

Yet to his chamber at the last
He came, and to the floor he cast
His wrapping mantle, and alone
He strove to think of all things done,
And strove once more to bring again
The longing sweet, the joy and pain
That on that morn he called desire;
For wretched fear had dulled that fire:
And, whereas erewhile he had deemed
That life was joy, and it had seemed
A never-ending game to be,
A fair and rich eternity
Before him, now was it indeed
A troublous fight, where he should need
Help on the left hand and the right,
Nor yet so 'scape the certain night.

But mid these thoughts he heard withal
The chamberlain to pages call,
To bear the bridal wine to him;
And as he might he strove to dim
His anxious thought, and with a smile
The coming curious eyes beguile.
They entered now, and whiles that he
Drank from the gold cup feverishly,
The minstrels, ere his draught was done,
Struck up The King of England's Son,
And soon amid that ordered word
The lessening sound of feet he heard,
And then the song itself must die.
But from the bridechamber nearby
Now for a space rose clear and sweet
The damsels' song, Fair Marguerite;
And when that ended all was still,
And he with strained, divided will,
Trembling with love, yet pale with fear,
To the bridechamber door drew near,
Muttering some well-remembered charm
That erst had kept his soul from harm.
Yet misty seemed the place; the wall—
Its woven waters seemed to fall,
Its trees, its beasts, its loom-wrought folk,
Now seemed indeed as though they woke,
And moved unto him as he went.
The room seemed full of some strange scent;
And strains of wicked songs he heard,
And half-said God-denying word:
He reeled, and cried aloud, and strove
To gain the door that hid his love;
It seemed to him that, were he there,

All would again be calm and fair.
But in the way before his eyes
A cloudy column seemed to rise,
Cold, odorous, impalpable,
And a voice cried, "I love thee well,
And thou hast loved me ere to-night,
And longed for this o'ergreat delight,
And had no words therefor to pray.
Come, have thy will, and cast away
Thy foolish fear, thy foolish love,
Since me at least thou canst not move,
Now thou with ring hast wedded me:
Come, cast the hope away from thee
Wherewith unhappy brooding men
Must mock their threescore years and ten;
Come, thou that mockest me, I live!
How with my beauty canst thou strive?
Unhappy if thou couldst! for see
What depth of joy there is in me!"

Then round about him closed the mist;
It was as though his lips were kissed,
His body by soft arms embraced,
His fingers lovingly enlaced
By other fingers; until he
Midst darkness his own ring did see.

Nought else awhile; then back there came
New vision: as amidst white flame,
The flower-girt goddess wavered there,
Nor knew he now where they twain were,
Midst wild desire that nigh did rend
His changed heart; then there came an end
Of all that light and ecstasy;
His soul grew blind, his eyes could see;
And, moaning from an empty heart,
He saw the hangings blown apart
By the night wind, the lights flare red
In the white light the high moon shed
O'er all the place he knew so well,
And senseless on the floor he fell.

Ah, what a night to what a morn!
Ah, what a morrow black with scorn,
And hapless end of happy love!
What shame his helpless shame to prove!
For who, indeed, alone could bear
The dreadful shame, the shameful fear,
Of such a bridal? Think withal,
More trusted such a tale would fall
Upon those folks' ears than on most,

Who, as I said erst, saw a host
Of wild things lurking in the night;
To whom was magic much as right
As prayers or holy psalmody.

So nothing else it seemed might be,
When Laurence for three nights had striven
To gain the fair maid to him given,
But that her sire should know the thing
And help him with his counselling.
So, weary, wasted with his shame,
Unto his house the bridegroom came,
And when the twain were left alone
He told him how the thing had gone.
The old man doubted not the sooth
Of what he said, but, touched with ruth,
Yet spent no time in mourning vain.

"Son," said he, "idle were the pain
To seek if thou some deed hast wrought
Which on thine head this grief hath brought—
Some curse for which this doth atone,
Some laugh whereby is honour gone
From the dread powers unnameable:
Rather, who now can help thee well?"

"Small heed, my father," Laurence said,
"Gave I to such things, and small dread
To anything I could not see,
But it were God who fashioned me:
From witch-wives have I bought ere now
Wind-bags indeed, but yet did trow
Nothing therein, but dealt with these
My shipmen's clamour to appease."

"Well," said he, "that perchance is worse
For thee, yea, may have gained this curse.
But come, I know a certain man
Who in these things great marvels can,
And something of an age are we,
Yoke-fellows in astronomy—
A many years agone, alas!"

So therewithal the twain did pass
Toward the great church, and entered there,
And, going 'twixt the pillars fair,
Came to a chapel, where a priest
Made ready now the Holy Feast:
"Hist," said the old man, "there he is;
May he find healing for all this!
Kneel down, and note him not too much,

No easy man he is to touch."

So down upon the floor of stone
They knelt, until the mass was done,
Midst peasant folk, and sailors' wives,
Sore careful for their husbands' lives;
But when the mass was fully o'er
They made good haste unto the door
That led unto the sacristy:
And there a ring right fair to see
The old man to a verger gave
In token, praying much to have
With Dan Palumbus speech awhile:
The verger took it with a smile,
As one who says, 'Ye ask in vain;'
But presently he came again,
And said, "Fair sir, come hither then,
The priest will see you of all men!"

With eyes made grave by their intent
From out the lordly church they went
Into the precinct, and withal
They passed along the minster wall,
And heard amid the buttresses
The grey hawks chatter to the breeze,
The sanctus bell run down the wind;
Until the priest's house did they find,
Built 'neath the belfry huge and high,
Fluttered about perpetually
By chattering daws, and shaken well
From roof to pavement, when the bell
Flung out its sound o'er night or day.

"Sirs, Dan Palumbus takes his way
E'en now from out the sacristy,"
The verger said, "sirs, well be ye!
For time it is that I were gone."
Therewith he left the twain alone
Beside the door, and, sooth to say,
In haste he seemed to get away
As one afeard; but they bode there,
And round about the house did peer,
But found nought dreadful: small it was,
Set on a tiny plot of grass,
And on each side the door a bay
Brushed 'gainst the oak porch rent and grey;
A yard-wide garden ran along
The wall, by ancient box fenced strong;
And in the corner, where it met
The belfry, was a great yew set,
Where sat the blackbird-hen in spring,

Hearkening her bright-billed husband sing.
A peaceful place it should have been
For one who of the world had seen
O'er much, and quiet watch would keep
Over his soul awaiting sleep.

But now they heard the priest draw nigh,
And saw him and his shadow high
Wind round the wind-worn buttresses;
So coming by the last of these
He met them face to face: right tall
He was; his straight black hair did fall
About his shoulders; strong he seemed,
His eyes look far off, as he dreamed
Of other things than what they saw;
Strange lines his thin pale face did draw
Into a set wild look of pain
And terror. As he met the twain
He greeted well his ancient friend,
And prayed them within doors to wend.
Small was his chamber; books were there
Right many, and in seeming fair.
But who knows what therein might be
'Twixt board and board of oaken tree?

Palumbus bade them sit, and sat,
And talked apace of this and that,
Nor heeded that the youth spake wild,
Nor that his old friend coughed and smiled,
As ill at ease, while the priest spake,
Then from his cloak a purse did take,
And at the last pushed in his word
Edgewise, as 'twere. Palumbus heard
As one who fain had been born deaf,
Then rose and cried, "Thou fill'st the sheaf,
Thou fill'st the sheaf! this is my doom,
Well may the sexton make my tomb!"
And up and down he walked, muttering,
'Twixt closed teeth, many a nameless thing.

At last he stopped and said, "O ye,
I knew that ye would come to me,
And offer me great store of gold:
Full often good help have I sold,
And thus this tide should I have done;
But on this mountain of grey stone
I stood last night, and in my art
I dealt; and terror filled my heart,
And hope, and great uncertainty;
Therefore I deem that I shall die;
For cool and bold erst have I been,

Whatever I have heard and seen;
But the old Master of my fear
Seems afar now, and God grown near;
And soon I look to see his face.
Therefore, if but for a short space,
Would I be on his side, and do
A good deed; all the more for you;
Since thou art part of sweet days, friend,
That once we deemed would never end;
And in thine eyes meseems, O youth,
Kindness I see and hope and truth;
And thou and he may speak a word
For me unto my master's Lord:—
Well, I must reap that I did sow—
But take your gold again and go:
And thou for six days fast and pray,
And come here on the seventh day
About nightfall; then shalt thou learn
In what way doth the matter turn,
And fully know of time and place,
And be well armed thy foe to face."

So homeward doubtful went the twain,
And Laurence spent in fear and pain
The six long days; and so at last,
When the seventh sun was well-nigh past,
Came to that dark man's fair abode;
The grey tower with the sunset glowed,
The daws wheeled black against the sky
About the belfry windows high,
Or here and there one sank adown
The dizzy shaft of panelled stone;
And sound of children nigh the close
Was mingled with the cries of those;
And e'en as Laurence laid his hand
Upon the latch, and there did stand
Lingering a space, most startling clear
The sweet chime filled the evening air.
He entered mid the great bell's drone,
And found Palumbus all alone
Mid books laid open:
"Rest," said he;
"Time presses not for thee or me:
Surely shall I die soon enow."
Silent, with hands laid to his brow,
He sat then, nor did Laurence speak,
Fearing perchance some spell to break:
At last the priest caught up a book,
And from its leaves a letter took,
And unknown words there were on it
For superscription duly writ,

And sealed it was in solemn wise.
He said:
"Thou knowest where there lies
Five leagues hence, or a little less,
North of the town, a sandy ness
That shipmen call St. Clement's Head;
South of it dreary land and dead
Lies stretched now, and the sea bears o'er
Ruin of shingle evermore,
And saps the headland year by year,
And long have husbandmen had fear
Of its short-lived and treacherous soil,
And left it free from any toil.
There, with thy face turned toward the rand,
At the hill's foot take thou thy stand,
Just where the turf the shingle meets,
Wherewith the sea the marshland eats;
But seaward if thy face thou turn,
What I have learned then shalt thou learn
With like reward—watch carefully
And well, and a strange company
Shall pass thee as thou standest there,
And heed thee not—some foul some fair,
Some glad some sorry; rule thy heart,
And heed them nothing for thy part,
Till at the end of all thou seest
A great lord on a marvellous beast
Unnameable; on him cry out,
And he thereon shall turn about
And ask thy need; have thou no fear,
But give him what I give thee here,
And let him read, and thou shalt win
Thine happiness, and have no sin.
But as for me, be witness thou
That in the scroll I give thee now,
My death lies, and I know it well,
And cry to God against his hell."

In languid voice he spake as one,
Who knows the task that must be done,
And how each word from him should fall,
And gives no heed to it at all;
But here he stopped a little space,
And once more covered up his face;
But soon began his speech again
In a soft voice, and freed from pain:

"And for the folk that thou shalt see,
Whence cometh all that company,—
Marvel thou not thereat, for know
That this is sure; long years ago,

Leagues seaward of that barren place,
The temple of a glorious race,
Built with far mightier walls than these,
Stood fair midst groves of whispering trees.
Thence come these folk remembering
Their glory once so great a thing—
I have said: 'Could they be once more
As they have been,—but all is o'er,
What matters what is, what has been,
And what shall be, when I have seen
The last few hours of my last day?-
Depart.  Ah me, to cast away
Such power as I on earth have had!
I who could make the lover glad
Above his love's dead face, at least
A little while—now has all ceased
With that small scrap of black and white:
Think of me, God, midst thy delight,
And save me! yea, or do thy will!
For thou too hast beheld my skill."

The scroll did Laurence hold in hand,
And silent he a space did stand,
Gazing upon Palumbus, who
Sat open-eyed, as though he knew
Nought of what things were round about;
So, stealthily, and in great doubt
Of strange things yet to come to pass,
Did Laurence gain the darkening grass,
And through the precinct and the town
He passed, and reached the foreshores brown,
And gathered heart, and as he might
Went boldly forward through the night.
At first on his left hand uprose
Great cliffs and sheer, and, rent from those,
Boulders strewn thick across the strand,
Made weary work for foot and hand;
But well he knew the path indeed,
And scarce of such light had he need
As still the summer eve might shed
From the high stars or sunset dead.
Soft was the lovely time and fair,
A little sea-wind raised his hair,
That seemed as though from heaven it blew.
All sordid thoughts the sweet time slew,
And gave good hope such welcoming,
That presently he 'gan to sing,
Though still amid the quiet night
He could not hear his song aright
For the grave thunder of the sea
That smote the beach so musically,

And in the dim light seemed so soft
As each great wave was raised aloft
To fall in foam, you might have deemed
That waste of ocean was but dreamed,
And that the surf's strong music was
By some unknown thing brought to pass;
And Laurence, singing as he went,
As in some lower firmament,
Beneath the line that marked where met
The world's roof and the highway wet,
Could see a ship's light gleam afar
Scarce otherwise than as a star,
While o'erhead fields of thin white cloud
The more part of the stars did shroud.

So on he went, and here and there
A few rough fisher-caries there were,
Launching their ordered keels to sea
Eager to gain, if it might be,
The harbour-mouth with morning-light,
Or else some bird that flies by night
Wheeled round about with his harsh cry;
Or as the cliffs sank he could spy
Afar some homestead glittering
With high feast or some other thing.
Such gleams of fellowship had he
At first along the unquiet sea,
But when a long way off the town
The cliffs were wholly sunken down,
And on the marshland's edge he went,
For all sounds then the night-jar sent
Its melancholy laugh across
The sea-wind moaning for the loss
Of long-drowned lands, that in old time
Were known for great in many a clime.

But the moon rose, and 'neath its light,
Cloud-barred, the wide wastes came in sight,
With gleaming, sand-choked, reed-clad pools,
And marsh-lights for the mock of fools;
And o'er the waste beneath the moon
The sea-wind piped a dreary tune,
And louder grew, and the world then
No more seemed made for sons of men,
And summer seemed an empty name,
And harvest-time a mock and shame:
Such hopeless ruin seemed settled there,
On acres sunny once and fair.

But Laurence now could well behold
The sandy headland bare and bold

Against the sea, and stayed his feet
Awhile, to think how he should meet
These nameless things, his enemies,
The lords of terror and disease;
Then trembling, hastened on, for thought
Full many an image to him brought,
Once seen, with loathing cast aside,
But ready e'en for such a tide,
Come back with longing's added sting,
And whatso horrors time could bring.
Now thrusting all these thoughts apart
He hastened on with hardy heart,
Till on the doubtful place he stood
Where the sea sucked the pasture's blood,
And with back turned unto the sea
He strove to think right strenuously
Of this and that well-liking place;
The merry clamour of the chase,
Pageant of soldier or of priest,
Or market-place or crowded feast,
Or splintered spears for ladies' sake,
Until he 'gan to dream awake:
Then, midst of all his striving, still
His happiest thoughts must turn to ill,
As in a fevered, restless dream.
He thought about some flowery stream,
Himself in gilded boat thereon—
A livid cloud came o'er the sun,
A great wave swept from bank to bank;
Or flower-crowned amid friends he drank,
And as he raised the red wine up
Fell poison shrieked from out the cup;
The garland when his heart was full
He set upon a fleshless skull;
The lute turned to a funeral bell,
The golden door led down to hell.
Then back from dreams his soul he brought,
And of his own ill matters thought,
And found his fear the lesser grew
When all his heart therein he threw.

Yet awful was the time indeed,
And of good heart sore had he need:
The wind's moan louder than before,
Some wave cast higher up the shore,
The night-bird's brushing past his head,—
All little things grew full of dread;
Yet did he waver nought at all,
Or turn, for whatso thing might fall.

The moon was growing higher now,

The east wind had been strong to blow
The night sky clear from vexing cloud,
And in the west his flock did crowd;
Sharper things grew beneath the light,
As with a false dawn; thin and bright
The horned poppies' blossoms shone
Upon a shingle-bank, thrust on
By the high tide to choke the grass;
And nigh it the sea-holly was,
Whose cold grey leaves and stiff stark shade
On earth a double moonlight made:
Above him, specked with thorn and whin,
And clad with short grey grass and thin,
The hill ran up, and Laurence knew
That down the other slope there grew
A dark pine-wood, whose added sound
Scarce noted, yet did more confound,
With changing note, his wearied mind.

But now with drowsiness grown blind,
Once more he tottered on his place,
And let fall down his weary face;
But then remembering all his part,
Once and again woke with a start,
And dozed again; and then at last,
Shuddering, all slumber from him cast,
Yet scarce knew if he lived or no:
For by his scared wild eyes did go
A wondrous pageant, noiselessly,
Although so close it passed him by;
The fluttering raiment by him brushed,
As through its folds the sea-wind rushed.

By then his eyes were opened wide.
Already up the grey hill-side
The backs of two were turned to him:
One like a young man tall and slim,
Whose heels with rosy wings were dight;
One like a woman clad in white,
With glittering wings of many a hue,
Still changing, and whose shape none knew.
In aftertime would Laurence say,
That though the moonshine, cold and grey,
Flooded the lonely earth that night,
These creatures in the moon's despite
Were coloured clear, as though the sun
Shone through the earth to light each one,
And terrible was that to see.

But while he stood, and shudderingly
Still gazed on those departing twain,

Yet 'gan to gather heart again,
A noise like echoes of a shout
Seemed in the cold air all about,
And therewithal came faint and thin
What seemed a far-off battle's din,
And on a sight most terrible
His eyes in that same minute fell,
The images of slaughtered men,
With set eyes and wide wounds, as when
Upon the field they first lay slain;
And those who there had been their bane
With open mouths as if to shout,
And frightful eyes of rage and doubt,
And hate that never more should die.
Then went the shivering fleers by,
With death's fear ever in their eyes;
And then the heaped-up fatal prize,
The blood-stained coin, the unset gem,
The gold robe torn from hem to hem,
The headless, shattered golden God,
The dead priest's crushed divining-rod;
The captives, weak from blow and wound,
Toiling along; the maiden, bound
And helpless, in her raiment torn;
The ancient man's last day forlorn:
Onward they pressed, and though no sound
Their footfalls made upon the ground,
Most real indeed they seemed to be.
The spilt blood savoured horribly,
Heart-breaking the dumb writhings were,
Unuttered curses filled the air;
Yea, as the wretched band went past,
A dreadful look one woman cast
On Laurence, and upon his breast
A wounded blood-stained hand she pressed.

But on the heels of these there came
A King, that through the night did flame,
For something more than steel or brass
The matter of his armour was;
Its fashion strange past words to say;
Who knows where first it saw the day?
On a red horse he rode; his face
Gave no more hope of any grace
Than through the blackness of the night
The swift-descending lightning might;
And yet therein great joy indeed
The brightness of his eyes did feed;
A joy as of the leaping fire
Over the house-roof rising higher
To greet the noon-sun, when the glaive

Forbids all folk to help or save.

Yet harmless this one passed him by,
And through the air deliciously
Faint pensive music breathed, and then
There came a throng of maids and men—
A young and fair and gentle band;
Whereof some passed him hand in hand,
Some side by side not touching walked,
As though of happy things they talked;
Noiseless they were like all the rest
As past him up the hill they pressed;
Yet she who brushed by him most close
Cast to his feet a fresh red rose.

Then somewhat of a space there was
Before the next band 'gan to pass,
So faint they moved for very woe;
And these were men and maids also,
And young were most, and most were fair;
And hand in hand some few went there,
And still were fain with love to see
Each other's bitter misery;
But most, just sundered, went along,
With faces drawn by hidden wrong,
Clenched hands and muttering lips that cursed
From brooding hearts their sin that nursed.
And she that went the last of all,
Black-robed, in passing by let fall
At Laurence's feet a black-bound wreath
Of bitter herbs long come to death.

Alone, afoot, when these were gone,
A bright one came, whose garments shone
In wondrous wise; a bow he bore,
And deadly feathered shafts' good store;
Winged was he and most Godlike fair;
Slowly he went, and oft would stare
With eyes distraught down on the grass,
As waiting what might come to pass;
Then whiles would he look up again,
And set his teeth as if with pain;
And whiles for very joy of heart
His eyes would gleam, his lips would part
With such a smile as though the earth
Were newly made to give him mirth;
Back o'er his shoulder would he gaze
Seaward, or through the marshland haze
That lay before, strain long and hard,
Till fast the tears fell on the sward:—
So towards the hill's brow wandered he.

Then through the moaning of the sea
There came a faint and thrilling strain,
Till Laurence strove with tears in vain,
I And his flesh trembled, part with fear,
Part as with some great pleasure near,
And then his dazzled eyes could see
Once more a noiseless company;
And his heart failed him at the sight,
And he forgot both wrong and right,
And nothing thought of his intent;
For close before him now there went
Fair women clad in ancient guise
That hid but little from his eyes
More loveliness than earth doth hold
Now, when her bones are growing old;
But all too swift they went by him,
And fluttering gown and ivory limb
Went twinkling up the bare hill-side,
And lonely there must he abide.

Then seaward had he nigh turned round,
And thus the end of life had found,
When even before his wildered sight
There glided forth a figure white,
And passed him by afoot, alone;
No raiment on her sweet limbs shone,
Only the tresses of her hair
The wind drove round her body fair;
No sandals were there on her feet,
But still before them blossoms sweet
Unnamed, unknown within that land,
Sprang up; she held aloft her hand
As to the trembling man she turned
Her glorious eyes, and on it burned
The dreadful pledge, the looked-for thing,
The well-wrought, lovely spousal ring.

Then Laurence trembled more and more;
Huge longing his faint heart swept o'er,
As one who would a boon beseech.
His fevered hand forth did he reach,
And then she stayed and gazed at him,
Just moving lightly each fair limb
As one who loiters, but must go;
But even as the twain stood so,
She saying nought, he saying nought,
And who knows what wild wave of thought
Beating betwixt them, from his girth
The dread scroll loosened fell to earth,
And to his ears where sounds waxed dim

Louder its rustle seemed to him
Than loudest thunder; down he bent,
Remembering now his good intent,
And got the scroll within his hand;
And when mid prayers he came to stand
Upright again, then was she gone,
And he once more was left alone.

Foredone, bewildered, downcast now,
Confused clamour heard he grow,
And then swept onward through the night
A babbling crowd in raiment bright,
Wherein none listened aught at all
To what from other lips might fall,
And none might meet his fellow's gaze;
And still o'er every restless face
Passed restless shades of rage and pain,
And sickening fear and longing vain.
On wound that manifold agony
Unholpen, vile, till earth and sea
Grew silent, till the moonlight died
Before a false light blaring wide,
And from amidst that fearful folk
The Lord of all the pageant broke.

Most like a mighty king was he,
And crowned and sceptered royally;
As a white flame his visage shone,
Sharp, clear-cut as a face of stone;
But flickering flame, not flesh, it was;
And over it such looks did pass
Of wild desire, and pain, and fear,
As in his people's faces were,
But tenfold fiercer: furthermore,
A wondrous steed the Master bore,
Unnameable of kind or make,
Not horse, nor hippogriff, nor drake.
Like and unlike to all of these,
And flickering like the semblances
Of an ill dream, wrought as in scorn
Of sunny noon, fresh eve, and morn,
That feed the fair things of the earth.
And now brake out a mock of mirth
From all that host, and all their eyes
Were turned on Laurence in strange wise,
Who met the maddening fear that burned
Round his unholpen heart, and turned
Unto the dreadful king and cried:
"What errand go ye on? Abide,
Abide! for I have tarried long;
Turn thou to me, and right my wrong!

One of thy servants keeps from me
That which I gave her not; nay, see
What thing thy Master bids thee do!"

Then wearily, as though he knew
How all should be, the Master turned,
And his red eyes on Laurence burned,
As without word the scroll he took;
But as he touched the skin he shook
As though for fear, and presently
In a great voice he 'gan to cry:
"Shall this endure for ever, Lord?
Hast thou no care to keep thy word?
And must such double men abide?
Not mine, not mine, nor on thy side?
For as thou cursest them I curse:—
Make thy souls better, Lord, or worse!"

Then spake he to the trembling man,
"What I am bidden, that I can;
Bide here, and thou shalt see thine own
Unto thy very feet cast down;
Then go and dwell in peace awhile."
Then round he turned with sneering smile,
And once more lonely was the night,
And colourless with grey moonlight.

But soon indeed the dawn drew near,
As Laurence stood 'twixt hope and fear,
Still doubting, now that all was gone,
If his own heart the thing had done,
Though on his coat the blood-mark was,
Though rose and wreath lay on the grass;
So long he waited wearily,
Until, when dawn 'gan stripe the sky,
If he were waking scarce he knew,
When, as he deemed, a white cloud drew
Anigh him from the marshland grey,
Over the empty ghost-trod way,
And from its midst a voice there' came:
"Thou who hast wrought me added shame,
Take back thine own and go thy ways;
And think, perchance, in coming days,
When all grows old about thee, how
From foolish hands thou needs must throw
A gift of unhoped great delight."
It vanished as the east grew bright,
And in the shadowless still morn
A sense of rest to him was born,
And looking down unto his feet,
His eyes the spousal-ring did meet.

He caught it up with a glad cry,
And kissed it over longingly,
And set it on his hand again;
And dreamlike now, and vague and vain,
Seemed all those images of fear,
The wicked sights that held him there;
And rather now his eyes could see
Her that was his now verily.

Then from that drear unhallowed place
With merry heart he set his face.
A light wind o'er the ocean blew,
And fresh and fair the young day grew;
The sun rose o'er the green sea's rim,
And gave new life and joy to him;
The white birds crying o'er his head
Seemed praising all his hardihead,
And laughing at the worsted foe;
So, joyous, onward did he go,
And in a little sheltered bay
His weariness he washed away,
And made afresh on toward the town:
He met the fish-wife coming down
From her red cottage to the strand,
The fisher-children hand in hand
Over some wonder washed ashore;
The old man muttering words of lore
About the wind that was to be;
And soon the white sails specked the sea,
And fisher-keel on fisher-keel
The furrowed sand again did feel,
And round them many a barefoot maid
The burden on her shoulders laid,
While unto rest the fishers went,
And grumbling songs from rough throats sent.

Now all is done, and he at last,
Weary, but full of joy, has passed
Over his threshold once again,
And scarce believed is all the pain
And all the fear that he has had,
Now night and day shall make him glad.

As for Palumbus, tossed about
His soul might be in dread and doubt,
In rest at least his body lay
Ere the great bell struck noon that day.
And soon a carver did his best
To make an image of that rest,
Nor aught of gold did Laurence spare
To make his tomb both rich and fair;

And o'er his clasped hands and his head
Thereafter many a mass was said.

So when the tale was clean done, with a smile
The old priest looked around a little while,
That grew, as young and old 'gan say their say
On that strange dream of time long past away;
So listening, with his pleased and thoughtful look
He 'gan turn o'er the worn leaves of his book,
Half noting at the first the flowers therein,
Drawn on the margin of the yellowing skin
Where chapters ended; or fair images
Of kings and lords amidst of war and peace
At books' beginnings; till within a space
His eyes grew fixed upon a certain place,
And he seemed reading. Was it then the name
Of some old town before his eyes that came,
And drew his thoughts there? Did he see it now?
The bridge across the river choked with snow;
The pillared market-place, not thronged this eve;
The muffled goodwives making haste to leave
The gusty minster porch, whose windows shone
With the firs t-litten candles; while the drone
Of the great organ shook the leaded panes,
And the wind moaned about the turret vanes?
—Nought changed there, and himself so changed mid change,
That the next land—Death's land—would seem nought strange
To his awakening eyes!
Ah! good and ill,
When will your strife the fated measure fill?
When will the tangled veil be drawn away,
And show us all that unimagined day?


## FEBRUARY

Noon—and the north-west sweeps the empty road,
The rain-washed fields from hedge to hedge are bare;
Beneath the leafless elms some hind's abode
Looks small and void, and no smoke meets the air
From its poor hearth: one lonely rook doth dare
The gale, and beats above the unseen corn,
Then turns, and whirling down the wind is borne.

Shall it not hap that on some dawn of May
Thou shalt awake, and, thinking of days dead,
See nothing clear but this same dreary day,
Of all the days that have passed o'er thine head?
Shalt thou not wonder, looking from thy bed,
Through green leaves on the windless east a-fire,

That this day too thine heart doth still desire?

Shalt thou not wonder that it liveth yet,
The useless hope, the useless craving pain,
That made thy face, that lonely noontide, wet
With more than beating of the chilly rain?
Shalt thou not hope for joy new born again,
Since no grief ever born can ever die
Through changeless change of seasons passing by?

The change has come at last, and from the west
Drives on the wind, and gives the clouds no rest,
And ruffles up the water thin that lies
Over the surface of the thawing ice;
Sunrise and sunset with no glorious show
Are seen, as late they were across the snow;
The wet-lipped west wind chilleth to the bone
More than the light and flickering east hath done.
Full soberly the earth's fresh hope begins,
Nor stays to think of what each new day wins:
And still it seems to bid us turn away
From this chill thaw to dream of blossomed May:
E'en as some hapless lover's dull shame sinks
Away sometimes in day-dreams, and he thinks
No more of yesterday's disgrace and foil,
No more he thinks of all the sickening toil
Of piling straw on straw to reach the sky;
But rather now a pitying face draws nigh,
Mid tears and prayers for pardon; and a tale
To make love tenderer now is all the bale
Love brought him erst.

But on this chill dank tide
Still are the old men by the fireside,
And all things cheerful round the day just done
Shut out the memory of the cloud-drowned sun,
And dripping bough and blotched and snow-soaked earth;
And little as the tide seemed made for mirth,
Scarcely they lacked it less than months agone,
When on their wrinkles bright the great sun shone;
Rather, perchance, less pensive now they were,
And meeter for that cause old tales to hear
Of stirring deeds long dead:
So, as it fell,
Preluding nought, an elder 'gan to tell
The story promised in mid-winter days
Of all that latter end of bliss and praise
That erst befell Bellerophon the bright,
Ere all except his name sank into night.

ARGUMENT

**Bellerophom bore unawares to Jobates King of Lycia the deadly message of King Prœtus: wherefore the Lycian King threw him often in the way of death, but the Fates willed him not to perish so, but gave him rather great honour and a happy life.**

Lo ye have erst heard how Bellerophon
Left Argos with his fortune all undone,
Well deeming why, and with a certain scorn,
Rather than anger, in his heart new-born,
To mingle with old courage, and the hope
That yet with life's wild tangle he might cope,
Nor be so wholly beaten in the end:
Whatever pain he gat from failing friend,
And earth made lonely for his feet again,
The brightness of his youth might nowise wane
Before it, or his hardihood grow dim.

So now the evening sun shines fair on him
In Lycia, as he goes up from the quays,
Well pleased beneath the new folk's curious gaze
With all the fair things that his eyes behold:
As goodly as the tale was that men told
Of King Jobates' city, goodlier
Than all they told it seemeth to him here,
And mid things new and strange and fairly wrought
Small care he hath for any anxious thought.
And so amid the shipmen's company
He came unto the King's hall, builded high
Above the market-place, and no delay
In getting speech of the great King had they,
For ever King Jobates' wont it was
To learn of new-corners things brought to pass
In outlands, and he served in noble wise
Such guests as might seem trusty to his eyes.
So in the midmost of his company
He passed in through the hall, and seemed to be
A very god chance-come among them there,
Though little splendid soothly was his gear;
A bright steel helm upon his brows he had,
And in a dark blue kirtle was he clad,
And a grey cloak thereover; bright enow
With gold and gems his great sword's hilt did glow,
But no such thing was in aught else he wore;
A spear great-shafted his strong right hand bore,
And in his left King Prœtus' casket shone:
Grave was his face now, though there played thereon
A flickering smile, that erst you might have seen

In such wise play, when small space was between
The spears he led and fierce eyes of the foe.

Thus through the Lycian court-folk did they go
Till to the King they came: e'en such a man
As sixty summers made not pinched or wan,
Though beard and hair alike were white as snow.
Down on the sea-farers did he gaze now
With curious peering eyes, and now and then
He smiled and nodded, as he saw such men
Amidst them as he knew in other days;
But when he met Bellerophon's frank gaze,
There his eyes rested, and he said: "O guest,
Though among these thy gear is not the best,
Yet know I no man more if thou art not
E'en that Bellerophon, who late hast got
Such praise mid men of Argos, that thy name
Two months agone to this our country came,
Adorned with many tales of deeds of thine;
And certainly as of a man divine
Thy mien is and thy face: how sayest thou?"

"So am I called," he said, "mid all men now,
Since that unhappy day that drave me forth,
Lacking that half that was of greatest worth,
And made me worthy—for my deeds, O King,
What I have done is but a little thing;
I wrought that I might live from day to day,
That something I might give for hire and pay
Unto my lord; from whom I bring to thee
A message written by him privily,
Hid in this casket; take it from my hand,
And do thou worthily to this my band,
And let us soon depart, for I am fain
The good report of other men to gain,
Wide through the world;—nor do thou keep me here
As one unto King Prœtus' heart right dear,
Because I deem that I have done amiss
Unto him, though I wot not how it is
That I have sinned: certes he bade me flee,
And ere he went my face he would not see;
Therefore I bid thee, King, to have a care
Lest on a troublous voyage thou shouldst fare."

"Sweet is thy voice," the King said; "many a maid
Among our fairest would be well a-paid
In listening to thy words a summer day.
Nor will our honour let thee go away
Whatso thy deed is, though I deem full well
But little ill there is of thee to tell.
Give forth the casket; in good time will we

This message of the King of Argos see,
And do withal what seemeth good therein.
Sit ye, O guests, for supper doth begin!—
Ho! marshals, give them room; but thou sit here,
And gather heart the deeds of Kings to bear
While yet thou mayst, and here with me rejoice,
Forgetting much; for certes in thy voice
Was wrath e'en now, and unmeet anger is
To mingle with our short-lived spell of bliss."

Then sat Bellerophon adown and thought
How fate his wandering footsteps erst had brought
To such another place, and of the end,
Whate'er it was, that fate to him did send.
Yet since the time was fair, and day by day
Ever some rag of fear he cast away,
And ever less doubt of himself he had,
In that bright concourse was he blithe and glad,
And the King blessed the fair and merry tide
That set so blithe a fellow by his side.

But the next day, in honour of the guest,
The King bade deck all chambers with his best,
And bid all folk to joyous festival,
And let the heralds all the fair youth call
To play within the lists at many a game;
"Since here last eve the great Corinthian came
That ye have heard of: and though ye indeed
Of more than manly strength may well have need
To match him, do your best, lest word he bear
Too soft that now the Lycian folk live here,
Forgetting whence their fathers came of yore
And whom their granddames to their grandsires bore."

So came the young men thronging, and withal
Before the altars did the oxen fall
To many a god, the well-washed fleeces fair
In their own bearers' blood were dyed, and there
The Persian merchants stood and snuffed the scent
Of frankincense, for which of old they went
Through plain and desert waterless, and faced
The lion-haunted woods that edged the waste.
Then in the lists were couched the pointless spears,
The oiled sleek wrestler struggled with his peers,
The panting runner scarce could see the crown
Held by white hands before his visage brown;
The horses, with no hope of gold or gain,
With fluttering hearts remembered not the rein
Nor thought of earth. And still all things fared so,
That all who with the hero had to do
Deemed him too strong for mankind; or if one

Gained seeming victory on Bellerophon,
He knew it for a courteous mockery
Granted to him. So did the day go by,
And others like it, and the talk still was
How even now such things could come to pass
That such a man upon the earth was left.

But when the ninth sun from the earth had reft
Silence, and rest from care, then the King sent
To see Bellerophon, who straightly went,
And found Jobates with a troubled face,
Pacing a chamber of the royal place
From end to end, who turned as he drew near,
And said in a low voice, "What dost thou here?
This is a land with many dangers rife;
Hast thou no heed to save thy joyous life?
The wide sea is before thee, get thee gone,
All lands are good for thee but this alone!"

And as the hero strove to catch his eye
And 'gan to speak, he passed him hurriedly,
And gat him from the chamber: with a smile
Bellerophon turned too within a while,
When he could gather breath from such a speech,
And said, "Far then King Prœtus' arm can reach:
So was it as I doubted; yet withal
Not everything to every king will fall
As he desires it, and the Gods are good;
Nor shall the Lycian herbage drink my blood:—
The Gods are good, though far they drive me forth;
But the four quarters, south, west, east, and north,
All are alike to me, who therein have
None left me now to weep above my grave
Whereso I fall: and fair things shall I see,
Nor may great deeds be lacking unto me:—
Would I were gone then!"
But with that last word
Light footsteps drawing swiftly nigh he heard,
And made a shift therewith his eyes to raise,
Then staggering back, bewildered with amaze,
Caught at the wall and wondered if he dreamed,
For there before his very eyes he seemed
To see the Lycian Sthenobœa draw nigh;
But as he strove with his perplexity
A soft voice reached his ears, and then he knew
That in one mould the Gods had fashioned two,
But given them hearts unlike; yea, and her eyes
Looked on his troubled face in no such wise
As had the other's; wistful these and shy,
And seemed to pray, Use me not cruelly,
I have not harmed thee.—Thus her soft speech ran:

"Far have I sought thee, O Corinthian man,
And now that I have found thee my words fail,
Though erst my heart had taught me well my tale."

She paused, her half-closed lips were e'en as sweet
As the sweet sounds that thence the air did meet,
And such a sense swept o'er Bellerophon
As whiles in spring had come, and lightly gone
Ere he could name it; like a wish it was,
A wish for something that full swift did pass,
To be forgotten.
Some three paces were
Betwixt them when she first had spoken there,
But now, as though it were unwittingly,
He slowly moved a little more anigh;
But she flushed red now ere she spake once more,
And faltered and looked down upon the floor.

"O Prince Bellerophon," at last she said,
"I dreamed last night that I beheld thee dead;
I knew thee thus, for twice had I seen thee,
Unseen myself, in this festivity;
And since I know how loved a man thou art,
Here have I come, to bid thee to depart,
Since that thou mayst do yet."
Nigher he came
And said, "O fair one, I am but a name
To thee, as men are to the Gods above;
And what thing, then, thy heart to this did move?"

So spake he, knowing scarce what words he said,
Strange his own voice seemed to him; and the maid
Spake not at first, but grew pale, and there passed
A quivering o'er her lips; but at the last,
With eyes fixed full upon him, thus she spake:

"Why should I lie? this did I for thy sake,
Because thou art the worthiest of all men,
The loveliest to look on. Hear me, then;
But ere my tale is finished, speak thou not,
Because this moment has my heart waxed hot,
And I can speak before I go my way—
Before thou leav'st me. On my bed I lay,
And dreamed I fared within the Lycian land,
And still about me there on either hand
Were nought but poisonous serpents, yet no dread
I had of them, for soothly in my head
The thought was, that my kith and kin they were;
But as I went methought I saw thee there
Coming on toward me, and thou mad'st as though

No whit about those fell worms thou didst know;
And then in vain I strove to speak to thee,
And bid thee get thee down unto the sea,
Where bode thy men ready at bench and mast;
But in my dream thou cam'st unto me fast,
And unto speech we fell of e'en such things
As please the sons and daughters of great kings;
And I must smile and talk, and talk and smile,
Though I beheld a serpent all the while
Draw nigh to strike thee: then—then thy lips came
Close unto mine; and while with joy and shame
I trembled, in my ears a dreadful cry
Rang, and thou fellest from me suddenly
And layst dead at my feet: and then I spake
Unto myself, 'Would God that I could wake,'
But woke not, though my dream changed utterly,
Except that thou wert laid stark dead anigh.
Then in this palace were we, and the noise
Of many folk I heard, and a great voice
Rang o'er it ever and again, and said,
Bellerophon who would not love is dead.
But I—I moved not from thee, but I saw
Through the fair windows many people draw
Unto the lists, until withal it seemed
As though I never yet had slept or dreamed,
That all the games went on, where yesterday
Thou like a god amidst of men didst play:
But yet through all, the great voice cried and said,
Bellerophon who would not love is dead.
This is the dream—ah, hast thou heard me, then?
Abide no more, I say, among these men:
Think'st thou the world without thy life can thrive,
More than my heart without thy heart can live?"

Almost before her lips the words could say,
She turned her eager glittering eyes away,
And hurried past, and as her feet did bear
Her loveliness away, he seemed to hear
A sob come from her; but for him, he felt
As in some fair heaven all his own he dwelt,
As though he ne'er of any woe had known,
So happy and triumphant had he grown.
But when he thus a little while had stood
With this new pleasure stirring all his blood,
He 'gan to think how that she was not there,
And 'thwart the glory of delight came care,
As uttermost desire so wrought in him,
That now in strange new tears his eyes did swim,
He scarce knew if for pleasure or for pain.
Of other things he strove to think in vain—
Nought seemed they;—the strange threatening of the King,

Nay the maid's dream—it seemed a little thing
That he should read their meaning more than this:
'Here in the land of Lycia dwells thy bliss;
So much she loved thee that she wished thee gone,
That thou mightst live, though she were left alone;
Or else she had not left thee; failing not
To see how all the heart in thee waxed hot
To cast thine arms about her and to press
Her heart to thine and heal its loneliness.'
Pity grew in him as he thought thereof,
And with its sweet content fed burning love,
Till all his life was swallowed by its flame,
And dead and past away were fear and shame,
Nor might he think that he could ever die.

But now at last he with a passionate sigh
Turned from the place where he had seen her feet,
And murmured as he went, "O sweet, O sweet,
O sweet the fair morn that thou breathest in,
When thou, awakening lone, dost first begin
For one more day the dull blind world to bless
With sight of thine unmeasured loveliness."

So speaking, through a low door did he gain
A little garden; the fair morn did wane,
The day grew to its hottest, the warm air
Was little stirred, the o'er-sweet lily there
With unbowed stem let fall upon the ground
Its fainting leaves; full was the air of sound
Of restless bees; from high elms far away
Came the doves' moan about the lost spring day,
And Venus' sparrows twittered in the eaves
Above his head. There 'twixt the languid leaves
And o'er-blown blossoms he awhile did go,
Nursing his love till faint he 'gan to grow
For very longing, and love, bloomed an hour,
Began to show the thorn about the flower,
Yet sweet and sweet it was, until the thought
Of that departing to his mind was brought,
And though he laughed aloud with scorn of it,
Yet images of pain and death would flit
Across his love, until at last anew
He 'gan to think that deeds there were to do
In his old way, if there he still would bide.
Deeds must have birth from hope; grief must he hide,
And into hard resolve his longing chill,
If he would be god-loved and conquering still:
So back he turned into the house, in mind,
Whatso might hap, the King once more to find,
And crave for leave to serve him; for he deemed,
Whate'er the King had warned or his love dreamed,

That he and youth 'gainst death were fellows twain
For years yet, whoso in the end should gain.

Deep buried in his thoughts he went, but when
He drew anigh the hall a crowd of men
Were round about it; armed they were, indeed,
But rent and battered was their warlike weed,
And some lacked wounding weapons; some men leant
Weakly 'gainst pillars; some were so much spent
They wept for weariness and pain; no few
Bore bandages the red blood struggled through;
E'en such they seemed, the hero thought, as folk
That erst before his Argive spears had broke,
And at his feet their vain arms down had cast:
So, wondering thereat, through these folk he passed
Into the hall, where on the ivory throne
Jobates sat, with flushed face, gazing down
Upon the shrinking captains; therewithal
E'en as he entered did the King's eyes fall
Upon him, and the King somewhat did start
At first, but then, as minding not the part
That he had played that morn, a gracious smile
Came o'er his face; then spake he in a while:
"Look upon these, O wise Bellerophon,
And ask of them what glory they have won—
Or ask them not, but listen unto me:
Over the mountain-passes that men see
Herefrom, a town there is, and therein dwell
Folk baser and more vile than men can tell;
A godless folk, without a law or priest;
A thankless folk, who at high-tide and feast
Remember not the Gods; no image there
Makes glad men's eyes, no painted story fair
Tells of past days; alone, unhelped they live,
And nought but curses unto any give:
A rude folk, nothing worth, without a head
To lead them forth,—and this morn had I said
A feeble folk and bondsmen of mine own.
But now behold from this same borel town
Are these men empty-handed now come back,
And midst these Solymi is little lack
This morn of well-wrought swords and silk attire
And gold that seven times o'er has felt the fire.
"Lo now, thou spak'st of wandering forth again—
Rather be thou my man, and 'gainst these men
Lead thou mine army; nay, nor think to win
But little praise if thou dost well herein,
For these by yesterday are grown so great
That if thou winnest them, midst this red heat
Of victory, a great deed shalt thou do,
And great will thy reward be; wilt thou go?

Methought thou hadst a mind to serve me here."

So, as Bellerophon drew more anear,
He thought within his heart, "Ah, then, I know
From all these things why he would have me go;
Yet since indeed I may not quite depart
From Lycia now, because my new-smitten heart
Is bound with bonds of love unto the land,
Safer am I in armour, sword in hand,
Than midst these silken hangings and fair things,
That well I wot hide many poison-stings:
The Gods are great, nor midst of men am I
Of such as, once being threatened, quickly die."

Then he spake out: "O King, wilt thou then pray
To all the Gods to give me a good day?
For when I was a youth and dwelt at home
Men deemed I knew somewhat of things to come,
And now methinks more dangers I foresee
Than any that have yet been forged for me."

The King frowned at that word, and flushed blood-red,
As if against his will; but quickly said,
In a mild voice: "Be of good cheer, O son;
For if the Gods help not Bellerophon
They will not have to say, that in this land
I prayed their good-will for thee with close hand.
No god there is that hath an altar here
That shall not smoke with something he holds dear
While thou art absent from us—but these men,
Worn as they are, are fain to try again,
As swiftly as may be, what from the Fates
In bloody fields the Lycian name awaits;
Mine armoury is not empty, yet there are
Unwounded men to furnish forth the war
Yea, and mine household-folk shall go with thee,
And none but women in mine house shall be,
Until the Lycian shield once more is clean
Through thee, as though no stain had ever been.
Canst thou be ready by the second day
Unto the Solymi to take thy way?"

"So be it," said the wise Corinthian;
"And here, O King, I make myself thy man—
May the Gods make us faithful; but if worse
Must happen, on his head fall all the curse
Who does the wrong!—Now for thy part see thou
That we who go have everything enow;
Nor think to hear too soon of victory,
For though a spliced staff e'en as strong may be
As one ne'er broken, lean thou not thereon

Till o'er the narrow way thy feet have won
And thou may'st try it on the level grass.
Now give me leave,. for I am fain to pass
Thy men in order by me, and to find
How best thy wounded honour I may bind."

When first the hero's hand the King's hand took,
But ill belike Jobates that did brook,
And well-nigh drew it back; yet still it lay
And moved not, and the King made haste to say:

"May the Gods bless us both, as I bless thee,
Who at this tide givest good help to me!
Depart, brave man; and, doing but thy best,
Howe'er fate goes, by me shalt thou be blest."

Then went Bellerophon, and laboured sore
To give the Lycian folk good heart once more,
Till day passed into night, and in fair dream
And hopeful waking, happy love did gleam,
E'en like the young sun, on the hero's head.
But when the next bright day was well-nigh dead,
Within the brazen porch Bellerophon
Stood thinking o'er all things that had been done.
Alone he was, and yearning for his love,
And longing for some deed the truth to prove
Of what seemed dreamlike now, midst all the stir
Of men and clash of arms; and wearier
He felt than need was, as the evening breeze
Raised up his hair. But while sweet images
His heart made now of what he once had seen,
There in the dusk, across the garden green,
A white thing fluttered; nor was steadier
His heart within him, as he thought of her,
And that perchance she came; and soon anigh
A woman drew, but stopping presently
Over against him, he could see her now
To be a handmaid, and, with knitted brow,
Was going thence, but through the dusk she cried:
"O fair my lord Bellerophon, abide
And hearken—here my lady sendeth me,
And saith these words withal:
Philonoë,
Born of the Lycian King, Both give thee this
Fair blade, and prayeth for thee health and bliss;
Saying, moreover; as for this same sword,
Draw it not forth before base man or lord,
But be alone when first it leaves the sheath .
Yet since upon it lieth life and death,
Surely thou wilt not long delay to see
The face of that bright friend I give to thee."

He felt the cold hilt meet his outstretched hand,
And she was gone, nor longer did he stand
Than but to look if any stood thereby,
Then gat him gone therefrom, and presently
Was lone within his chamber; there awhile
He stood regarding with a lovesome smile
The well-wrought sword, and fairly was it dight
With gold and gems; then by the taper's light
He drew it from the sheath, and, sooth to tell,
E'en that he hoped for therewithal befel,
Because a letter lay 'twixt blade and sheath,
Which straight he opened, and nigh held his breath
For very eagerness, the while he read:

Short is the time, and yet enow, it said,
Nightfall it will be when thou readest this.
If thou wouldst live yet, for the weal and bliss
Of many, gird this sword to thee, and go
Down to the quay, and there walk to and fro,
Until a seafarer thou meetest there,
With two behind him who shall torches bear;
He shall behold the sword, and say to thee,
'Is it drawn forth?' and say 'Yea, verily,
And the wound healed.' Then shall he bring thee straight
Unto his keel, which with loose sails doth wait
Thy coming, and shall give thee gold good store,
Nor bide the morn to leave the Lycian shore.
Farewell; I would have seen thee, but I feared—
I feared two things; first, that we might be heard
By green trees and by walls, and thus should I
Have brought the death on thee I bid thee fly;
The first—but for the second, since I speak
Now for the last time—Love has made me weak;
I feared my heart made base by sudden bliss
I feared—wilt thou be wroth who readest this?—
Mine eyes I saw in thine that other tide;
I thought perchance that here thou mightst abide,
Constrained by Love.

Now if I have said ill,
Shall not my soul of sorrow have its fill?
I sin, but bitter death shall pay therefor.

He read the piteous letter o'er and o'er,
Till fell the tears thereon like sudden rain,
For he was young, and might not love again
With so much pleasure, such sweet bitterness,
Such hope amid that new-born sharp distress
Of longing; half-content to love and yearn,
Until perchance the fickle wheel might turn.

The well-kissed sword within his belt he set,
But ye may well deem was more minded yet
To bide his fortune in the Lycian land,
What fear soe'er before his path might stand;
And great his soul grew, thinking of the tide
When every hindrance should be thrust aside,
And love should greet him; calm, as though the death,
He knew so nigh him, on some distant heath
Were sitting, flame-bound, waiting for the word
Himself should give; with hand upon his sword,
Unto the hall he took his way: therein
Was growing great and greater joyful din,
For there they drank unto the coming day;
And as through all that crowd he made his way,
The shouts rose higher round him, and his name
Beat hard about the stony ears of Fame.

So then beside the Lycian King he sat
A little while, and spake of this and that,
E'en as a man grown mighty; and at last
Some few words o'er that feasting folk he cast,
Proud, mingling sharp rebuke with confidence.
And bade them feast no more, but going thence
Make ready straight to live or die like men.
And therewithal did he depart again
Amidst them, and for half the night he went
Hither and thither, on such things intent
As fit the snatcher-forth of victory;
And then, much wondering how such things could be,
That aught but love could move a man at all,
Into a dreamless slumber did he fall,
Wherefrom the trumpet roused him in the morn,
Almost before the summer sun was born;
And midst the new-born longings of his heart,
From that fair place now must he needs depart
Unguarded and unholpen to his fate.

Nought happed to him 'twixt palace-court and gate
Of the fair city; thronged it was e'en then
With anxious, weeping women and pale men,
But unto him all faces empty were
But one, that nowise might he now see there:
Or ere he passed the great gate back he gazed'
To where the palace its huge pile upraised
Unto the fresh and windy morning sky,
As seeking if he might e'en now espy
That which he durst not raise his eyes unto
When 'neath its walls he went a while ago.

So through the gate the last man strode, and they

Who in the city seemed so great a stay
Unto that people, as the country-side
About their moving ranks spread bleak and wide,
Showed like a handful, and the town no less
Seemed given up to utter helplessness.

Seven days of fear wore by; Philonoë
Must vex her heart with all that yet might be,
And oft would curse herself that she it was
Through whom such death as his should come to pass,
And weep to think of all her life made lone.
But on the eighth day, at the stroke of noon,
A little band of stained and battered men
Passed through the gate into the town again,
And left glad hearts as well as anxious ones
Behind them, as they clattered o'er the stones
Unto the palace: there the King they found
Set on his throne, with ancient lords around,
And cried to him, "O King, rejoice! at last
Raised is thy banner, that ill men had cast
Unto the ground; as safely mayst thou lie
Within the city of the Solymi
As in this house thou buildedst for thy bliss,
For all things there are thine now, e'en as this."

Then the King rose, and filled a cup with wine,
And said, "All praise be unto things divine!
Yet ere I pour, how goes it with our folk?
Did many die before they laid the yoke
On these proud necks? when will they come again?"

"O King," they said, "though they fell not in vain,
Yet many fell; but now upon the way
Our fellows are: I think on the third day
They will be here, and needs must they be slow,
Because they have with them a goodly show;
Wains full of spoil, arms, and most fair attire,
Wrought gold that seven times o'er has felt the fire;
And men and women of thy stubborn foes
E'en as thou wilt their lives to keep or lose."

"What sayst thou next about Bellerophon,"
The King said, "that this day for me hath won?
Is he alive yet?"
Then the man waxed pale,
And said, "He liveth, and of small avail
Man's weapons are against him; on the wall
He stood alone, for backward did we fall
Before the fury of the Solymi,
Because we deemed ourselves brought there to die,,
And might not bear it: then it was as though

A clear bright light about his head did glow
Amidst the darts and clamour, and he turned
A face to us that with such glory burned
That those behind us drave us back again,
And cried aloud to die there in the pain
Rather than leave him, and with such a wave
Of desperate war swept up, they scarce could save
Their inmost citadel from us that tide,
Who at the first with mocks had bidden us bide
A little longer in a freeman's land,
Until their slaves had got their whips in hand
To drive us thence."
Now as he spake, at first
The King like one, who heareth of the worst,
And must not heed it, hearkened, but when he
Had heard his servant's tale out, suddenly
The wine he poured, and cried, "Jove, take thou this
In token of the greatness of our bliss,
In earnest of the gifts that thou shalt have,
Who thus our name, our noble friends didst save."
So spake he, looking downward, and his heart
In what his lips said, had perchance, some part,
However, driven on by long-sworn oath,
He dealt in things that sore he needs must loathe:
And he who erst had told him of the thing
Seemed fain to linger, as if yet the King
Had something more to say; but no fresh word
He had for him, but with great man and lord
Made merry, praising wind and wave
That brought Bellerophon their fame to save.

But joyous was the town to hear of this,
For in that place, midst all that men call bliss,
Cold fear was mingled; such a little band
They seemed, but clinging to a barbarous land,
With strange things round about them; if the earth
Should open not to swallow up their mirth
And them together, they must deem it good;
Or if the kennels ran not with their blood,
While a poor remnant, driven forth with whips,
Must sit beneath the hatchways of strange ships,
Of such account as beasts. So there dwelt they,
Trembling amidst their wealth from day to day,
Afraid of god and man, and earth and sky.
Judge, therefore, if they thought not joyously
Of this one fallen amongst them, who could make
The rich man risk his life for honour's sake,
The trembling slave remember what he was,
The poor man hope for what might come to pass.

So when the day carne when the gates were flung

Back on their hinges, and the people hung
About the pageant of their folk returned,
And many an eager face about him burned
With new and high desires they scarce could name,
He wondered how such glory on him came,
And why folk gazed upon him as a god,
And would have kissed the ground whereon he trod.
A little thing it seemed to him to fight
Against hard things, that he might see the light
A little longer and rejoice therein,
A little thing that he should strive to win
More time for love; and even therewithal
Into a dreamy musing did he fall
Amidst the shouts and glitter, and scarce knew
What things they were that he that day did do,
Only the time seemed long and long and long,
The noise and many men still seemed to wrong
The daintiness of his heart-piercing love,—
As through a world of shadows did he move.

Think then how fared his love Philonoë
Amid the din of that festivity!
For if while joy hung betwixt hope and fear
Life seemed a hateful thing to her and drear,
And all men hateful; if herself she cursed,
The hatefullest of all things and the worst;
If rest had grown a name for something gone
And not remembered; if herself alone
Seemed no more one, but made of many things
All wretched and at strife; if sudden stings
Of fresh pain made her start up from her place,
And set to some strange unknown goal her face,
And she must stifle wails with bitterest pain—
If all this was, ought she not now to gain
A little rest? now, when she heard the voice
Of triumph and the people's maddening noise
Round her returning love; still did she bear
Her grinding dread if with a wearier,
Yet with a calmer face, than now she bore
Desire so quickened by that fear past o'er.
She in her garden wandered through the day,
And heavy seemed the hours to pass away.
Her colour came and went, she trembled when
She heard some louder shout of joyous men;
She could not hear the things her maidens spake,
Nor aught could she seem gracious for their sake;
The sweetest snatch of some familiar song
She might not hearken; she abode not long
Within the shadow; weary of the sun
She grew full soon; the glassy brook did run
In vain across her feet; the ice-cold well

Quenched not her thirst; the half-blown roses' smell
Was not yet sweet enough: the sun sank low,
And then she murmured that the day must go
That should have been so happy: wearily
She laid her down that night, but nought slept she;
Yet in the morn the new sun seemed to bring
A joy to her, and some unnamed dear thing
Better than rest or peace; for in her heart
She knew that he in all her thoughts had part;
Yea, and she thought how dreamlike he would ride
Amidst his glory, and how ill abide
The clamour of the feast; yea, and would not
That night to him belike be dull and hot,
And that dawn hopeful?

'Neath the wall there was
A place where dewy was the daisied grass
E'en nigh the noon; a high tower great and round
Cast a long shadow o'er that spot of ground,
And blind it was of window or of door,
For, wrought by long-dead men of ancient lore,
No part it was of that stone panoply
That girt the town; so lilies grew thereby,
And woodbine, and the odorous virgin's-bower
Hung in great heaps about that undyked tower,
And lone and silent was the pleasance there.
Thither Love led Philonoë the fair,
And well she knew of him, and still her heart
At every little sound and sight would start,
And still her palms were tingling for the touch
Of other hands, and ever over-much
Her feet seemed light.

But when the bushes gleamed
With something more than the low sun that streamed
Athwart their blossoms, and a clear voice rung
Above the ousel's; then with terror stung,
She leaned her slim and perfect daintiness
'Gainst the grey tower, and even like distress
Her great joy seemed. Green clad he was that morn,
And to his side there hung a glittering horn,
A mighty unbent bow was in his hand,
And o'er his shoulders did the feathers stand
Of his long arrows; in his gleaming eyes
Such joy there was as he beheld the prize,
That in that shadow now he seemed to be
A piece of sunlight fallen down suddenly.

So face to yearning face they stood awhile,
And every word at first seemed poor and vile,
None better than another; nor durst they

Lips upon lips or palm to fingers lay,
More than if many people stood around,
With such strange fear and shame doth love abound.

At last she spake: "Thou comest, then, to say
How thou wilt now be wise and go away,
E'en as I bade; the prey has 'scaped the net;
Be wise, the fowler other wiles hath yet!"

"Yea," said he, "then thy word it was indeed
That needs must think about me in my need:
Strange, then, that now thou biddest me begone!
Belike thou know'st not of folk left alone,
And what life grows to them: yet art thou kind—
Thou deemest other friends I yet may find.
Alas, life goeth fast; not every day
Do we behold folk standing in the way
With outstretched hands to meet us."
"Ah," she said,
"How sweet thou art! Wand yet the dead are dead,
The absent are but dead a little while.
Then get thee gone from midst of wrong and guile,
And we shall meet once more in happier days,
When death lurks not amidst of rosy ways—
Ah, wilt thou slay me, then?—I knew not erst
How poor a life I had, and how accurst,
Before I felt thy lips—what thing is this
That makes me faint amidst of new-born bliss?"

"Rest in mine arms, O well-beloved," said he;
"I faint not, neither shall death come on me
While thus thou art: nay, nay, I think if I,
Hacked with an hundred swords, should come to lie,
Yet without thee I should not then depart."

"O love, alas! the sorer is my heart
The more I love," she said, "we are alone;
Our loving life is not for any one
But for our own selves—ah, deem all I said
Before those lips of thine on mine were laid
As said again and yet again! Some hate
Is round thee here, some undeserved strange fate
Awaits thee here in Lycia—yea, full sure
The hungry swords here may we twain endure;
But what then?—Of the dead what hast thou heard
That maketh thee so rash and unafeared?
Can the dead love, or is there any space
In their long sleep when they lay face to face
Soft as we do now? can their pale lips plead
The pleas of love? or can their fixed eyes lead
Heart unto heart? or hast thou heard that they

Can wait from weary day to weary day,
And hope, as I will, while thou gatherest fame?
Can they have pleasure there e'en in a name,
A memory? is their pain a pleasure there,
Are tears sweet, and the longing sobs that wear
The hours away, where life and hope are gone?
"How can I any longer be alone?
Can I forget thee now? the while I live?
O my beloved, must I strive and strive,
And move thee not? How sweet thou art to me!
How dull the coming day that knows not thee!"

"Fear not," he said; "not yet my days are done!
When on the deadly wall I stood alone,
And back the traitors fell from me, I felt
As though within me such a life there dwelt
As scarce could end—Lo now, if I depart
I lack the safeguard of thy faithful heart,
And meet new dangers that thou know'st not of.
Yea, listen, nor rebuke me—This our love;
Hast thou not heard how love may grow a-cold
Before the lips that called thereon wax old?
Ah, listen! seas betwixt us, and great pain,
And death of days that shall not be again;
And yearning life within us, and desire
That changes hearts as fire will quench the fire.
These are the engines of the Gods, lest we,
Through constant love, Gods too should come to be.
A little pain, a little fond regret,
A little shame, and we are living yet,
While love that should out-live us lieth dead—

"Ah, my beloved, lift that glorious head
And look upon me! put away the thought
Of time and death, and let all things be nought
But this love of to-day! and think of me
As if for ever I should seem to thee
As I am now—I will not go away,
Nor sow my love, to reap some coming day
I know not what: be merry, we shall live
To see our love high o'er all danger thrive."

For now she wept, but, starting midst her tears,
She stopped and listened like a bird that hears
A danger on the wind: the round tower's shade
A lesser patch upon the daisies made,
And all about the place 'gan folk to stir:
She turned and girt her loosened gown to her,
And with one sob, and a long faithful look,
The gathering tears from out her eyes she shook,
Nor bade farewell, but swiftly gat her gone.

But he beneath the tower so left alone
Stooped down and kissed her foot-prints in the grass,
And then with swift steps through the place did pass,
Thinking high things; nor knew he till that hour
How sweet life was, or love its fruit and flower.

So passed the days, nor often might it be
That such sweet hours as this the twain might see;
And they must watch that folk might not surprise
Their hearts' love through the windows of their eyes
When midst of folk they met: but glorious days
Were for Bellerophon, and love and praise
From all folk, though the great end lingered yet
When he sweet life, or glorious death, should get.

Now on a day was held of most and least
Unto Diana sacrifice and feast,
And on that tide the market empty was,
And through the haven might no dromund pass;
And then the wont was they should bear about
The goddess wrought in gold, with song and shout
And winding of great horns, amidst a band
Of bare-kneed maidens, bended bow in hand
And quiver at the back; and these should take,
As if by force, and for the city's sake,
Three damsels chosen by lot for that same end,
And bind their hands, and with them straightly wend
Unto the temple of Diana; there
The priest should lead them to the altar fair
And midst old songs should raise aloft the knife
As if to take from each her well-loved life;
Therewith the King, with a great company,
Through the great door would come and respite cry,
And offer ransom: a great golden horn,
A silver image of a flowering thorn,
Three white harts with their antlers gilt with gold,
A silk gown for a huntress, every fold
Thick wrought with gold and gems; then to and fro
An ancient song was sung, to bid men know
That of such things the goddess had no need;
Yet in the end the maidens all were freed,
The harts slain in their place, the dainty things
Hung o'er the altar from fair silver rings,
And then, midst semblance of festivity
And joyful songs, the solemn day went by.

All this they told Bellerophon, and said
Moreover, that the white-foot well-girt Maid
These gifts must have, because a merry rout
Of feasters, knowing neither fear nor doubt,

With love and riot did her grove defile
In the old days; and therefore nought more vile
Than three fair maids' lives would she have at first,
And with that burden was the city cursed
For many years; "But in these latter days,
She to whom we to-morrow give great praise,
Will take these signs of our humility,
And let the folk in other wise go free."

So on the morn joyful the city was,
Nor did men look for aught to come to pass
More than in other years; but lo, a change!
For there betid great portents dire and strange.
For first, when in the car of cedar-wood,
Decked with green boughs, the golden goddess stood,
And the white oxen strained at yoke and trace,
In no wise might they move her from the place,
Though they had drawn well twenty times that weight.
So when the priests had come in all their state
To pray her, and no lighter she would grow,
They said she did it for that folk might know
She fain would have a shrine built o'er the way,
And that all rites should there be wrought that day.
So was it done, and now all things seemed well
A little space, and nought there was to tell
Until the King had brought the ransom due,
And the loosed bonds men from the maidens drew;
Then fell the third maid down before the King,
And cried from foaming mouth a shameful thing
Unmeet for maids; then from the frightened folk
That filled the street a clamour there outbroke,
And some cried out to slay the woman there,
And some to burn her wanton body fair,
And some to cast her forth into the sea
And purge the town of that iniquity.
But when the King had bidden lead her forth,
And try if she indeed were one of worth,
Or if her maidenhood were nought and vain,
The tossing street grew somewhat stilled again,
And o'er the sinking tumult called a priest:
"Abide, let see if she will take the beast
E'en as her wont is! but if so it be
That of our old crime she has memory
And threatens us with something strange and new,
Yet mid your fear do all in order due,
Nor make two faults of one, that ye may bear
A double punishment from year to year."

Then were the harts brought forth; the first one stood
Fearless as he were lonely in the wood,
While to his throat drew nigh the sharp-edged knife,

Nor did the second strive to keep his life;
But when the third and biggest drew anigh,
He tossed his gilded antlers angrily
And smote his foot against the marble floor,
While from his throat came forth a low hoarse roar;
And as the girl whose office was to smite
His drawn-back throat came forth confused and white,
And raised a wavering hand aloft, then he
His branching horns from the priests' hands shook free,
And as the affrighted girl fell back, turned round,
And gathered up his limbs for one last bound;
But even therewith a soldier from the band
That stood about the King raised up his hand,
And in the beast's heart thrust his well-steeled spear,
And as he smote, like one who knew no fear,
He cried aloud:
"O foolish Artemis,
Men's ways thou knowest not, putting from thee this,
The gift once offered! think no more of us
That we will pray with eyes all piteous
Before thee, or give gifts from trembling hands;
But get thee gone straightway to other lands,
Where folk will yet abide thee—for we know
How long a way it is for thee to go
From heaven to earth, how far thine arms will reach,
And no more now thy good-will do beseech!"

He stooped, and from the beast his weapon drew,
Then turned and passed his fear-struck fellows through,
Or ere the swords from out the scabbards came;
And so folk say, that no man knew his name
Or whence he was.

But from the concourse broke
In pale and murmuring knots the frightened folk;
And if the priests had heart yet for a word
Of comfort, neither so had they been heard;
But they slunk off too, more perchance afraid
Because they were the nigher to the Maid.

Now had the morn begun with cloud and sun;
But, little heeded there of any one
Mid that beginning of fear's agony,
Slowly the clouds were swallowing up the sky;
So ere the sun had wholly sunk in them,
Great drops fell slowly from a black cloud's hem
Amid that troubled folk, who felt as though
They from that place of terror needs must go,
Yet, going, scarce could feel their unnerved feet;
Then gleamed a lightning-flash adown the street,
The clattering thunder, made ten times more loud,

Because of dread, hushed all the murmuring crowd,
And brought a many trembling to their knees,
And some set off a-running toward the quays,
That they might go they knew not where or why;
But therewithal such rain fell from the sky,
As though some river of the upper world
Had burst his banks, the furious south-wind hurled
The folk's wet raiment upward as it tore
Along the ground, and the white rain-spray bore
Seaward along: yet so it came to pass
That no more terror from the sky there was;
The wind grew steady, but from roof of grey
Fast fell the rain upon the ruined day,
Till trembling still, and shivering with the cold,
Home went all folk, and soon the Maid of gold
Stood lonely in the rain-beat way and drear,
Amid drenched cloths and garlands, once made fair
To make the day more joyous. You had thought
That now already had the Maiden brought
Upon the city all the dreaded ill,
So lifeless was it grown and lone and still.

But now to tell of Prince Bellerophon;
Upon that day so chanced it he had gone
Unto the hills, in chase the hours to spend
Until the tide of feasting should have end;
For since he was an alien in that place,
Beside the King he might not show his face
Unto the goddess; so that morn he stood
Upon a hill's top that from out a wood
Rose bare; thence looking east, he saw the sky
Grow black and blacker as the rain drew nigh,
And deemed it good to go, but, as he turned,
Afar a jagged streak of lightning burned,
Paling the sunshine that the dark woods lit,
And rocks about him; through his mind did flit
Something like fear thereat; and still he gazed
Out to the east, but not again there blazed
That fire from out the sky. Now was he come
To such a place, that thence fair field, and home
Of toiling men, and wood, and broad bright stream
Lay down below, and many a thing did gleam
Beneath the zenith's brightness, brighter yet
For horror of the far clouds' stormful threat,
And clear the air was with the coming rain—
So then as he would turn his head again,
Out in the far horizon like a spark
Some flame broke out against the storm-clouds dark,
And seemed to grow beneath his eyes; he stood,
And, gazing, saw across the day's dark mood
Another and another, nigh the first;

Then, as the distant thunder's threatening cursed
The country-side, and trembling beast and man,
The spark-like three flames into one thread ran,
That shot aloft amidst, yet further spread
At either end; and to himself he said:
"Ah, is it so? what tidings then draw near?
In warlike lands soon should I look to hear
Of armies marching on through war and wrack;
Good will it be in haste to get me back
Unto the foolish folk that trust in me."

Then did he mount and ride off hastily
Adown the slopes; but not so fast withal
But that upon him did the full storm fall
In no long time; and so through pelting rain
And howling wind he reached the gate again;
And so unto the palace went, to hear
From pale lips tales of all that day of fear;
And when about those bale-fires seen afar
He spake, and bade make ready for some war,
Folk listened coldly; for they thought to see
Some strange, portentous sign of misery
Set in the heavens upon the morrow morn,
And the old tale of war seemed well outworn.

Yet ere the night beyond its midst was worn,
Another tale unto their ears was borne
That cast into their hearts the ancient fear,
And the Gods' threatening easier seemed to bear
Than this that fell on them.

At dead of night
The grey clouds drew apart, the moon shone bright
Over a dripping world; and some folk slept
Wearied by fear, if some their tired limbs kept
Ready for flight; then clattering horse-hooves came
To the east gate, and one called out the name
Of him who had the guard; so said the man
That forth he went into the moonlight wan,
And saw nought but the tall black-shadowed trees
Waving their dripping boughs in the light breeze,
So went back scared. But in a while again
The galloping of horse did he hear plain,
But he and his sat fast and spake no word,
And scarce fhr fear might they hold spear or sword.
Nigher the sound came, till it reached the gate;
Then as the warders did abide their fate,
Thinking to see the gates burst open wide,
And death in some strange shape betwixt them ride,
The gates were smitten on with hasty blows,
And breathless cries of wild entreaty rose

Up through the night:
"Open, O open, ye
Who sit in peace, and let in misery!
Do ye not see the red sky at our backs?
And how the earth all quiet places lacks,
And shakes beneath the myriad hooves of steel?
Open, ah open, as ye hope for weal!
For ships lie at your quays with sails all bent
And oars made ready—Open, we are spent!
Do ye not hear them? Open, Lycian men!"

With staring eyes still sat the warders when
That cry they heard, and knew not what should be;
And the great gates of oak, clenched mightily
With iron end-long and athwart, seemed fair
Unto their eyes; but as they cowered there
A clash of steel again their dull ears heard
That came from out the town, and more afeard
They grew, if it might be; then torches came
Into the place of guard, and mid their flame
A shining one in arms, with wrathful eyes
'Neath his bright helm, who cried:
"Why in this guise
Sit ye, O Lycians? Get each to his home!
For know that yesterday three keels did come
Laden with spindles and all women's gear,
And none need lack e'en such a garment here
As well befits him—lutes the Gods have sent,
And combs and golden pins, to that intent
That ye may all be merry—what say I?
Ye may be turned to women verily,
Because the Gods are wise, and thriftless deed
Mislikes them, and forsooth is little need
That thews and muscles go with suchlike hearts
As ye have, while all wise and manly parts
Are played by girls, weak-handed, soft, and white.

"Get to the tower-top, look ye through the night,
And ye shall see the cleared sky made all red
And murky 'neath the moon with signs of dread;
Come forth and meet them! What! the Gods ye fear,
And what they threaten? Life to you is dear?
Ah, fools, that think not how to all on earth
The very death is born along with birth;
That some men are but dying twenty years,
That some men on this sick-bed of all tears
Must lie for forty years, for eighty some,
Or ever they may reach their peaceful home!
Ah, give to birth the name of death, and wait
With brave hearts rather for the stroke of fate,
And hope, since ye gained death when ye were born,

That ye from death by dying may be torn—
Unless ye deem that if this day ye live,
The next a deathless life to you will give.

"Come, then! these few behind me may ye see
Who think it worse to live on wretchedly
Than cast the die amidst of noble strife
For honoured death or fearless glorious life—
Yea, yea! and is the foe upon us then?"

For even as he spake they heard again
The smiting on the door, and as the sword
Leapt from the exile's sheath with his last word,
Again the cry, made dim by the thick door,
Smote on their ears:
"Lycians, are ye no more
Within your guarded town? A voice we heard
As if of one who bade us not be feared—
He was a god belike, and no more men
Dwell in your town: ah, will ye open then?
Do ye not hear that noise upon the wind,
And do ye think that ye fair days shall find
If our red blood shall stain your ancient gate?"

Then, as if these were maddened by some fate,
Down rained the blows upon the unyielding oak,
And the scared guards shrank back behind the folk
Bellerophon brought with him; therewith he
Sheathed his bright blade, and shot back mightily
The weight of iron bolt, and therewithal
Stepped aside swiftly; back the gates did fall
Upon their hinges, and a wretched throng
Stood, horse and foot, the glimmering spears among,
Cowering and breathless, and with eyes that turned
Over their shoulders, as though still they yearned
To see no more the quiet moonlit way
Beyond the open gates. But now, when they
Were ordered somewhat, and the gates again
Shut fast, Bellerophon cried out:
"O men,
Full fast ye fled, meseems! and who were these,
That made you tremble at the wet-leaved trees
And quivering acres of the bearded rye?"

Then spake an old man: "Fair sir, manfully
Thou speakest, and thy words are full of hope;
And yet with these no power thou hast to cope,
Who for each rye-head raise a spear aloft
Who know as much of fear, or pity soft,
As do the elm-trees; whom the Gods drive on
Until the world once happy they have won

And made it desert, peopled by the ghosts
Of those who happy died before their hosts;
Or else lived on in fear and misery
A little while before God let them die—
Devils are these; but what scorn shall we get
When thou hast heard that these are women!—yet
Keep thou thy scorn till thou art face to face
With these a minute ere the fearful chase."

Loud laughed Bellerophon, and said, "See ye,
O tremblers, what foreknowledge was in me,
When I said e'en now ye should change your parts
With women! Throw the gates wide, fearful hearts,
And let us out, that with a word or two
All that is needed herein we may do!"

The old man said, "Laugh, then, while yet your eyes
Are still unblasted with the miseries
These days have brought on us!—Lo, if I tell
Half of the dreadful things that there befell,
Ye will not listen,—if I tell the shape
Of these fell monsters, for whom hell doth gape,
Still will ye say that but my fear it is,
That speaketh in me,—yea, but hearken this;
For certainly such foes are on you now
As, bound together by a dreadful vow,
Will slay yourselves, and wives, and little ones,
And build them temples with the blanched bones,
Unto the nameless One who gives them force."

Then cried Bellerophon, in wrath: "To horse!
To horse, O Lycians! Ere the moon is down
The dawn shall come to light us; in the town
Bide thou, O captain, and guard gate and wall;
And leave us to what hap from Fate may fall!
We are enow—and for these cowards-here,
Let them have yet another death to fear
Unless they rule their tongues. Tell thou the King
That, when I come again, full many a thing
These lips will have to tell him; and meanwhile,
Since often will the Gods make strong the vile,
And bring adown the great, let him have care
That this his city is left nowise bare
Of men, and food, and arms. More might I say,
But now methinks the night's face looks towards day.
The moon sinks fast; so get we speedily
Unto that redness in the eastern sky,
That at the dawn with smoke shall dim the sun.'

A shout rose when his last clear word was done,
And at his back went rolling down the way

Mingled with clash of arms, for, sooth to say,
Hard had he laboured ere the dark night fell,
And thus had gathered men who loved him well,
Stout hearts to whom more fair it seemed to be
The face of death in stricken field to see
Than in that place to bide, till Artemis
Had utterly consumed all hope of bliss
With some unknown, unheard-of shape of fear.

So now his well-shod steed they brought him there;
Once more from out its sheath he drew his sword,
The gates swung backward at his shouted word,
And forth with eager eyes into the waves
Of darkness did he ride; the spears and glaives
Moved like a tossing winter grove behind
As on he led them, fame or death to find;
And grey night made the world seem over wide,
And over empty, in the darkling tide,
Betwixt the moonset and the dawn of day.

Then rose the sun; the fear that last night lay
Upon that people changed to certain fear
Well understood, of death that drew anear;
And now no more the timorous kept their eyes
Turned unto earth, lest in the sky should rise
The dreadful tokens of a changing world;
No more they thought to see strange things down-hurled
By Gods as unlike their vain images
As unto men are hell's flame-branched trees.
Last night for any war or pestilence,
Glad had they been to change that crushing sense
Of helplessness and lies; but now this morn,
Tormented by the rumour newly born,
The vague fear seemed the lightest; the Gods' hands
Less cruel than the deeds of those fell bands. —
Uprooted vines, fields trampled into mire,
The ring of spears around the stead afire,
Steel or the flame for choice; the torture hour
When time is gone, and the flesh hath no power
But to give agony on agony
Unto the soul that will not let it die,
So strong it is—the lone despair; the shame
Of a lost country and dishonoured name;
These last but little things to bear indeed,
When e'en the greatest helps not in our need,
And o'er the earth is risen furious hell.

Now, when this terror on the city fell,
At first went thronging to the clamorous quays
Rich men, with whatso things their palaces
Could give, that strong-backed slaves of theirs might bear.

And to and fro the great lords wandered there,
Making hard bargains 'neath the shipmen's grin,
Who had good will a life of ease to win
With one last voyage; here and there indeed,
Among the heaps of silver and rich weed
Piled on the deck, the hard-hand mariners
Thrust rudely 'gainst the wondering infant heirs,
And delicate white slaves, and proud-eyed wives,
And grumbled as they wrought to save their lives.
And here and there a ship was moving out
With white sails spreading amid oath and shout,
While her sweeps smote the water heavily,
And on the prow stood, yearning for the sea
And other lands beyond, some trembling lord.
But presently thereof the King had word;
And when he knew that thus the matter went,
A trusty captain to the quays he sent,
And stout men armed, who lined the water-side.
So there perforce must every man abide,
For shut and guarded now was every gate.

But if, amid the fear of coming fate,
You ask how fared the sweet Philonoë,
With mind a shrinking tortured thing to see,
How shall you wonder! Tales of dread she heard
With scornful eyes, and chid with eager word
Her timorous women; and with bright flushed face
And glittering eyes, she went from place to place,
As though foreknowledge of the joy to come
Pierced through all grief. Of those that saw her, some
Would say, "Alas! this ill day makes her mad."
And some, "A message certes hath she had
From the other world, and is foredoomed to die."
But some would gaze upon her wrathfully,
While sitting with bent head on woe intent,
They watched her fluttering raiment as she went
Her daily ways as in fair time of peace.

So did the longest of all days decrease
Through hours of straining fear; full were the ways
With homeless country folk, with 'wildered gaze
Fixed on the eager townsmen questioning;
And carts with this or that poor homely thing,
And cumbered women worn and desolate,
Blocked up the road anigh the eastern gate.
Thronged with pale faces were the walls that day
Of folk so scared they could not go away,
But still must watch until the horror came,
Or watch at least that smoke above the flame
Till sundown lit the sky with dreadful light;
And still the tales of horror and affright

Grew greater, and the cumbered city still
Weighed down with wealth could summon up no will
To fight or flee, or with closed lips to wait
Amidst her gold the evil day of fate.
Night came at last, a night of all unrest:
Upon the armed men now the people pressed
At gate and quay, until they needs must yield,
And many a bark o'erladen slowly reeled
Beneath the moonlight o'er the harbour green;
While as the breathing of the night wind keen
Sang down the creek, great sounds of fear it bore,
And redder was the sky than heretofore.

A fearful night, when some at last must think
That they of no more horror now might drink
Than they had drank; wherefore, with stress of fear
Made brave, some men must catch up shield and spear,
And leaderless go forth unto the flame
All eyes were turned to; but when daylight came,
With its grey light came naked death again,
And honourless did all things seem and vain
That man might do; the gates were left ajar,
And through the streets helpless in weed of war
The warders went: nought worth the King was made,
When by each man the truth of all was weighed,
And all seemed wanting: help there was in none.

Yet when 'mid these things nigh the day was done,
And the foe came not, once more hope was born
Within men's hearts too wearied and outworn
To gather fresh fear; then the walls seemed good,
The great gates more than iron and oaken wood,
And with returning hope there came back shame;
And they, bethinking them of their old name,
'Gan deem that spear to spear was no ill play,
What wrath of goddesses soever lay
Upon the city; and withal indeed,
There came fresh rumours to their honour's need,
And they bethought them of the godlike one
Who in their midst so great a deed had done,
And who erewhile rode forth so carelessly
Their very terror with his eyes to see.
So at the sunset into ordered bands
Once more the men were gathered; women's hands
Bore stones up to the ramparts that no more
That crowd of pale and anxious faces bore,
But helms and spear-heads; and the King came forth
Amidst his lords, and now of greater worth
Than common folk he seemed once more to be.
And in some order, if still timorously
The Lycians waited through the night; the sky

Showed lesser tokens of the foe anigh,
So still hope grew.

At dawn of day the King
Bade folk unto Diana's image bring
Things precious and burnt-offerings; and the smoke
Curled o'er the bowed heads of the praying folk
There in the streets, and though nought came to pass
To tell that well appeased the goddess was,
And though they durst not strive to move her thence,
Yet did there fall on men a growing sense
That now the worst was over: and at noon,
Just as the King amid the trumpets' tune
Went to his house, a messenger pierced through
The wondering crowd, and toward Jobates drew,
Nor did him reverence, nor spake aught before
He gave unto the King the scroll he bore.
Then from his saddle heavily down-leapt,
Stiffened, as one who not for long has slept,
While the King read the scroll; then those anigh
Amid the expectant silence heard him cry,
"Praise to the Gods, who are not angry long!
Hearken, all ye, how they have quenched our wrong.

Good health and good-hap to the Lycian King
And all his folk, and every wished-for thing
Wisheth hereby Bellerophon, and saith:
From out the valley of the shade of death
Late am I come again to make you glad,
Because no evil journey have we had.
And now the land is cleansed of such a pest
As has not been before; be glad and rest,
And look to see us back in seven days' space,
For yet awhile must we abide to chase
The remnant of the women that ye feared.

Silence a moment followed that last word,
Then such a joyous shout, as good it is
That those can know not who still dwell in bliss;
Then turning here and there, with varied noise
The people through all places did rejoice,
Till pleasure failed for weariness; but still
Did old and young, and men and women fill
The temples with their praises; till, when earth
Had fallen into twilight mid their mirth,
With prayers and hymns they brought the great-eyed, white,
Slow-going oxen through the gathering night,
And yoked them to Diana's car again;
Nor this time were they yoked thereto in vain,
Down went the horned heads, beam and axle-tree
Creaked as they drew, and folk cried out to see

The wheels go round; heart opened unto heart
With unhoped joy, and hate was set apart,
Envy and malice waited for some day
More common, as the goddess took her way
Amid the torch-lit, flower-strewn, joyous street,
Unto the house made ready for her feet.

But mid the noise of great festivity
That filled the night, slept on Philonoë,
Amid that sea of love past hope and fear,
And woke at sunrise no more sound to hear
Than singing of the birds in thick-leaved trees
Ere yet the sun might silence them; like these
Did she rejoice, nor strange to her it was
That all these things her love should bring to pass.
Rising, she said, "To-day thou workest this,
And unto many givest life and bliss;
To-morrow comes: therewith perchance for me
A time when thou my faithful heart mayst see."
Then she alone her fair attire did on,
And mid the sleepers went her way alone
Into the garden, and from flower to flower
Passed, making sweeter even that sweet hour;
And as by soft folds of her fluttering gown
Her body's fairness was both hid and shown,
E'en so in simpleness her soul indeed
Lay, not drawn back, but veiled beneath the weed
Of earthly beauty that the Gods had lent
Till they through years should work out their intent.

O'er the freed city passed the time away,
Until it drew unto the promised day
Of their return who all that peace had won.
And now the loved name of Bellerophon
Rang ever in the maiden's ears; and she,
As in the middle of a dream, did see
The city made all ready for that hour,
When in a fair-hung townward-looking bower,
Pale now, amid her maidens she was set,
New pain of longing for her heart to get.

Some dream there was of hurrying messengers
Bright with a glory that was nowise theirs,
And strains of music bearing back again
The heart to vague years long since lived in vain;
Then still a moving dream—of robes of gold,
Armour unsullied by the bloody mold
That bought this peace; a dream of noble maid
And longing youth in snowy robes arrayed;
Of tinkling harps and twinkling jewelled hands,
And gold-shod feet to meet the war-worn bands,

That few and weary, flower-crowned, made the dream
Less real amid the dainty people seem—
A wild dream of strange weapons heaped on wains,
And rude wrought raiment vile with rents and stains,
And dream-like figures by the axle-trees—
Women or beasts? and in the hands of these
Trumpets of wood, and conch-shells, and withal
Clamour of blast and horrid rallying call,
And such a storm of strange discordant cries,
As stilled the townsfolk mid their braveries,
For therewith came the prisoners of the fight.

A dreadful dream!—with blood-stained hair and white,
Clad in most strange habiliment of war,
Sat an old woman on a brazen car;
White stared her eyes from a brown puckered face
Upon the longed-for dainties of that place,
But wrath and fear no more in them were left,
For death seemed creeping on her; an axe-heft
Her chained hands held yet; and a monstrous crown,
Of heavy gold, 'twixt her thin feet and brown
Was laid as she had cast it off in fight,
When she was fain amidst her hurried flight
To hide all signs of her fell royalty.
An unreal dream—about her seemed to be,
Figures of women, clad in warlike guise,
In scales of brass, beasts' skins, and cloths of dyes,
Uncouth and coarse, made vile with earth and blood.
A dream of horror! nought that men deem good
Was seen in them, were they or young or old:
Great-limbed were some and mighty to behold,
With long black hair and beast-like brows, and low;
Bald-headed, old, and wizened did some go,
Yet all adorned with gold; this, in rich gown
Of some slain woman, went with eyes cast down;
That yelling walked, with armour scantly clad,
And at her belt a Lycian's head yet had
Hung by the flaxen hair; this old and bent
From bushy eyebrows grey, strange glances sent,
Grinning as from their limbs the people shrank;
But most the cup of pain and terror drank,
That they had given to drink so oft ere now
If any sign thereof their eyes might show,
And whatso mercy they of men might have,
No hope for them their gross hearts now did save.

A dreadful dream! Philonoë's slim hands
Shut from her eyes the sight of those strange bands;
Yet dreamlike must her heart behold them still,
Amid new thoughts of God, and good and ill,
And her eyes filled with tears. But what was this

That smote her yearning heart with sudden bliss,
Yet left it yearning? her fair head she raised,
And with wide eyes down on the street she gazed,
Yet cried not out; though all cry had been drowned
Amid those joyous shouts, as, laurel-crowned,
And sword in hand, and in his battered gear
On his black horse he came, and raised to her
Eyes that her heart knew. Nay, she moved not aught,
Nor reached her arms abroad, as he was brought
Beneath her place, too soon to go away;
And open still her hands before her lay
As down the street passed on the joyous cries,
Nor were there any tears in her soft eyes;
Only her lips moved softly, as she cast
One look upon the people going past,
Struggling and slow behind the last bright spears,
Whose steady points had so thrust back their fears.

But amid silence 'neath the eyes of men,
Another time that day they met again;
And that was at the feast in the great hall,
For thither must the King's folk, one and all,
Women as men, give welcome unto him
Through whom they throve. Belike all things grew dim
Before the hero's eyes but her alone,
Belike a strange light in the maid's eyes shone,
Made bright with pain; but yet hand met not hand,
Though each to each so close the twain must stand,
And though the hall was hushed to hear her say
Words that she heeded not of that fair day.
But when her clear and tender speech had end,
And mouths of men a mighty shout did send
Betwixt the pillars, still her lips did move,
As though they two were lone, with words of love
Unheard, but felt by him.

So passed the day,
And other days and nights fell fast away;
But now when this great trouble had gone by,
And things again seemed no more now to lie
Within his mighty hands, she 'gan to fear
Her father's wiles again; the days grew drear,
The nights too long, nor might she see his face,
Nor might they speak in any lonely place;
And hope at whiles waxed dim, and whiles she saw
The fate her heart so dreaded on them draw,
While she must sit aside with folded hands,
While for her sake he shunned the peaceful lands.

And all the while there must at last be borne
That darkest hour that brings about the morn.

Now as the days passed, to his treasury
Would the King go, King Prœtus' gift to see,
And stand with knitted brows to gaze on it,
While many thoughts about his heart would flit.
And on a day he said, "Time yet there is
To slay the man who saved our life and bliss.
Once did I cast him unto death, and he
Must win nought thence but utter victory;
And when the Gods helped me with ruin and fear
Another time, yet that brought nowise near
The end this binds me to; yet once again
Shall it be tried before I call it vain,
And strive no more, but bear the punishment
That on oath-breakers and weak fools is sent."

Then gat he to the doom-hall of the town,
And midst his lords and wise men sat him down
And judged the people; if at whiles to him
The clamour of the jarring folk waxed dim
Amid the thoughts of his own life that rose
Within him and about his heart did close,
Yet none the less a great King there he seemed;
As of a god's his heart the people deemed.

Now in good peace and joy the summer wore,
Nor did folk mind how it was told of yore
That in the days to come great dangers three,
Within the bounds of Lycia should there be;
For fear of ill was grown an empty name.
Into fair autumn slipped the summer's flame
More fruitful than its wont, and barn and garth
Ran over with the good things of the earth.
Crowded the quays were, but no merchandise,
No bale of fair-wrought cloth or odorous spice,
Bore pestilence within it at that tide;
In peace and health the folk dwelt far and wide.

But when the way's dust easier now was seen
Upon the bordering grape-bunches, whose green
Was passing slow through red to heavy black,
And the ploughed land all standing crop did lack,
Though yet the share the fallow troubled not;
Now, when the nights were cool, and noons still hot,
And in the windless woods the acorn fell,
More tidings were there of that land to tell.

For on a day as in the doom-hall sat
Jobates, and gave word on this and that,
A clamour by the outer door he heard
Of new-come folk, mixed with the answering word

Of those his guards, who at the door did stand;
So when his say was said, he gave command
To bring in one of those about the door;
Then was a country carle brought forth before
The ivory seat, and scared he seemed to be;
And sodden was his face for misery,
As on the King he stared with open eyes.

"What wilt thou?" said Jobates. "What thing lies
Upon thee that my power can take away?
For in mine house the Gods are good to-day."

Twice did the man's lips open as to speak,
But no sound came; the third time did outbreak
A husky, trembling sound from them, but nought
To tell the wondering folk what thing he sought.
Then said the King, "The man is mazed with fear;
Go ye and bring him wine; we needs must hear
What new thing now has happed beneath the sun.
Take heart! for thou art safe!"
So was it done:
The man raised up the bowl with trembling hand,
And drank, and then a while he yet did stand
Silent amid the silence; then began
In a weak voice:
"A poor and toiling man
I am indeed; therefore a little thing,
My woe may seem to thee; yet note, O King,
That the world changes; unimagined ill
Is born therein, and shall grow greater still.
"In early summer I was well enow
Among such men as still have need to sow
Before they reap, to reap before they eat,
Nor did I think too much of any threat
Time had for me; but therewith came the tide
When those fell women harried far and wide;
I saved myself, my wife, and little ones,
And with nought else lay on this city's stones
Until peace came; then went I to the west
Where dwelt my brother in good peace and rest,
And there the four of us must eat our bread
From hands that grudged not mayhap, with small dread
And plenteous toil. A vineyard hath he there,
Whose blossoming in March was full and fair,
And May's frost touched it not, and July's hail
Against its bunches green might not prevail;
Up a fair hill it stretched; exceeding good
Its sunny south-turned slopes are; a thin wood
Of oak-trees crowns the hill indeed, wherein
Do harbour beasts most fain a feast to win
At hands of us and Bacchus; but a wall

Well built of stones guardeth the garth from all
On three sides, and at bottom of the hill
A full stream runs, that dealeth with a mill,
My brother's too, whose floury duskiness
Our hungry souls with many a hope did bless;
Within the mill-head there the perch feed fat,
And on the other side are meadows flat,
And fruitful; shorn now, and the rooting swine
Beneath the hedge-row oak-trees grunt and whine,
And close within the long grass lies the quail,
While circling overhead the kite doth sail,
And long the partridge hath forgot the mowers.
A close of pot-herbs and of garland flowers
Goes up the hill-side from the green-banked stream,
And a house built of clay and oaken beam
Stands at its upper end, whose hillward side
Is midst the vines, that half its beams do hide.—
Nay, King, I wander not, I mind me well
The tale from end to end I have to tell,
Have patience!
"Fair that house was yesterday,
When lusty youth and slim light-handed may
Were gathered from the hamlets thereabout;
From the stream-side came laughing scream and shout,
As up the bank the nets our maidens drew,
And o'er their bare feet washed with morning dew
Floundered the cold fish; for grape-gathering tide
It was that morn, and folk from far and wide
Came to our help, and we must feast them there,
And give them all we had of good and fair.
"King, do I babble? thou for all thy crown
And robes of gold hadst gladly sat thee down
At the long table 'neath the apple-trees-
And now—go find the bones of one of these,
And be called wise henceforth!
"The last guest came,
The last shout died away that hailed his name,
The ring of men about the homestead door
Began to move; the damsels hung no more
Over the fish-tubs, but their arms shook dry
And shod their feet, and came up daintily
To mingle with the girls new-come thereto,
And take their baskets and the edge-tools due;
The good wife from the white well-scalded press
Brushed off the last wasp; while her mate did bless
The Gods, and Bacchus chiefly, as he poured
Upon the threshold ancient wine long stored
Under the earth; and then broke forth the song
As to the vineyard gate we moved along.
"Hearken, O King! call me not mad, or say
Some evil god-sent dream upon me lay;

Else could I tell thee thus how all things fell?
Nay, speak not, or the end I may not tell.
"Yea, am I safe here? will he hear of it
And come to fetch me, even if I sit
Deep underground, deep underneath the sea,
In places thou hast built for misery
Of those that hate thee; yet for safeguard now
Of me perchance? O King, abide not thou
Until my tale is done, but bid them go
Strengthen thy strong gates—deem thy high walls low
While yet the sun they hide not!"
At that word
He turned and listened as a man who heard
A doubtful noise afar, but still the King
Sat quiet midst his fear of some great thing,
And spake not, lest he yet should lose the tale.

Then said the man: "How much may now avail
Thy power and walls I know not, for I thought
Upon the wind a certain noise was brought—
But now I hear it not, and I will speak
What said I?—From all mouths there did outbreak
A plaintive song made in the olden time,
Long sung by men of the wine-bearing clime;
Not long it was, and ere the end was o'er
In midst the laden vine-rows did we pour,
And fell to work as glad as if we played;
And merrier grew the laugh of man and maid
As the thin baskets filled upon that morn;
And how should fear or thought of death be born
In such a concourse! Now mid all this, I
Unto the upper end had drawn anigh,
And somewhat lonely was I, when I heard
A noise that seemed the cry of such a bird
As is a corncrake; well, I listened not,
But worked away whereas was set my lot,
Midst many thoughts; yet louder 'gan to grow
That noise, and not so like a bird seemed now
As a great spring of steel loosed suddenly.
I put my basket down, and turned to see
The other folk, nor did they heed the noise,
And still amid their labour did rejoice;
But louder still it seemed, as there I stood
Trembling a while, then turned, and saw the wood
Like and unlike what I had known it erst;
And as I gazed the whole sky grew accurst
As with a greenish vapour, and I turned
Wild eyes adown the hill to see what burned;
There did my fellows 'twixt the vine-rows pass
Still singing; smitten then I thought I was
By sudden sickness or strange coming death;

But even therewith in drawing of a breath
A dreadful shriek rose from them, find mine eyes
Saw such a shape above the wall arise
As drove all manhood from me, and I fell
Grovelling adown; nor have I words to tell
What thing it was I saw; only I know
That from my feet the firm earth seemed to go,
And like a dream showed that fair country-side,
And, grown a mockery, needs must still abide,
An unchanged picture 'gainst the life of fear
So fallen upon me. The sweet autumn air
With a faint sickening vapour now was filled,
And all sounds else but that sound were clean stilled,
Yea, even the voice of folk by death afeard,
That in the void that horror might be heard,
And nought be heeded else.
                                    "Hearken, O King,
The while I try to tell thee of the thing
What like it was—well, lionlike, say I?
Yea, as to one who sees the teeth draw nigh
His own neck—like a horror of the wood,
Goatlike, as unto him who in drear mood
Sees monsters of the night bemock his love,
And cannot hide his eyes or turn to move—
Or serpent-like, e'en as to such an one
A serpent is, who floating all alone
In some untroubled sea all void and dim
Beholds the hoary-headed sea-worm swim,
Circling about him, ere he rise to strike—
Nay, rather, say the world hath not its like—
A changer of man's life, a swallowing dread,
A curse made manifest in devil-head.

"Long lay I there, meseems; no thought I had
Either of death, or yet of being made glad
In time to come, for all had turned to pain,
Nor might I think of aught to call a gain—
Right wondrous is the life of man, O King!
So strong to bear so many a fearful thing,
So weak of will—See now, I live, who lay
How long I know not, on that wretched day,
As helpless as a dead man, but for this,
That pain still grew with memory of what bliss
Passed life had been to me; until, God wot,
So was I helped, that memory now was not,
And all was blank.
                          "Well, once more did I wake,
Empty at first, till stirred the sickening ache
Of that great fear; then softly did I rise,
And gazed about the garth with half-dead eyes,
A heart whence everything but fear was gone."

He stopped a while and hung his head adown,
As if remembering somewhat; then he drew
Nigher the King, and said: "This thing is true,
Though thou believe it not—that I was glad
Within the hour that yet my life I had,
Though this I saw—the garth made waste and bare,
Burnt as with fire, and for the homestead fair
The last flames dying o'er an ash-heap grey—
Gone was the mill, the freed stream took its way
In unchecked shallows o'er a sandy bed.
"I knew not if my kin were slain or fled,
Yet was I glad awhile that nought was there
But me alone, till sense and dread 'gan stir
Within my heart; then slowly I began
To move about, and saw no child of man—
Unless maybe those ash-heaps here and there
I durst not go anigh, my fellows were.
Could I but flee away now! down I gat
Unto the stream, yet on the bank I sat
A long while yet, bewildered; till at last
I gathered heart, and through the stream ran fast,
And on and on, and cried, 'Are all men gone?
Is there none left on earth but I alone,
And have I nought to tell my tale unto?'

"So did I run, until at last I knew
That among men I was, who, full of fear,
Were striving somewhat of the words to hear
My heart spake, but my lips would utter not;
And food and drink from them perchance I got,
Perchance at last I told the story there;
I know not, but I know I felt the air
And seemed to move—they must have brought me then
To thee, O King—but these are not the men,
These round about—there is no more to say.
Meseems I cannot sleep or go away,
Yet am I weary."
Slowly came from him
The last words, and his eyes, all glazed and dim,
Began to close; he tottered, and at last
Sank on the ground, and into deep sleep passed,
Nor might men rouse him; so they bore him thence,
Till death should reach him or returning sense.

So next of those who brought him thereunto
Was question made what of those things they knew;
Who answered e'en as for their fear they might;
For some had seen a fire the late-past night,
And some the morn before a yellow smoke;
And one had heard the cries of burning folk;

And one had seen a man stark naked fly
Adown the stream-side, and as he went by
Saw that he bled, and thought that on his flesh
Were dreadful marks, that were as done afresh
By branding irons. One, too, said he saw
A dreadful serpent by the moonlight draw
His dry folds o'er the summer-parched way
Unto a pool that 'neath the hill-side lay.
And men there were who said that they had heard
The sound of lions roaring, and, afeard,
Had watched all-armed, with barred doors, through the night.
Then as men's faces paled with sore affright,
Unto the doom-hall came more folk, and more,
And tales of such-like things they still told o'er,
Of fresh deaths and of burnings, and still nought
They had to tell of what this fear had wrought.

Now ye shall know that Prince Bellerophon
In a swift ship had sailed a while agone
'Gainst a Tyrrhenian water-thief, who then
Wrought great scathe on the peaceful merchantmen
That sought those waters; so the King sent forth
Another captain that he held of worth,
And eighty men with him in company,
Well armed, the truth of all these things to see.

At sunset from the town did they depart,
And none among them seemed to lack good heart,
And wise they were in war; but ere the sun
Through all the hours of the next day had run,
One ancient brave man only of the band
Came back again, no weapon in his hand,
No shield upon his neck—but carrying now
His son's dead body on his saddle-bow,
A lad of eighteen winters, fair and strong;
But when men asked what thing had wrought that wrong,
Nought might he answer, but with bowed-down head
Still sat beside the armed body dead,
As one who had no memory; but when folk
Searched the youth's body for the deadly stroke,
No wound at all might they find anywhere;
So still the old man sat with hopeless stare,
And though he seemed right hale and sound of limb,
And ate and drank what things were brought to him,
Yet speechless did he live for three more days,
Then to the silent land he went his ways.

Now a great terror on the city fell,
Even as that whereof we had to tell
In the past summer; day by day there came
Folk fleeing to the gates, who thought no shame

To tell how dreams had scared them, or some sign
In earth, or sky, or milk, or bread, or wine,
Or in some beast late given unto a god;
And on the beaten ways once more there trod
The feet of homeless folk; the country-side
Grew waste and bare of men-folk far and wide;
And whatso armèd men the King did send,
But little space upon their way did wend
Ere they turned back in terror; nigher drew
The belt of desolation, yet none knew
What thing of ill it was that wrought this woe,
More than the man who first the tale did show.

Meanwhile men's eyes unto the sea were turned
Watching, until the Sea-hawk's image burned
Upon the prow Bellerophon that bore,
And his folk cast the hawser to the shore,
And long it seemed to them did he delay.
Yet since all things have end, upon a day
The Sea-hawk's great sweeps beat the water green,
And her long pennon down the wind was seen,
As nigh the noontide toward the quays she passed,
With sound of horns and singing; on the mast
Hung the sea-robbers' fair shields, lip to lip,
And high above the clamour of the ship,
Out from the topmast, a great pennoned spear
The terror of the seas aloft did bear,
The head of him who made the chapmen quake.

New hope did that triumphant music wake
Within men's hearts, as now with joyous shout
The bay-crowned shipmen shot the gangway out
Unto the shore, and once more as a god
The wise Bellerophon among them trod,
As to the Father's house he took his way,
The tenth of all the spoil therein to lay.
But when he came into the greatest square
Where was the temple, a great throng was there,
And on the high steps of the doom-hall's door,
A clear-voiced, gold-clad herald stood, before
A row of spears; and now he cried aloud,
Over the raised heads of the listening crowd:

"Hearken, O Lycians! King Jobates saith;
Upon us lies the shadow of a death
I may not deal with; old now am I grown,
And at the best am but one man alone;
But since such men there are, as yet may hope
With this vague unseen death of man to cope,
He whereby such a happy end is wrought
Shall nowise labour utterly for nought

As at my hands; lest to the gods we seem
To hold too fast to wealth, lest all men deem
We are base-born and vile: so know hereby,
That to the man who ends this woe will I
Give my fair daughter named Philonoë,
And this land's rule and wealth to share with me.
And if it be so that he may not take
The maiden, let him give her for my sake
To whom he will; or if that may not be,
A noble ransom shall he have of me
And be content.—May the gods save us yet,
And in fair peace these fears may we forget!"

He ended, and the folk about the place,
Seeing the shipmen come, on these did gaze,
And in their eyes were mingled hope and doubt;
But at the last the shadow of a shout
They raised for Prince Bellerophon; and he
Stood at the door one moment silently,
And wondered; for he knew nought of the things
That there had fallen while the robber-kings
He chased o'er ridge and furrow of the sea;
Because folk deemed ill-omened it would be
To tell thereof ere all things due were paid
Unto the Father, and the fair tenth laid
Before his altar. Yet he could not fail
To see that in some wise the folk must ail;
Such haggard eyes, such feverish faces were
About him; yea, the clamour and the cheer
That greeted him were eager with the pain
Of men who needs must hope yet once again
Before they fall into the jaws of death.

So as the herald spake, he held his breath,
His heart beat fast, and in his eyes there burned
The light of coming triumph, as he turned
Unto a street that led from out the place,
And up the steep way saw the changeless grace
Of the King's palace, and the sun thereon,
That calmly o'er its walls of marble shone,
For all the feverish fears of men who die:
One moment thus he stood, and smiled, then high
Lifted his sword, and led the spear-wood through
The temple-door and toward the altar drew.

But when all rites to Jove were duly done,
Unto the King went up Bellerophon,
To tell him of his fare upon the sea;
So in the chamber named of porphyry
He found Jobates pacing to and fro,
As on the day when first he bade him go

And win the Solymi.
"O King," he said,
"All hail to thee! the water-thief is dead,
His keel makes sport for children of the sea."

"And I, Bellerophon, have news for thee,
And see thou to it! The gods love so well
The fair wide world, that fear and death and hell
In this small land will they shut up for aye.
And thou—when thou hadst luck to get away,
Why must thou needs come back here, to abide
In very hell? I say the world is wide,
And thou art young; far better had it been,
When o'er the sea-thief's bulwarks first were seen
Men's wrathful eyes, the war-shout to have stayed;
Then might ye twain, strong in each other's aid,
Have won some fair town and good peace therein:
For here with us stout heart but death shall win."

Now on a table nigh the King's right hand
Bellerophon beheld a casket stand
That well he knew; thereby a letter lay,
Whose face he had not seen before that day,
And as he noted it a half-smile came
Across his face, for a look like to shame
Was in the King's eyes as they met his own.

Cheerly he spake: "O King, I have been thrown
Into thine hands, and with this city fair
Both weal and woe have I good will to share.
Young am I certes, yet have ever heard
That whether men live careless or afeard
Death reaches them; of endless heaven and hell
Strange stories oft have I heard people tell;
Yet knew I no man yet that knows the road
Which leadeth either to the blest abode
Or to the land of pain. Not overmuch
I fear or hope the gates of these to touch
Unless we twain be such men verily
As on the earth make heaven and hell to be;
And if these countries are upon the earth,
Then death shall end the land of heaven and mirth,
And death shall end the land of hell and pain.
Yea, and say all these tales be not in vain,
Within mine hand do I hold hope—within
This gold-wrought scabbard—such a life to win
As will not let hope fall off utterly,
Until such time is come that I must die
And no more need it. But the time goes fast;
Into mine ears a tale the townsmen cast
With eager words, almost before my feet

The common earth without Jove's fane could meet;
I heard thy herald too say mighty things—
How sayest thou about the oaths of kings?"

The King's eyes glistened: "O Corinthian,"
He said, "if there be such a twice-cursed man
As rules the foolish folk and punisheth,
And yet must breathe out lies with every breath,
Let him be thrice cursed, let the Gods make nought
Of all his prayers when he in need is caught!"
"What sayest thou," then said Bellerophon,
"If a man sweareth first to such an one,
And then to such another, and the twain
Cannot be kept, but one still maketh vain
The other?"
Then the King cast down his eyes:
"What sayest thou, my son? What mysteries
Lie in these words of thine? Go forth and break
This chain of ours, and then return to take
Thy due reward—oft meseems so it is
That these our woes are forged to make thy bliss."

Then laughed Bellerophon aloud, and said,
"The Gods are kind to mortals, by my head!
But so much do they love me certainly
That more than once I shall not have to die;
And I myself do love myself so well
That each night still a pleasant tale shall tell
Of the bright morn to come to me. But thou,
Think of thy first vow and thy second vow!
For so it is that I may come again
Despite of all: and what wilt thou do then?
Ponder meanwhile if from ill deeds can come
Good hap to bless thee and thy kingly home!"

And even with that last word was he gone,
And the King, left bewildered and alone,
Sat down, and strove to think, and said at last:
"Good were it if the next three months were passed;
I should be merrier, nigher though I were
Unto that end of all that all men fear."

Then sent he for his captain of the guard,
And said to him, "Now must thou e'en keep ward
Closer than heretofore upon the gates,
Because we know not now what thing awaits
The city, and Bellerophon will go
The truth of all these wondrous things to know:
So let none pass unquestioned; nay, bring here
Whatever man bears tales of woe or fear
Into the city; fain would I know all—

Nay, speak, what thinkest thou is like to fall?"

"Belike," the man said, "he will come again,
And with my ancient master o'er us reign;
E'en as I came in did he pass me by,
And nowise seemed he one about to die."

"Nay," said the King, "thou speak'st but of a man;
Shall he prevail o'er what made corpses wan
Of many a stout war-hardened company?"

"Methinks, O King, that such might even be,"
The captain said; "he is not of our blood;
He goes to meet the beast in other mood
Than has been seen among us, nor know I
Whether to name him mere man that shall die,
Or half a god; for death he feareth not,
Yet in his heart desire of life is hot;
Life he scorns not, yet will his laughter rise
At hearkening to our timorous miseries,
And all the self-wrought woes of restless men."

"Ah," said the King, "belike thou lov'st him then?"

"Nay, for I fear him, King," the captain said,
"And easier should I live if he were dead;
Besides, it seems to me our woes began
When down our streets first passed this godlike man,
And all our fears are puppets unto him;
That he may brighter show by our being dim,
The Gods have wrought them as it seems to me."

"What wouldst thou do then that the man might be
A glorious memory to the Lycian folk,
A god who from their shoulders raised a yoke
Dreadful to bear; then, as he came, so went,
When he had fully wrought out his intent?"

"Nay, King, what say'st thou? Hast thou then forgot
Whereto he goes this eve? Nay, hear'st thou not
His horse-hooves' ring e'en now upon the street?
Look out! look out! thine eyes his eyes shall meet,
And see the sun upon his armour bright!
Yet the gold sunset brings about the night,
And the red dawn is quenched in dull grey rain."

Then swiftly did the King a window gain,
And down below beheld Bellerophon,
And certes round about his head there shone
A glory from the west. Then the King cried:
"O great Corinthian, happy mayst thou ride,

And bring us back our peace!"
The hero turned,
And through his gold hair still the sunset burned,
But half his shaded face was grey. He stayed
His eager horse, and round his mouth there played
A strange smile as he gazed up at the King,
And his bright hauberk tinkled ring by ring.
But as the King shrank back before his gaze,
With his left hand his great sword did he raise
A little way, then back into the sheath
He dropped it clattering, and cried:
"Life or death,
But never death in life for me, O King!"
Therewith he turned once more; with sooty wing
The shrill swifts down the street before him swept,
And from a doorway a tired wanderer leapt
Up to his feet, with wondering look to gaze
Upon that golden hope of better days.

Then back the King turned; silent for awhile
He sat beneath his captain's curious smile,
Thinking o'er all the years gone by in vain.
At last he said:
"Yea, certes, I were fain
If I my life and honour so might save
That he not half alone, but all should have."

"Yea," said the captain, "good the game were then,
For thou shouldst be the least of outcast men;
So talk no more of honour; what say I, —
Thou shouldst be slain in short time certainly,
Who hast been nigh a god before to-day!
Be merry, for much lieth in the way
'Twixt him and life: and, to unsay the word
I said before, be not too much afeard
That he will come again. The Gods belike
Have no great will such things as us to strike,
But will grow weary of afflicting us;
Because with bowed heads, and eyes piteous,
We take their strokes. When thou sitt'st down to hear
A minstrel's tale, with nothing great or dear
Wouldst thou reward him, if he thought it well
Of wretched folk and mean a tale to tell;
But when the godlike man is midst the swords
He cannot 'scape; or when the bitter words,
That chide the Gods who made the world and life,
Fall from the wise man worsted in the strife;
Or when some fairest one whose fervent love
Seems strong the world from out its curse to move,
Sits with cold breast and empty hands before
The hollow dreams that play about death's door—

When these things pierce thine ears, how art thou moved!
Though in such wise thou lov'st not nor art loved,
Though with weak heart thou lettest day wear day
As bough rubs bough; though on thy feeble way
Thou hast no eye to see what things are great,
What things are small, that by the hand of fate
Are laid before thee. Shall we marvel then,
If the Gods, like in other things to men,
(For so we deem them) think no scorn to sit
To see the play, and weep and laugh at it,
And will not have poor hearts and bodies vile
With unmelodious sorrow to beguile
The long long days of heaven—but these, in peace,
Trouble or joy, or waxing, or decrease,
Shall have no heed from them—ah, well am I
To be amongst them! never will I cry
Unto the Gods to set me high aloft;
For earth beneath my feet is sweet and soft,
And, falling, scarce I fall.
"Behold, O King,
Beasts weep not ever, and a short-lived thing
Their fear is, and their generations go
Untold-of past; and I who dwell alow,
Somewhat with them I feel, and deem nought ill
That my few days with more of joy may fill;
Therefore swift rede I take with all things here,
And short, if sharp, is all my woe and fear.
"Now happier were I if Bellerophon,
This god on earth, from out our land were gone,
And well I hope he will not soon return
Who knows? but if for some cause thou dost yearn
For quiet life without him, such am I
As, risking great things for great things, would try
To deal with him, if back again he comes
To make a new world of our peaceful homes.
Yet, King, it might well be that I should ask
Some earthly joy to pay me for the task;
And if Bellerophon returns again
And lives, with thee he presently will reign,
And soon alone in thy place will he sit;
Yea, even, and if he hath no will for it.
His share I ask then, yet am not so bold
As yet to hope within mine arms to fold
Philonoë thy daughter, any more
Than her, who on the green Sicilian shore
Plucked flowers, and dreamed no whit of such a mate
As holds the keys of life, and death, and fate—
Though that indeed I may ask, as in time,
The royal bed's air seem no outland clime
To me, whose sire, a rugged mountaineer,
Knew what the winter meant, and pinching cheer."

Into the twinkling crafty eyes of him
The King looked long, until his own waxed dim
For thinking, and unto himself he said:
"To such as fear is trouble ever dead,
How oft soe'er the troublous man we slay?"

At last he spake aloud: "Quick fails the day;
These things are ill to speak of in the night;
Now let me rest, but with to-morrow's light
Come thou to me, and take my word for all."

The mask of reverence he had erst let fall
The Captain brought again across his face,
And smiling left the lone King in his place.
Who when all day had gone, sat hearkening how
Without, his gathering serving-men spake low,
And through the door-chinks saw the tapers gleam.

But now while thus they talked, and yet the stream
Of golden sunsetting lit up the world,
Ere yet the swift her long dusk wings had furled
In the grey cranny, fair Philonoë went
Amid her maids with face to earth down-bent
Across the palace-yard, oppressed with thought
Of what those latter days to her had brought;
Daring, unlike a maid's sweet tranquil mind,
And hushed surprise, so strange a world to find
Within her and around her: life once dear,
Despised yet clung to; fear and scorn of fear;
A pain she might not strive to cast away,
Lest in the heart of it all life's joy lay;
Joy now and ever. Toward the door she came
Of the great hall; the sunset burned like flame
Behind her back, and going ponderingly
She noted her grey shadow slim to see
Rise up and darken the bright marble wall;
Then slower on the grass her feet did fall
Till scarce she moved; then from within she heard
A voice well loved cry out some hurried word.
She raised her face, and in the door she seemed
To see a star new fallen, therefrom there gleamed
Such splendour, but although her dazzled eyes
Saw nought, her heart, fulfilled of glad surprise,
Knew that his face was nigh ere she beheld
The noble brow as wise as grief-taught eld,
As fair as a god's early unstained youth.

A little while they stood thus, with new ruth
Gathering in either's heart for the other's pain,
And fear of days yet to be passed in vain,

And wonder at the death they knew so nigh
And disbelief in parting, should they die,
And joy that still they stood together thus.
Then, in a voice that love made piteous
Through common words and few, she spake and said:

"What dost thou, Prince, with helmet on thine head
And sword girt to thee, this fair autumn eve?
Is it not yet a day too soon to leave
The place thou tamest to this very noon?"
He said, "No Lycian man can have too soon
His armour on his back in this our need,
Yea, steel perchance shall come to be meet weed
For such as thou art, lady. Who knows whence
We next may hear tales of this pestilence?
Fair is this house: yet maybe, or today
The autumn evening wind has borne away
From its smooth chambers sound of woe and tears,
And shall do yet again. Death slayeth fears,
Now I go seek if Death too slayeth love."

A little toward him did one slim hand move,
Then fell again mid folds of her fair gown;
She spake:
"Farewell, a great man art thou grown;
Thou know'st not fear or lies; so fare thou forth:
If the Gods keep not what is most of worth
Here in the world, its memory bides behind;
And we perchance in other days may find
The end of hollow dreams we once have dreamed,
Waking from which such hopeless anguish seemed."

Pale was her face when these words were begun,
But she flushed red or ere the end was done
With more than sunset. But he spake and said:
"Farewell, farewell, God grant thee hardihead,
And growing pleasure on from day to day!"

Then toward the open gate he took his way,
Nor looked aback, nor yet long did she turn
Her eyes on him, though sore her heart did yearn
To have some little earthly bliss of love
Before the end.

But right and left did move
Her damsels as he passed them, e'en as trees
Move one by one when the light fickle breeze
Touches their tops in going toward the sea;
And their eyes turned upon him wonderingly
That such a man could live, such deeds be done;
But now his steed's hooves smote upon the stone,

He swung into his saddle, and once more
Cast round a swift glance at the great hall door
And saw her not; alone she stood within,
Striving to think what hope of things to win
Had left her life; her maidens' prattling speech
Within the porch her wildered ears did reach,
But not the hard hooves' clatter as he rode
Along the white wall of that fair abode,
Nor yet the shout that he cast back again
Unto the King; dark grew each window-pane,
She seemed to think her maids were talking there,
She doubted that some answer came from her;
She knew she moved thence, that a glare of light
Smote on her eyes, that old things came in sight
She knew full well; that on her bed she lay,
And through long hours was waiting for the day;
But knew not what she thought of; life seemed gone,
And she had fought with Gods, and they had won.

Next morn, the captain, as it was to be,
Held speech with King Jobates privily.
And when he came from out the royal place
A smile of triumph was there on his face,
As though the game were won; but as he went
Unto the great gate on his luck intent,
A woeful sound there smote upon his ear,
And crossed his happy mood with sudden fear;
For now five women went adown the street,
That e'en the curious townsmen durst not meet,
Though they turned round to look with wild scared eyes,
And listened trembling to those doleful cries;
Because for Pallas' sacred maids they knew
Those wild-eyed wailing ones that closer drew
Scant rags about them, as with feet that bled
And failing limbs they tottered blind with dread,
Past house and hall. Now such-like had been these,
And guarded as the precious images
That hold a city's safety in their hands,
And dainty things from many distant lands
Were gathered round them in the house that stood,
Fair above all, within the hallowed wood,
Ten leagues from out the city; wondrous lore,
Folk deemed, within that house they pondered o'er,
And had been goddesses, but that they too
The hope of death if not its terror knew.

White grew the captain's face these folk to see,
Yet midst his fear he muttered: "Well be ye,
O Gods, who have no care to guard your own!
Perchance ye too weary of good are grown;
Look then on me, I shall not weary you—

I who once longed great things and high to do
If ye would have it so;—come, bless me then,
Since ye are grown aweary of good men!"
So to his folk he turned, and bade them take
The holy women for the goddess' sake,
And give them into some kind matron's care.
So did they, and when bathed and clad they were,
He strove in vain to know their tale; for they
Had clean forgot all things before that day,
And only knew that they by some great curse
Had late been smitten, and mid fear of worse
Were leaving life behind. So when he knew
That with these woful women he might do
Nought else, because their hearts were dead before
Their bodies, midst the fear and tumult sore
He went unto the gate, and waited there
If he perchance some other news might hear;
But nought befell that day to tell about,
And tidingless night came, and dark died out.

But just before the rising of the sun
The gate was smitten on, and there sat one
On a grey horse, and in bright armour clad.
Young was he, and strong built; his face seemed glad
Amidst of weariness, and though he seemed
Even as one who of past marvels dreamed.
Now turned the captain to him hastily,
And said: "Fair fellow, needs thou must with me,
Nor speak thou good or bad before the King
Has heard thee;" therewith, scarcely wondering,
He rode beside the captain, and the twain
In no long time the palace gate did gain,
Which opened at a word the captain spake,
And past the warders standing half awake
They came unto the King: sleeping he lay,
While o'er his gold bed crept the daylight grey;
But softly thereunto the captain went,
And to his sleeping head his own down bent
And whispered; then as one who has just heard
Right in his ears the whisper of death's word,
He started up with eyes that, open wide,
Still saw not what the strange new light might hide;
Upright he sat, and panting for a while,
Till heeding at the last the captain's smile,
And low and humble words, he smiled and said:
"Well be ye! for I dreamed that I was dead
Before ye came, and waking thought that I
Was dead indeed, and that such things were nigh
As willingly men name not. What wouldst thou?
What new thing must the Lycians suffer now?"

"King," said the captain, "here I have with me
A man-at-arms who joyful seems to be;
Therefore I deem somewhat has come to pass,
Since for these many days no face here has
Made e'en a show of gladness, or of more
Than thinking good it were if all were o'er,—
The slow tormenting hope—the heavy fear.
Speak thou, good friend! the King is fain to hear
The tale thou hast to tell."
Then spake the man:
"Good hap to me, indeed, that thus I can
Make glad the Lycian folk, and thee, O King!
But nowise have I wrought the happy thing,
But some immortal as meseems
"Now I
With other two made up my mind to try
The chance of death or glorious life herein,
In good hope either rest from fear to win
Or many days of pleasure; so I armed
In this my father's gear, that had been charmed
Years long agone by spells, well worn I doubt
To nothing now, if one might clean tell out
The truth of all; then in Diana's fane
Anigh our house I met the other twain,
And forth we went at dawn, two days ago.
Not hard it was our rightful road to know,
For hour by hour of dreadful deaths we heard,
And still met fleeing folk, so sore afeard
That they must scowl upon us questioning.
And so at last we deemed the dreadful thing,
What death soever he dealt otherwhere
From time to time, must have his chiefest lair
Within Minerva's consecrated lands,
That stretch from where her mighty temple stands
Midst its wild olive-groves, until they meet
The rugged mountain's bare unwooded feet.
Thither we turned, and at the end of day
We reached the temple, and with no delay
Sought out the priests and told them of our rede.
"They answered us that heavy was their need,
That day by day they dreaded death would come
And take them from the midst of that fair home,
And shortly, that when midnight was passed o'er,
Their lives in that house they would risk no more,
But get them gone. 'All things are done,' said they,
'The sacred maids, who have not seen the day,
But in these precincts, count the minutes now
Until the midnight moon the way shall show;
Ten horse-loads of the precious things we have,
That somewhat of our past lives we may save
To bring us o'er the sea. So sorry cheer,

Fair sons, of meat or lodging get ye here,
For all is bare and blank as some hill-side;
Nor, if ye love your lives, will ye abide
Another minute here: for us, indeed,
One answer more from Pallas do we need;
And, that being got at, nothing stays us then.'

"Worn were the faces of these holy men,
And their eyes wandered even as they spake,
And scarcely did they move as men awake
About that place, whose mighty walls of stone
Seemed waiting for the time when all was gone,
Except the presence of the Dreadful Maid,
Careless of who was glad and who afraid.

"Shortly we answered; we would bide and see
What thing within the precinct there might be
Until the morn, and if we lived till then,
Further afield would seek this death of men.
They heard us wondering, or with scorn, but gave
Such cheer to us as yet they chanced to have;
And we, being weary, fell asleep withal
Within a chamber nigh the northern wall
Of the great temple. Such a dream I had,
As that I thought fair folk, in order glad,
Sang songs throughout a place I knew to be
A town whereof had tales been told to me
When I was but a youngling: years agone
Had I forgot it all, and now alone
The nameless place had come to me.—O King,
I dreamed, I say, I heard much people sing
In happy wise; but even therewithal
Amidst my dream a great voice did there call,
But in a tongue I knew not; and each face
Was changed to utter horror in that place;
And yet the song rose higher, until all tune
Was strangled in it, and to shrill shrieks soon
It changed, and I sat upright in my bed,
Waked in an instant, open-mouthed with dread.
I know not why—though all about I heard
Shrill screams indeed, as though of folk afeard,
Mixed with a roar like white flame that doth break
From out a furnace-mouth: the earth did shake
Beneath my bed, and when my eyes I turned
Without the window, such a light there burned
As would have made the noon-tide sunshine grey.
There on the floor one of my fellows lay,
Half-armed and groaning like a wounded man;
And circling round about the other ran,
With foaming lips as one driven mad with fear.
"Then I, who knew not what thing drew anear,

And scarce could think amid my dread, sat still
Trembling a little space of time, until
To me from out the jaws of death was born,
Without a hope it seemed, a sudden scorn
Of death and fear; for all the worst I knew,
And many a thing seemed false that had been true,
And many a thing now seemed of little worth
That once had made the mean and sordid earth
All glorious.
"So with fixed and steady face
I armed myself; and turned to leave the place,
And passed from out it into the great hall
Of the very temple, where from wall to wall
There rolled a cloud of white and sulphurous smoke;
And there the remnant of the temple folk,
That had not heart enow to flee away,
Like dying folk upon the pavement lay,
And some seemed dead indeed. High o'er that gear
Stood golden Pallas, with her burnished spear
Glittering from out the smoke-cloud in that light,
That made strange day and ghastly of the night;
And her unmoved calm face that knew no smile
Cast no look down, as though she deemed too vile
The writhing tortured limbs, the sickening sound
Of dying groans of those that lay around,
Or to the pillars clung in agonies
Past telling of; but now I turned mine eyes,
Grown used to death within a little space,
Unto the other end of that fair place,
Where black the wood of polished pillars showed
Against the dreadful light, that throbbed and glowed,
Changing, and changing back to what it was.
So, through their rows did I begin to pass,
And heavier grew the smoke-cloud as I went;
But I, upon the face of death intent,
And what should come thereafter, made no stay
Until two fathom of white pavement lay
Betwixt me and the grass: the lit-up trees
Sparkled like quick-fire in the light night breeze,
And turned the sky black, and their stems between
The black depths of the inner wood were seen;
Like liquid flame a brook leapt out from them,
And, turning, ran along the forest hem:
'Twixt that and me —How shall I tell thereof,
And hope to 'scape hard word and bitter scoff?

"Let me say first that, changing horribly
That noise went on and seemed a part of me,
E'en as the light; unless by death I won
Quiet again; earth's peace seemed long years gone,
And all its hopes poor toys of little worth.

Therefore I turned not, nor fell down to earth,
And still within my hand I held my sword,
And saw it all as I see thee, fair lord.

"And this I saw: a mass, from whence there came
That fearful light, as from a heart of flame;
But black amid its radiance was that mass,
And black and claw-like things therefrom did pass,
Lengthening and shortening, and grey flocks of hair
Seemed moving on it with some inward air
The light bore with it; but in front of me
An upreared changing dark bulk did I see,
That my heart told me was the monster's head,
The seat of all the will that wrought our dread;
And midst thereof two orbs of red flame shone
When first I came, and then again were gone,
Then came again, like lights on a dark sea
As the thing turned. And now it seemed to me,
Moreover, that, despite the dreadful sound
That filled my very heart and shook the ground,
Mute was the horror's head, as the great shade
That sometimes, as in deep sleep we are laid
Seems ready to roll over us, and crush
Our souls to nought amidst its shadowy hush:
Nor might I know how that dread noise was wrought.

"But, when unto the place I first was brought
Where now I stayed, and stared, I knew not well
If the thing moved; but deemed that I might tell
Ten fathoms o'er betwixt us, and midway
'Twixt me and it a temple-priest there lay,
Face foremost, armed, and in his hand a spear;
And as with fixed eyes I stood moveless there,
Striving to think how I should meet the thing,
Amidst that noise I heard his armour ring
As smitten by some stroke; and then I saw
Unto that hideous bulk the body draw,
And yet saw not what drew it; till at last
Into the huge dark mass it slowly passed.
Nor did the monster change; unless, methought
A little nigher thereto I was brought
And still my eyes were fixed on it; with hand
Upon my drawn-back sword I still did stand,
Mid thoughts of folk who meet dread things alone
In dreadful lands, and slowly turn to stone.
So stood I: quicker grew my fevered breath,
Long, long, the time seemed betwixt life and death,
And I began to waver therewithal,
And at the last I opened lips to call
Aloud, and made no sound; then fell my brand
Clanging adown from out my feeble hand,

And rest seemed sweet again; one step I made
Aback, to gain a huge pier's deep black shade,
Then at my fallen sword in vain I stared,
And could not stoop to it—
"And then there blared
A new sound forth, I deemed a trumpet-blast,
And o'er mine eyes a dull thick veil seemed cast,
And my knees bent beneath me, and I fell
A dead heap to the earth, with death and hell
Once more a pain, and terrible once more,
Teaching me dreadful things of hidden lore,
Showing strange pictures to my soul forlorn
That cursed the wretched day when I was born.

"There lay I, as it seemed, a weary tide,
Nor knew I if I lived yet, or had died,
E'en as the other folk, of utter fear,
When in mine ears a new voice did I hear,
Nor knew at first what words it said to me;
Till my eyes opened, and I seemed to see,
Grown grey and soft, the marble pillars there,
And 'twixt their shafts afar the woodland fair,
As if through clear green water; then I heard
Close by my very head a kindly word:
'Be of good cheer! the earth is earth again,
And thou hadst heart enow to face the bane
Of Lycia, though the Gods would not that thou
Shouldst slay him utterly: but rise up now
If so thou mayst, and help me, for I bleed,
And of some leech-craft have I speedy need,
Though no life-blood it is that flows from me.'

"Then clearer grew mine eyes, and I could see
An armed man standing over me, and I
Rose up therewith and stood unsteadily,
And gazed around, and saw that the fell light
Had vanished utterly; fast waned the night
And a cold wind blew, as the young dawn strove
With the low moon and the faint stars above,
And all was quiet. But that new-come man,
Standing beside me in the twilight wan,
Seemed like a god, come down to make again
Another earth all free from death and pain.
Tall was he, fair he seemed unto me then
Beyond the beauty of the sons of men:
But as our eyes met, and mine, shamed and weak,
Dropped before his, once more he 'gan to speak:

"'Be not ashamed,' he said, 'but look around,
And thou shalt see thy fear lie on the ground,
No more divine or dreadful.'

"Then I saw
A tangled mass of hair, and scale, and claw,
Lie wallowing on the grey down-trodden grass;
Huge was it certes, but nought like the mass
Of horror mid the light my fear still told
My shuddering heart of, nor could I behold
Clearly the monster's shape in that dim light;
Yet gladly did I turn me from the sight
Unto my fellow, and I said:
"'Hast thou
Some other shape unto mine eyes to show?
And is this part of the grim mockery
Whereto the Gods have driven me forth to die?
Or art thou such a dream as meets the dead
When first they die?'
"I am a man,' he said,
'E'en as thou art; thou livest, if I live;
And some god unto me such strength did give,
That this my father's father's sword hath wrought
Deliverance for the Lycians, and made nought
This divine dread—but let us come again
When day is grown; and I have eased the pain
Of burning thirst that chokes me, and thine hands
Have swathed my hurts here with fair linen bands,
For somewhat faint I grow.'
"So then we passed
Betwixt the pillars till we reached at last
The chamber where I erst had slept, and there
We drank, and then his hurts with water fair
I bathed, and swathed them; and by then the day
Showed how my fellows on the pavement lay
Dead, yet without a wound it seemed; and when
Into the pillared hall we came again,
From one unto the other did we go
That lay about the place, and even so
It was with them; then the new-corner sighed
And said: 'Belike it was of fear they died,
Yet wish them not alive again, for they
Had found death fearful on another day;
But gladly had I never seen this sight,
For I shall think thereof at whiles by night,
And wonder if all life is worth such woe—
But now unto the quarry let us go.'

"So forth we went, but when we came whereas
The beast lay, slantwise o'er the wind-swept grass
Shone the low sun on what was left of him,
For all about the trodden earth did swim
In horrible corruption of black blood,
And in the midst thereof his carcase stood,
E'en like a keel beat down and castaway

At dead ebb high up in a sandy bay.
But when I gathered heart close up to go
And touch that master of all horror, lo,
How had he changed! for nothing now was there
But skin, beset with scale and dreadful hair
Drawn tight about the bones: flesh, muscle strong,
And all that helped the life of that great wrong,
Had ebbed away with life; his head, deep cleft
By the fair hero's sword-edge, yet had left
Three teeth like spears within it; on the ground
The rest had fallen, and now lay around
Half hidden in the marsh his blood had made;
Hollow his sides did sound when, still afraid
Of what he had been, with my clenched hand
I smote him. So a minute did we stand
Wondering, until my fellow said to me:

"In the past night didst thou do valiantly,
So smite the head from off him, and then go
This finished work unto the King to show,
And tell him by that token that I come,
Who heretofore have had no quiet home
Either in Corinth or the Argive land.
Here till to-morrow bide I, to withstand
What new thing yet may come; for strange to me
Are all these things, nor know I if I be
Waking or sleeping yet, although methinks
My soul some foretaste of a great bliss drinks.
So get thee to the work, and then go forth;
These coming days in sooth will show the worth
Of what my hand hath wrought!'
"Weary he seemed
And spake, indeed, well-nigh as one who dreamed;
But yet his word I durst not disobey;
With no great pain I smote the head away
From off the trunk, and humbly bade farewell
Unto my godlike saviour from deep hell;
I gat my horse, and to the saddle bound
The monster's head, whose long mane swept the ground,
Whose weight e'en now was no light pack-horse load,
And so with merry heart went on my road,
And made on toward the city, where I thought
A little after nightfall to be brought;
But so it was, that ere I had gone through
The wasted country and now well-nigh drew
Unto the lands where people yet did dwell,
So dull a humour on my spirit fell,
That at the last I might not go nor stand;
So, holding still the reins in my right hand,
I laid me down upon the sunburnt grass
Of the road-side, and just high noon it was.

"But moonrise was it when I woke again;
My horse grazed close beside with dangling rein;
But when I called him, and he turned to me,
No burden on his back I now might see,
And wondered; for right firmly had I bound
The thing unto him; then I searched around
Lest he perchance had rolled, and in such wise
Had rid him of that weight; and as mine eyes
Grew used to the grey moonlight, I could trace
A line of greyish ashes, as from place
To greener place, the wandering beast had fed;
But nothing more I saw of that grim head.
Then much I wondered, and my fear waxed great,
And I 'gan doubt if there I should not wait
The coming of that glorious mighty one,
Who for the world so great a deed had done.
But at the last I thought it good to go
Unto the town e'en as he bade me do,
Because his words constrained me. Nought befell
Upon the road whereof is need to tell,
And so my tale is done; and though it be
That I no token have to show to thee,
Yet doubt not, King Jobates, that no more
The Gods will vex the land as heretofore
With this fell torment. Furthermore, if he
Who wrought this deed is no divinity
He will be here soon; so must thou devise,
O Lycian King, in whatso greatest wise
Thou wilt reward him—but for me, I pray
That thou wilt give me to him from to-day,
That serving him, and in his company,
Not wholly base I too become to be."

The King and captain for a little while
Gazed each at each; an ugly covert smile
Lurked round the captain's mouth, but the King stared
Blankly upon him, e'en as though he heard
A doom go forth against him; and again
The man who brought the news stared at the twain
With knitted brows, as greatly marvelling
Why they spake nought, until at last the King
Turned eyes upon him, and the captain spake:

"Certes, O King, brightly the day doth break
If this man sayeth sooth; nor know I one
To do this deed except Bellerophon;
And so much certes hast thou honoured him
That nothing now thy glory can wax dim
Because of his; and though indeed the earth
Hold nought within it of such wondrous worth
As that which thou wilt give him in reward,

Not overmuch it is for such a sword,
And such a heart, the people's very friend."

So spake he, and before his speech had end
His wonted face at last the King had got,
And spake unto the man:
"We doubt thee not;
Thy tale seems true, nor dost thou glorify
Thyself herein—certes thou wouldst abye
A heavy fate if thou shouldst lie herein—
So here shalt thou abide till sight we win
Of him who wrought this deed; then shalt thou have
A good reward, as one both true and brave
As for a son of man, for he, meseems,
Who made an end of our so fearful dreams
Is scarcely man, though friend to me a man—
But now this tale of thine, that well began
And went on clearly, clearly has not told
The very shape of what thou didst behold."

"No," said the man, "when I stood therebeside
Methought its likeness ever would abide
Within my mind! but now, what shall I say—
Hast thou not heard, O King, before to-day,
That it was three-formed? So men said to me,
Before its very body I did see
That, lion-like, the beast's shape was before,
And that its goat-like hairy middle bore
A dragon's scaly folds across the waste
Itself had made. But I, who oft have faced
The yellow beast, and driven goats afield,
And shaken the black viper from my shield,
Can liken it to these things in no whit.
Nay, as I try e'en now to think of it,
Meseems that when I woke in the past night,
E'en like a dream dissolved by morning light,
Its memory had gone from me; though, indeed,
Nought I forgot of all my dreadful need.
Content thee, King, with what I erst have told;
For when I try his image to behold
Faint grows my heart again, mine eyes wax dim,
Nor can I set forth what I deemed of him
When he lay dead.—Hearken,—what thing draws nigh?"
For from outside there rang a joyous cry,
That grew, still coming nearer, till they heard
From out the midst thereof a well-known word,
The name Bellerophon: then from his bed
The King arose, and clad himself, and said:

"Go, captain, set the King Bellerophon
Without delay upon the royal throne,

And tell him that I come to make my prayer,
That, since for a long time I have sat there,
And know no other trade than this of King,
He of his bounty yet will add a thing
To all that he hath given, and let me reign
Along with him. Send here my chamberlain,
That I may clothe me in right fitting guise
To do him honour in all goodly wise."

So spake his lips, but his eyes seemed to say;
'Long is it to the ending of the day,
And many a thing may hap ere eventide;
And well is he who longest may abide.'

So from the presence did the captain pass,
When now the autumn morn in glory was,
And when he reached the palace court, he found
The eager people flocking all around
The door of the great hall, and variously
Men showed their joyance at that victory.
But in the hall there stood Bellerophon
Anigh the daïs, and the young sun shone
On his bright arms, and round from man to man
In eager notes the hurried question ran,
And, smiling still, he answered each; but yet
Small share that circle of his tale did get,
Because distraught he was, and seemed to be
As he who looks the face of one to see
Who long delays; but when the captain's staff
Cleft through the people's eager word and laugh,
And, after that, his fellow of the night
Bellerophon beheld, his face grew bright
As one who sees the end. Withal he said
As they drew nigh:
"Has the King seen the head,
Knows he what it betokens? For, behold!
Before the sun of that day grew acold
Whereon thou left'st me, all that heap was gone
Thou sawest there, both hair and flesh and bone;
So when this dawn I mounted my good steed,
I looked to thee to show forth that my deed,
Lest all should seem a feigned tale or a dream."

"Master," the other said, "thou well mayst deem,
That what thy will loosed, my will might not hold;
E'en as thy tale, so must my tale be told,
And nought is left to show of that dread thing."

E'en as he spake did folk cry on the King,
And now to right and left fell back the crowd,
And down the lane of folk gold raiment glowed,

And blare of silver trumpets smote the roof.
Then said the captain:
"Certes, no more proof
The King will ask, to show that thou hast done
The glorious deed that was for thee alone;
Be glad, thy day is come, and all is well!"

But on his sword the hero's left hand fell,
And he looked down and muttered 'neath his breath,
"Trust slayeth many a man, the wise man saith;
Yet must I trust perforce." He stood and heard
The joyful people's many-voicèd word
Change into a glad shout; the feet of those
Who drew anear came closer and more close,
Till their sound ceased, and silence filled the hall;
And then a soft voice on his ears did fall,
That seemed the echo to his yearning thought:

"Look up, look up! the change of days hath brought
Sweet end to our desires, and made thee mine!"

He raised his eyes, and saw gold raiment shine
Before him in the low sun; but a face
Above it made the murmuring crowded place
Silent and lone; for there she stood, indeed,
His troublous scarce-kept life's last crown and meed
Her sweet lips trembled, her dear eyes 'gan swim
In tears that fell not, as she reached to him
One hand in greeting, while a little raised
And restless was the other, as she gazed
Into his eyes, and lowly was her mien;
But yet a little forward did she lean,
As though she looked for sudden close embrace,
Yet feared it 'neath the strange eyes of that place.

But though his heart was melted utterly
Within him, he but drew a little nigh,
And took her hand, and said:
"What hour is this
That brings so fair a thing to crown my bliss?
What land far off from that which first I knew?
How shall I know that such a thing is true,
Unless some pain yet falls on thee and me?
Rather this hour is called eternity,
This land the land of heaven, and we have died
That thus at last we might go side by side
For ever, in the flower-strewn happy place."

Then closer to her drew his bright flushed face;
Well-nigh their lips met, when Jobates cried:
"Good hap, Corinthian! for thou hast not died;

The pale land holds no joy like thou wilt have
If yet awhile the Gods thy dear life save.
Yet mayst thou fear, indeed, for such thou art,
That yet the Gods will have thee play thy part
In heaven and not on earth—But come on now,
And see if this my throne be all too low
For thy great heart; sit here with me to-day,
And in the shrines of the Immortals pray,
With many offerings, lest they envy thee,
And on the morrow wed Philonoë,
And live thy life thereafter."
So he spake,
Smiling, and yet a troubled look did break
Across the would-be frankness of his smile.
But still the hero stood a little while
And watched Philonoë, as she turned and went
Adown the hall, and then a sigh he sent
From out his heart, and turned unto the King
As one who had no thought that anything
Of guile clung round him, and said:
"Deem thou not,
O King, that ruin from me thou hast got,
Although I take from thee my due reward;
For still for thee my hand shall hold the sword,
Nor will I claim more than thou givest me,
And great is that, though a king's son I be."

So on the throne was set Bellerophon,
And on his head was laid the royal crown
Instead of helm; and just as safe he felt
As though mid half-fed savage beasts he dwelt.
Yet when he went out through the crowded street,
Shouting because of him, when blossoms sweet
Faint with the autumn fell upon his head,
When his feet touched the silken carpet spread
Over the temple-steps; when the priests' hymn
Rang round him in the inner temple dim,
He smiled for pleasure once or twice, and said:
"So many dangers, yet I am not dead;
So many fears, yet sweet is longing grown,
Because to-morrow morn I gain my own!
So much desire, and but a night there is
Betwixt me and the perfecting of bliss!"

So fell the noisy day to feastful night,
For sleep was slow to hush the new delight
Of the freed folk; and in the royal house
Loud did the revellers grow, and clamorous,
And yet that too must have an end at last,
And to their sleeping-places all folk passed
Not long before the shepherds' sleep grew thin.

But listening to the changing of the din,
Philonoë lay long upon her bed,
Nor would sweet sleep come down to bless her head,
No, not when all was still again; for she,
Oppressed with her new-found felicity,
Had fallen to thoughts of life and death and change,
And through strange lands her wearied heart did range,
And knew no peace; therefore at last she rose
When all was utter stillness and stood close
Unto the window. Such a night it was
That a thin wind swept o'er the garden-grass
And loosened the sick leaves upon the trees;
Promise of rain there was within the breeze,
Yet was the sky not wholly overcast,
But o'er the moon yet high the grey drift passed,
And with a watery gleam at whiles she shone,
And cast strange wavering shadows down upon
The trembling beds of autumn blossoms tall,
And made the dusk of the white garden wall
Gleam like another land against the sky.

She turned her from the window presently,
And went unto her dainty bed once more;
But as she touched its silk a change came o'er
Her anxious heart, and listening there she stood,
Counting the eager throbbing of her blood;
But nought she heard except the night's dim noise;
Then did she whisper (and her faint, soft voice
Seemed hoarse and loud to her)—"Yet will I go
To Pallas' shrine, for fain I am to know
If all things even yet may go aright,
For my heart fails me."
To the blind dusk night
She showed her loveliness awhile half-veiled,
When she had spoke, as though her purpose failed;
Then softly did she turn and take to her
A dusky cloak, and hid her beauty rare
In its dark folds, and turned unto the door;
But ere she passed its marble threshold o'er
Stayed pondering, and she said:
"Alas, alas!
To-morrow must I say that all this was
And is not—this sweet longing?—what say men—
It cometh once and cometh not again,
This first love for another? holds the earth
Within its circle aught that is of worth
When it is dead?—and this is part of it,
This measureless sweet longing that doth flit,
Never to come again, when all is won.
And is our first desire so soon foredone,
Like to the rose-bud, that through day and night

In early summer strives to meet the light,
And in some noon-tide of the June, bursts sheath,
And ere the eve is past away in death?
Belike love dies then like the rest of life?
—Or fails asleep until it mix with strife
And fear and grief?—and then we call it pain,
And curse it for its labour lost in vain.
"Sweet pain! be kind to me and leave me not!
Leave me not cold, with all my grief forgot,
And all the joy consumed I thought should fill
My changing troubled days of life, until
Death turned all measuring of the days to nought!
"And thou, O death, when thou my life hast caught
Within thy net, what wilt thou with my love,
That now I deem no lapse of time can move?
O death, maybe that though I seem to pass
And come to nought, with all that once I was,
Yet love shall live I called a part of me,
And hold me in his heart despite of thee,
And call me part of him, when I am dead
As the world talks of dying."
So she said,
But scarcely heard her voice, and through the door
Of her own chamber passed; light on the floor
Her white feet fell, her soft clothes rustled nought,
As slowly, wrapped in many a changing thought,
Unto the Maiden's shrine she took her way
That midmost of the palace precincts lay;
But in a chamber that was hard thereby,
Although she knew it not, that night did lie
Her love that was, her lord that was to be.

Through the dark pillared precinct, silently
She went now, pausing every now and then
To listen, but heard little sound of men;
Though far off in the hill-side homesteads crowed
The waking fowl, or restless milch-kine lowed
In the fair pastures that her love had saved;
And from the haven, as the shipmen heaved
Their sail aloft, a mingled strange voice came.

So as she went, across her flitted shame
Of her own loneliness, and eager love
That shut the world out so, and she 'gan move
With quicker steps unto the temple-stead,
Scarce knowing what her soft feet thither led.

Within an open space the temple was,
And dark-stemmed olives rose up from the grass
About it, but a marble path passed o'er
The space betwixt the cloister and its door

Of some ten yards; there on its brink she stayed,
And from the cloister watched the black trees swayed
In the night breeze. E'en as a bather might
Shrink from the water, from the naked night
She shrank a little—the wind wailed within
The cloister walls, the clouds were gotten thin
About the moon, and the night 'gan to wane—
Then, even as she raised her skirts again
And put her foot forth, did she hear arms clash,
And fear and shame her heart did so abash,
She shrank behind a pillar; then the sound
Of footsteps smote upon the hardened ground,
And 'gainst the white steps of the shrine she saw
From out the trees a tall dark figure draw
Unto the holy place: the moon withal
Ran from a cloud now, and her light did fall
Upon a bright steel helm: she trembled then,
But her first thought was not of sons of men;
Of the armed goddess, rather, did she think,
And closer in her hiding-place did shrink.

Then though the moon grew dull again, yet she
Ten shapes of armed men at the last could see
Steal up the steps and vanish from the night,
And a sharp pang shot through her; but affright
She felt not now of gods: she murmured low;
"What do these men-at-arms in such guise now
Amidst the feast? God help me, we are caught
Within a brazen net!"
And with that thought
No more delay she made but girt her gown
Unto her, and with swift feet went adown
The marble steps, and so from tree to tree,
Through all the darkest shadow, silently
Gained the dark side of the brass temple door;
And through its chink she saw the marble floor
Just feebly lit by some small spark of light
She saw not, and the gleam of armour white,
And knew that she unto the men was close.

E'en as some sound that loud and louder grows
Within our dreams and yet is nought at all
She heard her heart, as clinging to the wall
She strove to listen vainly; but at last
All feebleness from out her did she cast
With thought of love—and death that drew anear-
And therewithal a low voice did she hear,
She thought she knew.
"Milo the Colchian?"
It said as asking, and another man
Said "Here" in a hoarse voice and low; once more

The first voice said; "The Clearer of the Shore,
Known by no other name the people say,
Art thou here too?" a new voice muttered "Yea."
And then again the first:
"My tale told o'er
And none found wanting—since ye know wherefore
We here are met, few words are best to-night:
Within the ivory chamber, called the White,
Lies the ill monster's bane, asleep belike,
Or, at the worst without a sword to strike,
Or shield to ward withal; his wont it is
To have few by him; on this night of bliss
Those few of night-cropped herbs enow have drunk,
And deep in slumber like short death are sunk:
So light our work is; yet let those who lack
Heart thereunto e'en at this hour go back;
Though—let these take good heed that whatsoe'er
We risk hereafter they in likewise share,
Except the risk of dying by his sword."

He ceased awhile, and a low muttered word
Seemed to say, "We are ready:" then he said:

"When he is slain, then shall ye bear his bed
Into this shrine, and burn what burned may be
In little space; but into the deep sea
Thou Clearer of the Shore, with thy two men
Shalt bear him forth.—Fellows, what say we then,
When on the morn the city wakes to find
Its saviour gone? This:—'Men are fools and blind,
And the Gods all-wise; this man born on earth
By some strange chance, yet was of too great worth
To live, and go as common men may go;
Therefore the Gods, who set him work to do,
When that was done, had no more will to see
His head grow white; or with man's frailty
Burn out his heart; they might not hear him curse
His latter days, as unto worse and worse
He fell at last; therefore they took him hence
To make him sharer in omnipotence,
And crown him with their immortality,
Nor may ye hope his body more to see.
These ashes of the web wherein last lay
His godlike limbs that took your fear away,
(Limbs now a very god's), this fire-stained gold
That, unharmed, very god might nowise hold,
Are left for certain signs—so shall ye rear
A temple to him nigh the gate; and bear
Gifts of good things unto the one who wrought
Deliverance for you, when ye e'en were brought
Unto the very gate of death and hell.'

"Fellows, spread vaguely this tale that I tell!
But thou, O Chremes, when the work is done
Get straight unto the forest all alone,
And with some slaughtered beast come back again
Ere noon, as though of hearers thou wert fain;
Folk know thee for a wanderer through the wood,
So make thy tale up as thou deemest good
Of voices heard by thee at dead of night;
So shall our words live and all things be right.
"Come, then; the night is changing; good it were
That dawn's first glimmer did not find us here!"

So spake he, and then opened wide the door,
And all seemed lonely there as heretofore;
So one by one adown the steps they stole,
Setting their anxious faces to the goal
Of the White Chamber.

But Philonoë,
Fair-footed, tender-limbed, and where was she?
Her sick heart did but note the name and place
They spoke of, ere she moved her woe-worn face
From the cold brass, and stayed to hear no more,
But stole away as silent as before,
Keeping love back till all were lost or won;
Nor knew she what she set her feet upon
Till, panting, through his chamber-door she passed;
There through the dusk a quick glance round she cast
And saw his men asleep, nor knew if they
Were dead, or if in sleep indeed they lay;
Then with such haste as a spent man, borne down
A swift stream, catches at some bare bough brown,
From off the wall she took sword, shield, and spear,
Hauberk and helm, and drew his bed anear,
And stayed not now, nor thought, but on his breast,
Laid bare before her, a light hand she pressed,
And as he started upright in the bed
Beneath her touch, bowed down to him and said:

"Speak not, but listen to Philonoë,
Thy love, and save thy life for thee and me!
Thy foes are on thee! make no more delay
As thou art wise!—needs must I go away;
I do my part—one minute more shall show,
If love in death or life we are to know."

His lips yet trembled, yet his heart did ache
With longing, ere he felt he was awake
And knew that she was gone, and knew not where:
So driving back desire he armed him there
Over his nakedness, and hastily

Caught up his weapons, and turned round to see
What help was nigh: and when he saw his men
Lie on the floor as dead, well deemed he then
His hour was come; and yet he felt as though
He scarce might tell if it were hard to go,
So short all life seemed that must end at last;
But therewith nowise hope from him he cast,
But on the golden bed he took his stand,
And poised the well-steeled spear in his right hand,
And waited listening.

Mid the fallen leaves' sound,
Driven by the autumn wind along the ground,
Footfalls of stealthy men he seemed to hear;
Yet nowise might that minute teach him fear,
Who life-long had not learned to speak the name;
Calm to his lips his steady breath still came,
Well-nigh he smiled; wide open were his eyes,
As though they looked to see life's mysteries
Unfolded soon before them; as he gazed
Through the dusk room, he heard the light latch raised
And saw the door move.

Even therewithal
A gleam of bright light from the sky did fall,
As from a fleecy cloud the white moon ran,
And smiling, stern, unlike the face of man,
His helmed head high o'er the black-shadowed floor
Showed strange and dreadful, as the ivory door
Swung back on well-oiled hinges silently.

Silence a little space yet,—then a cry
Burst from his lips, and through the chamber rang
A shriek of fear therewith, and a great clang
Of falling arms, and the bright glittering brand
Instead of the long spear was in his hand.
But for his foes, across the threshold lay
Their leader slain, and those his fellows, they
Hung wavering by the door, and feared the night,
And feared the godlike man, who in his might
Seemed changed indeed according to the tale
They were to tell: but as with faces pale
And huddled spears they hung there, in their doubt
If he were God or man, a mighty shout
Came from his lips again, and there was cast
Across the windy night a huge horn's blast,
Hoarse, loud, and long-enduring; and they fled
This way and that, pursued by nought but dread.

But strange tales of that night of fear they told
In after days. Some said they did behold,

As through the mighty outer door they ran,
A woman greater than a child of man,
All armed and helmed: some told of a bright flame
Glowing about the hero, when they came
Unto the door, and said that his one word
Had slain their leader swifter than a sword.

But for Bellerophon, awhile he stood
Nigh to the door until his wrathful mood
Changed into scorn; and then the moonlight wan
With kindled light he helped, and then the man
His spear had reached in strong arms he upraised;
But when he saw the eyes that on him gazed
With dead stare, then he knew the captain's face.
"Fool," said he, "fear hath brought thee to this case,
Long hadst thou lived for me—but is this all?
Will not the voice of Sthenobœa call
O'er the green waves to ghosts of lovers dead,
Ere yet the bridal wreath is on my head?"

E'en as he spake he heard the horn once more,
And then a sound as if on a low shore
The sea were breaking, then a swelling shout
That louder grew, till his own name leapt out
From midst of it, and then he smiled and cried:

"Prœtus, thy casket held a goodly bride,
A noble realm for me! O love, I come;
Surely thine heart has won me a fair home,
Instead of that straight house I should have had
If these eyes had not made thy dear heart glad."

Therewith he sheathed his sword, and stepping o'er
His cumbered threshold, made for the great door,
Whither the wakened house now thronging ran:
Men armed and unarmed, child and ancient man;
For death it was to wind that mighty horn,
But when in dangerous battle it was borne
By the king's, hand. Now nigher as he drew
Unto the door he 'gan to see therethrough
The points of steel tossing amid the light
Of torches, and the wind of waning night
Bore sound of many men on it; but dim
The pillared hall was yet. Then close to him
A slim close-mantled woman came and said:

"Go forth and speak—we twain are not yet dead.
I think we shall not die at all, dear heart;
Farewell!"
His soul and body seemed to part,
As swiftly, shadow-like, she passed him by,

And toward her chamber went: unwittingly
He gained the great door's platform, and looked down
Upon the tumult of the gathering town.
While at his back a dark mass clustered now,
With helmet on the head, and spear and how;
So, gathering earthly thoughts, he stood and cried:

"What will ye, good men, that ye make this tide
More noisy than the day? What will ye do?
Speak out, that we may rest, some one of you!"

Then stood a man forth, clad in armour bright,
And cried aloud: "O, well betide the night
That hides thee not from us, Bellerophon!
Surely we deemed some horror had been done,
And deemed the Gods had ta'en thee from our hands;
Because the horn, the terror of far lands,
The gift of Neptune, did we seem to hear."

Then said the hero: "Ah, then all the fear
The beast divine brought with it is not gone
Masters, ye dreamed belike—nor dreamed alone
Strange dreams; for I dreamed too,—that all-armed men
Beset my door to take my life; and when
I went therefrom e'en now, why yet I dreamed
E'en as I went upright—because meseemed
Over my threshold lay a man new slain.
Be merry, O my masters; go again
Unto your well-hung beds; to-morrow comes,
Whereon ye praise the Gods for your saved homes
With great rejoicings, and raise hands for me
And my beloved midst your festivity."

He ceased, and a great shout the twilight rent,
And one by one unto their homes they went.
Then turned the Prince unto the palace band,
And saw a certain one on his right hand,
Making as he would speak, and knew him straight
To be the man who had the heart to wait
The beast now slain. Smiling on him, he said:
"What, hast thou dreamed the monster was not dead?
Good is it that the grain is gathered in,
Else should men dream that they the crop did win
Last week, and let it stand afield to rot!"

"Nay," said the man, "O master, I dreamed not;
But from yon flanking tower, waking, I saw
A shadowy figure toward the great horn draw,
And blow a blast thereon, then vanish quite,
Not like a mortal thing, into the night."

Then spake a grey old man: "Yea, think thereon
As of a portent, O Bellerophon,
Of wondrous things to come, that thou shalt see,
As showing forth how great thy days shall be;
For doubt not this was Pallas, who would show
How great a gift she gives the city now."

Again from these there rang a joyous shout;
But the Prince hung his head, as if in doubt
Of the new time with hidden lies begun.
At last he said:
"Go, friends, ere yet the sun
Has slain the stars outright; what things soe'er
May hap, the Gods will have of me good care,
This night at least!"
So through the house they went
Each to his place, when nigh the night was spent.
But when to his own door Bellerophon
Was come, the captain's body was clean gone,
And the drugged men were waking. Then he thought,
"Was it a dream, indeed, that these things brought
Before mine eyes? Nay, my lips tremble yet
With that sweet touch. My breast may more forget
This hauberk's weight, than that sweet clinging hand.
I dreamed not, and this haunted Lycian land
Holds for me good and evil infinite.
So be it, and the new returning light
Shall bring new rede to guard my troubled ways.
May the Gods give beginning of good days!"

Then on the bed he sat to think of her,
But ere the end of the grey time was there
His head had fallen aside; sleeping he lay,
And let the bright sun bring about the day.

He woke at last, and fresh and joyous felt,
As forth he went; no sword within his belt
He set that morn; he bore no biting spear;
But clad he was in gold and royal gear,
Such as a King might bear in Saturn's reign;
And in such wise the great hall did he gain,
And on the ivory throne he sat him down,
And felt the golden circle of the crown,
But light as yet, upon his unused head.
Then to his presence were strange people led;
Hunters from far-off corners of the realm,
Shipmen with hands well hardened by the helm,
Merchants who in strange tongues must bid him thrive,
And dainty cherished things unto him give
And still he wearied, and their words forgot,
And wondered why the other King came not.

But yet, before the ending of the morn,
The casket that his own hands once had borne,
Was brought unto him by a man, who spake
In this wise:
"King Jobates bids thee take,
O King Bellerophon, what lies herein,
And saith that since thine office doth begin
This day, right good it were to judge of this—
If the man did so utterly amiss
To strive to keep his oath. He bids thee say
Withal if thou wilt have what yesterday
He gave unto thine hands—and, taking it,
Forget wild dreams that o'er the year did flit."

Then King Bellerophon looked down, and drew
A letter from that casket that he knew,
And opened it and read; and in such wise
It gave the key to half-deemed mysteries.

King Prœtus to Jobates, King of men,
Sends goodly greeting.—Dost thou mind thee when
I saved thee from the lions? then I had
One gift from thee which has not made me glad,
Thy daughter; though a goddess, all men said,
Had scarce been fairer at my board and bed.—
Another thing thou gav'st me then,—an oath
To do my bidding once, if lieve or loath
It were to thee. Now bring all to an end,
And slay the man who bears this—once my friend,
And still too close unto my memory,
That on my skirts his treacherous blood should lie.
Take heed, though, that I say, myself, at whiles,
"The Gods are full of lies and luring smiles,
And know no faith." And this Bellerophon
May be a god; being even such an one
As seemeth kind beyond the wont of men,
Just and far-seeing, brave in those times when
Men's hearts grow sick with fear. Lo, such is he,
And yet a monster! He shall dwell with thee
Life-long, perchance; and once or twice Desire
Shall burn up all these things, as with a fire;
And he shall tread his kindness under foot,
And turn a liar e'en from his heart's root,
And turn a wretched fool. Yea, what say I?
Turn a mere trembling coward, loth to die,
Rather than be all this. So take him, then,
While yet thou deem'st him first of mortal men,
And in forefront of battle let him fall;
Or, lonely, on some foeman's spear-swept wall,
If it may be;—that he may leave behind

A savour, sweet in some men's mouths, nor find
That he has fallen to hell while yet he lives.

Such counsel to thee, friend, King Prœtus gives—
A hapless man. But happy mayst thou dwell,
As thou shalt keep thy faith. Live hale and well!

Not clear he saw these latter words of it,
For many a memory through his heart did flit,
Blinding his eyes belike: at last his head
He raised, and to the messenger he said:

"Say to Jobates that I deem the man
Did even with his oath as such men can,
Who fear the Gods so much they may not tell
What gifts men give them. Say that all is well,
That I will take the gift he gave to me,
And long right sore that World's Desire to see."

So the man went, and left Bellerophon
Pensive, and pondering on the days long gone
That brought him unto this: his happy love
The heart within him did to pity move;
He thought, "Alas! and can it ever be
That one can say, 'Thou art enough for me—
And I, and I—wilt thou not suffer it,
That I, at least, before thy feet may sit
Until perchance I grow enough for thee?'
Alas, alas! and can it ever be
That thus a heart shall plead and plead, in vain?"

So did he murmur; but withal a strain
Of merry music made him lift his head
Slaying all thought of suffering folk or dead;
And even as a man new made a god,
When first he sets his foot upon the sod
Of Paradise, and like a living flame
Joy wraps him round, he felt, as now she came,
Clear won at last, the thing of all the earth
That made his fleeting life a little worth.

My heart faints now, my lips that tell the tale
Falter to think that such a life should fail;
That use, and long days dropping one by one,
As the wan water frets away the stone,
Should change desires of men, and what they bring,
E'er while their hearts with sickening longing cling
Unto the thought that they are still the same,
When all they were is grown an empty name.

O Death-in-life, O sure pursuer, Change,

Be kind, be kind, and touch me not, till strange,
Changed too, thy face shows, when thy fellow Death
Delays no more to freeze my faltering breath!

The dull day long had faded into night
Ere all was done; taper and fire-light
Cast on the wall's fair painted images
Shadows confused of some, amidst of these,
The old men on the dais; down below
Amid the youths was stir and murmur now;
Some said they fain had known a little more
Of that Bellerophon ere all was o'er;
Some said, that if the man lived, sure it was
That happiness of his would soon o'erpass,
Because he kept back something of the stake:
Some said the story back their thoughts did take
To Argos, and the deeds there, and the end
Whereto the feet of Sthenobœa did wend
So surely from the first, not without praise
Of some, they said: some wondered of the days
That Prœtus had, and if the godlike man
And he, who clung to joy as cowards can,
E'er met again, and what things they forgat
And what remembered, if it came to that.

But one youth who had sat alone and sad,
While others friends and loves beside them had,
Rose up amid their talk, and slowly turned
To where the many lights that thereby burned
Scarce reached, and in that dimness walked awhile;
And when he came back, with a quivering smile
On his sad face, gazed at the elders there,
As though he deemed his place among them were,
Who had nigh done with life; and one or two
Among the youths looked up, as if they knew
The pain that ailed him.

Many-peopled earth!
In foolish anger and in foolish mirth,
In causeless wars that never had an aim,
In worshipping the kings that bring thee shame,
In spreading lies that hide wrath in their breast,
In breaking up the short-lived days of rest,
In all thy folk care nought for, how they cling
Each unto each, fostering the foolish thing,
Nought worth, grown out of nought, that lightly lies
'Twixt throat and lips, and yet works miseries!
While in this love that touches every one,
Still wilt thou let each man abide alone,
Unholpen, with his pain unnameable!
Is it, perchance, lest men should come to tell

Each unto other what a pain it is,
How little balanced by the sullied bliss
They win for some few minutes of their life,
Lest they die out and leave thee void of strife,
Empty of all their yearning and their fear,
'Twixt storm and sunshine of thy changing year?

Late February days; and now, at last,
Might you have thought that winter's woe was past;
So fair the sky was, and so soft the air.
The happy birds were hurrying here and there,
As something soon would happen. Reddened now
The hedges, and in gardens many a bough
Was overbold of buds. Sweet days, indeed,
Although past road and bridge, through wood and mead,
Swift ran the brown stream, swirling by the grass,
And in the hill-side hollows snow yet was.

Within sound of the city, yet amid
Patches of woodland that its white walls hid,
The house was, where the elders sat this tide,
The young folk with them; by the highway-side
The first starred yellow blossoms of the spring
Some held in hand; some came in, hurrying
From deeper in the woods, and now in fold
Of skirt and gown its treasures did they hold;
And soon to garland-making youth and maid
Were sat down: then the Swabian smiled, and said:

"However it be that I, so old and grey,
A priest too, yet again must have to say
More words of Venus, judge ye, maids: in sooth,
I, wandering once in long-past days of youth,
Came to the place my tale shall tell of now.
Vague tales, wherein I was well fain to trow,
Being dreamy and a youth, I oft had heard
Thereof, yet somewhat I did grow afeard
Before that cavern, although not alone
I was there, and the morn was such an one
As this fair morn has been: my fellow there
Was an old forester with thin white hair—
Lo you, like mine now!—but his deep-set eyes,
Bright mid his wrinkles, made him seem right wise—
As I would fain seem, maidens.—Ye may wot
That many a tale of that place had he got,
Because nearby, child boy and man, had he
Dwelt ever: so on a felled oaken tree
We sat beside the cave's mouth there of old,
While he this story, that I looked for, told.

ARGUMENT

**This story tells of a certain man who by strange adventure fell into the power of Venus, and who, repenting of his life with her, was fain to return to the world and amend all, but might not; for his repentance was rejected of men, by whomsoever it was accepted.**

A certain summer afternoon day hung
Doubtful 'twixt storm and sunshine, and the earth
Seemed waiting for the clouds to spread, that clung
About the south-east, ere its morning mirth,
Ere all the freshness of its hopeful birth,
Should end in dreadful darkness, and the clash
Of rain-beat boughs and wildering lightning-flash.

Such a tide brooded o'er the ancient wood,
Wild with sour waste and rough untended tree,
Which, long before the coming of the Rood,
Men held a holy place in Germany;
Yea, and still looked therein strange things to see,
Still deemed that dark therein was uglier
Than in all other wilds, more full of fear.

Grim on that day it was, when the sun shone
Clear through the thinner boughs, and yet its light
Seemed threatening; such great stillness lay upon
The wide-head oaks, such terror as of night
Waylaying day, made the sward yet more bright,
As, blotting out the far-away blue sky,
The hard and close-packed clouds spread silently.

Now 'twixt the trees slowly a knight there rode,
Musing belike; a seemly man and fair,
No more a youth, but bearing not the load
Of many years; he might have seen the wear
Of thirty summers: why he journeyed there
Nought tells the tale, but Walter doth him name,
And saith that from the Kaiser's court he came.

Dull enow seemed his thoughts, as on he went
From tree to tree, with heavy knitted brow,
And eyes upon the forest grass intent;
And oft beneath his breath he muttered low,
And once looked up and said: "The earth doth grow
Day after day a wearier place belike;
No word for me to speak, no blow to strike:

"Once I looked not for this and it has come;
What shall the end be now I look for worse?

Woe worth the dull walls of mine ancient home,
The ragged fields laid 'neath the ancient curse!
Woe worth false hope that dead despair doth nurse
Woe worth the world's false love and babbling hate—
O life, vain, grasping, uncompassionate!"

He looked around as thus he spake, and saw
That he amidst his thoughts had ridden to where
The close wood backward for a space did draw,
Leaving a plain of sweet-grown sward all clear,
Till at the end thereof a cliff rose sheer
From the green grass, o'er which again arose
A hill-side clad with fir-trees dark and close.

Now nigh the cliff a little river ran,
And bright with sun were hill and mead, although
Already, far away, the storm began
To rumble, and the storm lift moving slow,
Over a full third of the sky to grow,
Though still within its heart the tumult stayed,
Content as yet to keep the world afraid.

There had he drawn rein, and his eyes were set
Upon a dark place in the sheer rock's side,
A cavern's mouth; and some new thought did get
Place in his heart therewith, and he must bide
To nurse the thing; for certes far and wide
That place was known, and by an evil fame;
The Hill of Venus had it got to name.

And many a tale yet unforgot there was
Of what a devilish world, dream-like, but true,
Would snare the o'er-rash man whose feet should pass
That cavern's mouth: old folk would say they knew
Of men who risked it; nor came back to rue
The losing of their souls; and others told
Of how they watched, when they were young and bold,

Midsummer night through: yea, and not in vain;
For on the stream's banks, and the flowery mead,
Sights had they seen they might not tell again;
And in their hearts that night had sown the seed
Of many a wild desire and desperate need;
So that, with longings nought could satisfy,
Their lives were saddened till they came to die.

For all the stories were at one in this,
That still they told of a trap baited well
With some first minutes of unheard-of bliss;
Then, these grasped greedily, the poor fool fell
To earthly misery, or no doubtful hell.

Yet, as these stories flitted by all dim,
The knight's face softened, sweet they seemed to him.

He muttered: "Yea, the end is hell and death,
The midmost hid, yet the beginning Love.
Ah me! despite the worst Love threateneth,
Still would I cling on to the skirts thereof,
If I could hope his sadness still could move
My heart for evermore.  A little taste
Of the king's banquet, then all bare and waste

"My table is; fresh guests are hurrying in
With eager eyes, there to abide their turn,
That they more hunger therewithal may win!
Ah me! what skill for dying love to yearn?
Yet, O my yearning! though my heart should burn
Into light feathery ash, blown here and there,
After one minute of that odorous flare."

With that once more he hung his head adown;
The name of Love such thoughts in him had stirred,
That somewhat sweet his life to him was grown,
And like soft sighs his breathing now he heard;
His heart beat like a lover's heart afeard;
Of such fair women as he erst had seen,
The names he named, and thought what each had been.

Yet, as he told them over one by one,
But dimly might he see their forms, and still
Some lack, some coldness, cursed them all, and none
The void within his straining heart might fill;
For evermore, as if against his will,
Words of old stories, turned to images
Of lovelier things, would blur the sight of these.

Long dwelt he in such musings, though his beast
From out his hand had plucked the bridle-rein,
And, wandering slowly onward, now did feast
Upon the short sweet herbage of the plain;
So when the knight raised up his eyes again,
Behind his back the dark of the oakwood lay,
And nigh unto its end was grown the day.

He gazed round toward the west first, and the stream,
Where all was bright and sunny, nor would he
Have deemed himself deep fallen into a dream
If he had seen the grass swept daintily
By raiment that in old days used to be;
When white 'neath Pallas' smile and Juno's frown
Gleamed Venus from the gold slow slipping down.

But void was all the meadow's beauty now,
And to the east he turned round with a sigh,
And saw the hard lift blacker and blacker grow
'Neath the world's silence, as the storm drew nigh;
And to his heart there went home suddenly
A sting of bitter hatred and despair,
That these things, his own heart had made so fair,

He might not have; and even as he gazed,
And the air grew more stifling yet and still,
Down in the east a crooked red line blazed,
And soon the thunder the eve's hush did fill,
Low yet, but strong, persistent as God's will.
He cried aloud: "A world made to be lost,
A bitter life 'twixt pain and nothing tossed!"

And therewithal he stooped and caught the rein,
And turned his horse about till he did face
The cavern in the hill, and said: "Ah, vain
My yearning for enduring bliss of days
Amidst the dull world's hopeless, hurrying race,
Where the past gain each new gain makes a loss,
And yesterday's gold love to-day makes dross!"

And as he spake, slowly his horse 'gan move
Unto the hill: "To-morrow and to-day,
Why should I name you, so I once hold Love
Close to my heart? If others fell away,
That was because within their souls yet lay
Some hope, some thought of making peace at last
With the false world, when all their love was passed."

But strangely light therewith his heart did grow,
He knew not why; and yet again he said:
"A wondrous thing that I this day must trow
In tales that poets and old wives have made!
Time was when duly all these things I weighed.
Yet, O my heart—what sweetens the dull air?
What is this growing hope, so fresh and fair?"

Then therewithal louder the thunder rolled,
And the world darkened, for the sun was down;
A fitful wind 'gan flicker o'er the wold,
And in scared wise the woods began to moan,
And fast the black clouds all the sky did drown;
But his eyes glittered,—a strange smile did gleam
Across his face, as in a happy dream.

Again he cried: "Thou callest me; I come;
I come, O lovely one! Oh, thou art nigh;
Like a sweet scent, the nearness of thine home

Is shed around; it lighteth up God's sky—
O me, thy glory!" Therewith suddenly
The lightning streamed across the gathering night,
And his horse swerved aside in wild affright.

He heeded not except to spur him on;
He drew his sword as if he saw a foe,
And rode on madly till the stream he won,
And, even as the storm-wind loud 'gan blow,
And the great drops fell pattering, no more slow,
Dashed through the stream and up the other bank,
And leaped to earth amid his armour's clank,

And faced the wild white rain, and the wind's roar,
The swift wide-dazzling lightning strange of hue,
The griding thunder, saying: "No more, no more,
Helpless and cruel, do I deal with you,
Or heed the things the false world calleth true.
Surely mine eyes in spite of you behold
The perfect peace Love's loving arms enfold."

Then, whirling o'er his head his glittering sword,
Into the night he cast it far away;
And turning round, without another word
Left the wild tumult of the ruined day,
And into the darkness that before him lay
Rushed blindly, while the cold rain-bearing wind
Wailed after him, and the storm clashed behind.

A few steps through black darkness did he go,
Then turned and stayed, and with his arms outspread
Stood tottering there a little while, as though
He fain would yet turn back; some words he said
If the storm heard, then fell, and as one dead
Lay long, not moving, noting not how soon
Above the dripping boughs outshone the moon.

He woke up with the tears upon his cheek,
As though awakened from some dream of love,
And as his senses cleared felt strange and weak,
And would not open eyes or try to move,
Since he felt happy and yet feared to prove
His new-born bliss, lest it should fade from him
E'en as in waking grows the love-dream dim.

A half hush was there round about, as though
Beast, bird, and creeping thing went each their ways,
Yet needs must keep their voices hushed and low,
For worship of the sweet love-laden days.
Most heavenly odours floated through the place,
Whate'er it was, wherein his body lay,

And soft the air was as of deathless May.

At last he rose with eyes fixed on the ground,
And therewithal his armour's clinking seemed
An overloud and clean unlooked-for sound:
He trembled; even yet perchance he dreamed,
Though strange hope o'er his wondering heart there streamed;
He looked up; in the thickest of a wood
Of trees fair-blossomed, heavy-leaved, he stood.

He turned about and looked; some memory
Of time late past, of dull and craving pain,
Made him yet look the cavern's mouth to see
Anigh behind him: but he gazed in vain,
For there he stood, as a man born again,
'Mid a close break of eglantine and rose,
With no deed now to cast aside or choose.

Yet, as a man new born at first may hear
A murmur in his ears of life gone by,
Then in a flash may see his past days clear,
The pain, the pleasure, and the strife, all nigh,
And stripped of every softening veil and lie,—
So did he hear, and see, and vainly strive
In one short minute all that life to live.

But even while he strove, as strong as sleep,
As swift as death, came deep forgetfulness,
Came fresh desire unnamed; his heart did leap
With a fresh hope, a fresh fear did oppress
The new delight, that else cried out to bless
The unchanging softness of that unknown air,
And the sweet tangle round about him there.

Trembling, and thinking strange things to behold,
The interwoven boughs aside he drew,
And softly, as though sleep the world did hold,
And he should not awake it, passed them through
Into a freer space; yet nought he knew
Why he was thither come, or where to turn,
Or why the heart within him so did burn.

Then through the wood he went on, and for long
Heard but the murmur of the prisoned breeze,
Or overhead the wandering wood-dove's song;
But whiles amid the dusk of far-off trees
He deemed he saw swift-flitting images,
That made him strive in vain to call to mind
Old stories of the days now left behind.

Slowly he went, and ever looking round

With doubtful eyes, until he heard at last
Across the fitful murmur of dumb sound,
Far off and faint the sound of singing cast
Upon the lonely air; the sound went past,
And on the moaning wind died soft away,
But, as far thunder startles new-born day,

So was his dream astonied therewithal,
And his lips strove with some forgotten name,
And on his heart strange discontent did fall,
And wild desire o'ersweet therefrom did flame;
And then again adown the wind there came
That sound grown louder; then his feet he stayed
And listened eager, joyous and afraid.

Again it died away, and rose again,
And sank and swelled, and sweeter and stronger grew,
Wrapping his heart in waves of joy and pain,
Until at last so near his ears it drew
That very words amid its notes he knew,
And stretched his arms abroad to meet the bliss,
Unnamed indeed as yet, but surely his.

SONG.

Before our lady came on earth
Little there was of joy or mirth;
About the borders of the sea
The sea folk wandered heavily;
About the wintry river side
The weary fishers would abide.
Alone within the weaving-room
The girls would sit before the loom,
And sing no song, and play no play;
Alone from dawn to hot mid-day,
From mid-day unto evening,
The men afield would work, nor sing,
'Mid weary thoughts of man and God,
Before thy feet the wet ways trod.

Unkissed the merchant bore his care,
Unkissed the knights went out to war,
Unkissed the mariner came home,
Unkissed the minstrel men did roam.

Or in the stream the maids would stare,
Nor know why they were made so fair;
Their yellow locks, their bosoms white,
Their limbs well wrought for all delight,
Seemed foolish things that waited death,
As hopeless as the flowers beneath

The weariness of unkissed feet:
No life was bitter then, or sweet.

Therefore, O Venus, well may we
Praise the green ridges of the sea
O'er which, upon a happy day,
Thou cam'st to take our shame away.
Well may we praise the curdling foam
Amidst the which thy feet did bloom,
Flowers of the gods; the yellow sand
They kissed atwixt the sea and land;
The bee-beset ripe-seeded grass,
Through which thy fine limbs first did pass;
The purple-dusted butterfly,
First blown against thy quivering thigh;
The first red rose that touched thy side,
And over-blown and fainting died;
The flickering of the orange shade,
Where first in sleep thy limbs were laid;
The happy day's sweet life and death,
Whose air first caught thy balmy breath—
Yea, all these things well praised may be,
But with what words shall we praise thee—
O Venus, O thou love alive,
Born to give peace to souls that strive?

Louder the song had grown to its last word,
And with its growth grew odours strange and sweet,
And therewithal a rustling noise he heard,
As though soft raiment the soft air did meet,
And through the wood the sound of many feet,
Until its dusk was peopled with a throng
Of fair folk fallen silent after song.

Softly they flowed across his glimmering way,
Young men and girls thin-clad and garlanded,
Too full of love a word of speech to say
Except in song; head leaning unto head,
As in a field the poppies white and red;
Hand warm with hand, as faint wild rose with rose,
Mid still abundance of a summer close.

Softly they passed, and if not swiftly, still
So many, and in such a gliding wise,
That, though their beauty all his heart did fill
With hope and eagerness, scarce might his eyes,
Caught in the tangle of their first surprise,
Note mid the throng fair face, or form, or limb,
Ere all amid the far dusk had grown dim.

A while, indeed, the wood might seem more sweet,

That there had been the passionate eyes of them
Wandering from tree to tree loved eyes to meet;
That o'er-blown flower, or heavy-laden stem
Lay scattered, languid 'neath the delicate hem
That kissed the feet moving with love's unrest,
Though love was nigh them, to some dreamed-of best.

A little while, then on his way he went,
With all that company now quite forgot,
But unforgot the name their lips had sent
Adown the wave of song; his heart waxed hot
With a new thought of life, remembered not,
Save as a waste passed through with loathing sore
Unto a life, which, if he gained no more

Than this desire, lonely, unsatisfied,
This name of one unknown, unseen, was bliss;
And if this strange world were not all too wide,
But he some day might touch her hand with his,
And turn away from that ungranted kiss
Not all unpitied, nor unhappy quite,
What better knew the lost world of delight?

Now, while he thought these things, and had small heed
Of what was round him, changed the place was grown
Like to a tree-set garden, that no weed,
Nor winter, or decay had ever known;
No longer now complained the dove alone
Over his head, but with unwearying voice
'Twixt leaf and blossom did the birds rejoice.

No longer strove the sun and wind in vain
To reach the earth, but bright and fresh they played
About the flowers of a wide-stretching plain,
Where 'twixt the soft sun and the flickering shade
There went a many wild things, unafraid
Each of the other or of the wanderer,
Yea, even when his bright arms drew anear.

And through the plain a little stream there wound,
And far o'er all there rose up mountains grey,
That never so much did the place surround,
But ever through their midmost seemed a way
To whatsoe'er of lovely through them lay.
But still no folk saw Walter; nay, nor knew
If those were dreams who passed the wild wood through.

But on he passed, and now his dream to prove
Plucked down an odorous fruit from overhead,
Opened its purple heart and ate thereof;
Then, where a path of wondrous blossoms led,

Beset with lilies and with roses red,
Went to the stream, and felt its ripples cold,
As through a shallow, strewn with very gold

For pebbles, slow he waded: still no stay
He made, but wandered toward the hills; no fear
And scarce a pain upon his heart did weigh;
Only a longing made his life more dear,
A longing for a joy that drew an ear;
And well-nigh now his heart seemed satisfied,
So only in one place he should not bide.

And so he ever wandered on and on,
Till clearer grew the pass 'twixt hill and hill;
Lengthened the shadows, sank adown the sun,
As though in that dull world he journeyed still
Where all day long men labour, night to fill
With dreams of toil and trouble, and arise
To find the daylight cold to hopeless eyes.

Some vague thought of that world was in his heart,
As, meeting sunset and grey moonrise there.
He came unto the strait vale that did part
Hill-side from hill-side; through the golden air,
Far off, there lay another valley fair;
Red with the sunset ran the little stream—
Ah me! in such a place, amid a dream,

Two sundered lovers, each of each forgiven,
All things known, all things past away, might meet.
Such place, such time, as the one dream of heaven,
Midst a vain life of nought.—With faltering feet
He stayed a while, for all grew over sweet;
He hid his eyes, lest day should come again
As in such dream, and make all blank and vain.

He trembled as the wind came up the pass,
Was it long time 'twixt breath and breath thereof?
Did the shade creep slow o'er the flower-strewn grass?
Was it a long time that he might not move,
Lest morn should bring the world and slay his love?
Surely the sun had set, the stream was still,
The wind had sunk adown behind the hill.

Nay, through his fingers the red sun did gleam,
In cadence with his heart's swift beating now
Beat the fresh wind, and fell adown the stream.
Then from his eyes his hands fell, and e'en so
The blissful knowledge on his soul did grow
That she was there, her speech as his speech, stilled
By very love, with love of him fulfilled.

O close, O close there, in the hill's grey shade,
She stood before him, with her wondrous eyes
Fixed full on his! All thought in him did fade
Into the bliss that knoweth not surprise,
Into the life that hath no memories,
No hope and fear; the life of all desire,
Whose fear is death, whose hope consuming fire.

Naked, alone, unsmiling, there she stood,
No cloud to raise her from the earth; her feet
Touching the grass that his touched, and her blood
Throbbing as his throbbed through her bosom sweet;
Both hands held out a little, as to meet
His outstretched hands; her lips each touching each;
Praying for love of him, but without speech.

He fell not and he knelt not; life was strong
Within him at that moment; well he thought
That he should never die; all shame and wrong,
Time past and time to come, were all made nought;
As, springing forward, both her hands he caught;
And, even as the King of Love might kiss,
Felt her smooth cheek and pressed her lips with his.

What matter by what name of heaven or earth
Men called his love? Breathing and loving there
She stood, and clung to him; one love had birth
In their two hearts—he said—all things were fair,
Although no sunlight warmed the fresh grey air
As their lips sundered. Hand in hand they turned
From where no more the yellow blossoms burned.

Louder the stream was, fallen dead was the wind,
As up the vale they went into the night,
No rest but rest of utter love to find
Amid the marvel of new-born delight,
And as her feet brushed through the dew, made white
By the high moon, he cried: "For this, for this
God made the world, that I might feel thy kiss!"

What, is the tale not ended then? Woe's me!
How many tales on earth have such an end:
I longed, I found, I lived long happily,
And fearless in death's fellowship did wend?'
On earth,—where hope is that two souls may blend
That God has made but she—who made her then
To be a curse unto the sons of men?

And yet a flawless life indeed that seemed
For a long while: as flowers, not made to die

Or sin, they were: no dream was ever dreamed,
How short soe'er, wherein more utterly
Was fear forgot or weariness worn by;
Wherein less thought of the world's woe and shame,
Of men's vain struggles, o'er the sweet rest came.

Men say he grew exceeding wise in love,
That all the beauty that the earth had known,
At least in seeming, would come back, and move
Betwixt the buds and blossoms overblown;
Till, turning round to that which was his own,
Blind would he grow with ecstasy of bliss,
And find unhoped-for joy in each new kiss.

Men say that every dear voice love has made
Throughout that love-filled loneliness would float,
And make the roses tremble in the shade
With unexpected sweetness of its note;
Till he would turn unto her quivering throat,
And, deaf belike, would feel the wave of sound
From out her lips change all the air around.

Men say he saw the lovers of old time;
That ORPHEUS led in his EURYDICE,
Crooning o'er snatches of forgotten rhyme,
That once had striven against eternity,
And only failed, as all love fails, to see
Desire grow into perfect joy, to make
A lonely heaven for one beloved's sake.

THISBE he saw, her wide white bosom bare;
Thereon instead of blood the mulberries' stain;
And single-hearted PYRAMUS anear
Held in his hand tufts of the lion's mane,
And the grey blade that stilled their longings vain
Smote down the daisies.—Changeless earth and old,
Surely thy heart amid thy flowers is cold!

HELEN he saw move slow across the sward,
Until before the feet of her she stood
Who gave her, a bright bane and sad reward,
Unto the PARIS that her hand yet wooed:
Trembled her lips now, and the shame-stirred blood
Flushed her smooth cheek; but hard he gazed, and yearned
Unto the torch that Troy and him had burned.

Then ARIADNE came, her raiment wet
From out the sea; to her a prison wall,
A highway to the love she could not get.
Then upon PHYLLIS' ivory cheeks did fall
The almond-blossoms. Then, black-haired and tall,

Came DIDO, with her slender fingers laid
On the thin edge of that so bitter blade.

Then, what had happed? was the sun darker now?
Had the flowers shrunk, the warm breeze grown achill?
It might be; but his love therewith did grow,
And all his aching heart it seemed to fill
With such desire as knows no chain nor will:
Shoulder to shoulder quivering there they lay,
In a changed world that had not night nor day.

A loveless waste of ages seemed to part,
And through the cloven dullness BRYNHILD came,
Her left hand on the fire that was her heart,
That paled her cheeks and through her eyes did flame,
Her right hand holding SIGURD'S; for no shame
Was in his simple eyes, that saw the worth
So clearly now of all the perished earth.

Then suddenly outbroke the thrushes' sound,
The air grew fresh as after mid-spring showers,
And on the waves of soft wind flowing round
Came scent of apple-bloom and gilliflowers,
And all the world seemed in its morning hours,
And soft and dear were kisses, and the sight
Of eyes, and hands, and lips, and bosom white.

Yea, the earth seemed a-babbling of these twain,
TRISTRAM and YSEULT, as they lingered there,
All their life days now nothing but a gain;
While death itself, wrapped in love's arms, must bear
Some blossom grown from depths of all despair,
Some clinging, sweetest, bitterest kiss of all,
Before the dark upon their heads should fall.

Others he saw, whose names could tell him nought
Of any tale they might have sorrowed through;
But their lips spake, when of their lives he sought,
And many a story from their hearts he drew,
Some sweet as any that old poets knew,
Some terrible as death, some strange and wild
As any dream that hath sad night beguiled.

But all with one accord, what else they said,
Would praise with eager words the Queen of Love;
Yet sometimes, while they spake, as if with dread,
Would look askance adown the blossomed grove;
Till a strange pain within his heart would move,
And he would cling to her enfolding arm,
Trembling with joy to find her breast yet warm.

Then a great longing would there stir in him,
That all those kisses might not satisfy;
Dreams never dreamed before would gather dim
About his eyes, and trembling would he cry
To tell him how it was he should not die;
To tell him how it was that he alone
Should have a love all perfect and his own.

Ah me! with softest words her lips could make,
With touches worth a lifetime of delight,
Then would she soothe him, and his hand would take,
And lead him through all places fresh and bright,
And show him greater marvels of her might,
Till midst of smiles and joy he clean forgot
That she his passionate cry had answered not.

Forgot to-day, and many days maybe:
Yet many days such questions came again,
And he would ask: "How do I better thee,
Who never knewst a sorrow or a pain?
Folk on the earth fear they may love in vain,
Ere first they see the love in answering eyes,
And still from day to day fresh fear doth rise."

Unanswered and forgot!—forgot to-day,
Because too close they clung for sight or sound;
But yet to-morrow:—"Changeless love, O say
Why, since love's grief on earth doth so abound,
No heart my heart that loveth so ere found
That needed me?—for wilt thou say indeed
That thou, O perfect one, of me hast need?"

Unanswered and forgot a little while;—
Asked and unanswered many a time and oft;
Till something gleamed from out that marvellous smile,
And something moved within that bosom soft,
As though the God of Love had turned and scoffed
His worshipper, before his feet cast down,
To tell of all things for his sake o'erthrown.

How many questions asked, nor answered aught?
How many longings met still by that same
Sweet face, by anguish never yet distraught,
Those limbs ne'er marred by any fear or shame;
How many times that dear rest o'er him came—
And faded mid the fear that nought she knew
What bitter seed within his bosom grew?

'Twixt lessening joy and gathering fear, grew thin
That lovely dream, and glimmered now through it
Gleams of the world cleft from him by his sin;

Hell's flames withal, heavens glory, 'gan to flit
Athwart his eyes sometimes, as he did sit
Beside the Queen, in sleep's soft image laid;
And yet awhile the dreadful dawn was stayed.

And in that while two thoughts there stirred in him,
And this the first: "Am I the only one
Whose eyes thy glorious kisses have made dim?
And what then with the others hast thou done?
Where is the sweetness of their sick love gone?"
Ah me! her lips upon his lips were laid,
And yet awhile the dreadful dawn was stayed.

And in that while the second thought was this:
"And if, wrapped in her love, I linger here
Till God's last justice endeth all our bliss,
Shall my eyes then, by hopeless pain made clear,
See that a vile dream my vain life held dear,
And I am lone? "—Ah, cheek to his cheek laid!
And yet awhile the dreadful dawn was stayed.

How long who knoweth?—and be sure meanwhile,
That could man's heart imagine, man's tongue say,
The strange delights that did his heart beguile
Within that marvellous place from day to day,
Whoso might hearken should cast clean away
All thought of sin and shame, and laugh to scorn
The fear and hope of that delaying morn.

But the third thought at last, unnamed for long,
Bloomed, a weak flower of hope within his heart;
And by its side unrest grew bitter strong,
And, though his lips said not the word, "Depart;"
Yet would he murmur: "Hopeless fair thou art!
Is there no love amid earth's sorrowing folk?"
So glared the dreadful dawn—and thus it broke.—

For on a night, amid the lily and rose,
Peaceful he woke from dreams of days bygone;
Peaceful at first; and, seeing her lying close
Beside him, had no memory of deeds done
Since long before that eve he rode alone
Amidst the wild wood; still awhile himseemed
That of that fair close, those white limbs he dreamed.

So there for long he lay in happy rest,
As one too full of peace to wish to wake
From dreams he knows are dreams. Upon her breast
The soft wind did the dewy rose-leaves shake;
From out a gleaming cloud the moon did break;
Till, mid her balmy sleep, toward him she turned,

And into his soul her touch his baseness burned.

Then fled all peace, as in a blaze of flame,
Rushed dreadful memory back; and therewithal,
Amid the thoughts that crowding o'er him came,
Clear vision of the end on him did fall;
Rose up against him a great fiery wall,
Built of vain longing and regret and fear,
Dull empty loneliness, and blank despair.

A little space in stony dread he lay,
Till something of a wretched hope at last
Amidst his tangled misery drave its way.
Slowly he rose, and, cold with terror, passed
Through blossomed boughs, whose leaves, upon him cast
As he brushed by, seemed full of life and sound,
Though noiselessly they fell upon the ground.

But soon he fled fast: and his goal he knew;
For each day's life once burdened with delight
Rose clear before him, as he hurried through
That lonely hell the grey moon yet made bright;
And midst them he remembered such a night
Of his first days there, when, hand locked in hand,
Sleepless with love, they wandered through the land;

And how, as thus they went, and as he thought
If he might still remember all her speech,
Whatso fresh pleasure to him might be brought,
A grove of windless myrtles they did reach,
So dark, that closer they clung each to each,
As children might; and how, the grove nigh done,
They came upon a cliff of smooth grey stone;

And how, because the moon shone thereabout
Betwixt the boughs grown thinner, he could see,
Gazing along her smooth white arm stretched out,
A cavern mid the cliff gape gloomily;
And how she said: "Hither I guided thee,
To show thee the dark danger and the death,
But if thou have heed, of thy love and faith."

Ah me! the memory of the sunrise sweet
After that warning little understood,
When stole the golden sun unto her feet,
As she lay sleeping by the myrtle-wood,
Watched by his sleepless longing!—"O how good
Those days were! fool, go back, go back again,
Shalt thou have lived and wilt thou die in vain?"

So cried he, knowing well now what it meant,

That long-passed warning; that there gaped the gate
Whereby lost souls back to the cold earth went:
Then through his soul there swept a rush of hate
'Gainst hope, that came so cruel and so late
To drive him forth from all the joys he knew,
Yet scarcely whispering why or whereunto.

Therewith he stayed: midst a bright mead he was,
Whose flowers across her feet full oft had met
While he beheld; a babbling stream did pass
Unto the flowery close that held her yet.
O bliss grown woe that he might ne'er forget!
But how shall he go back, just, e'en as now,
Oft, o'er again that bliss from him to throw?

He cried aloud with rage and misery,
But once again gat onward through the night;
Nought met him but the wind as he drew nigh
That myrtle-grove, black 'gainst the meadow bright;
Nought followed but the ghost of dead delight;
The boughs closed round him as still on he sped,
Half deeming that the world and he were dead.

But when he came unto the open space,
Grey with the glimmer of the moon, he stayed
Breathless, and turned his white and quivering face
Back toward the spot where he had left her, laid
Beneath the rose-boughs by their flowers down-weighed,
As if he looked e'en yet to see her come,
And lead him back unto her changeless home.

Nought saw he but the black boughs, and he cried:
"No sign, no sign for all thy kisses past!
For all thy soft speech that hath lied and lied!
No help, no cry to come back!—Ah, at last
I know that no real love from me I cast;
Nought but a dream; and that God knoweth too;
And no great gift He deems this deed I do.

"O me! if thou across the night wouldst cry,
If through this dusky twilight of the moon
Thou wouldst glide past and sob a-going by,
Then would I turn and ask no greater boon
Of God, than here with thee to dwell alone,
And wait His day!—but now, behold, I flee,
Lest thy kissed lips should speak but mocks to me!

"But now I flee, lest God should leave us twain
Forgotten here when earth has passed away,
Nor think us worthy of more hell or pain
Than such a never-ending, hopeless day!—

No sign yet breaketh through the glimmering grey!
Nought have I, God, for thee to take or leave,
Unless this last faint hope thou wilt receive!"

And with that word he rushed into the cave.
But when the depths of its chill dark he gained,
Turning he saw without the black boughs wave;—
And oh, amidst them swayed her form unstained! '
But as he moved to meet her, all things waned;
A void unfathomed caught him as he fell
Into a night whereof no tongue can tell.

Into bright sun he woke up suddenly,
And sprang up like a man with foes beset
Amidst of sleep; and crying an old cry
Learned in the tilt-yard, blind and tottering yet,
He stretched his hand out, that a tree-trunk met,
Dank with the dew of morn, and through his blood
A shiver ran, as hapless there he stood.

Until, though scarce remembering aught at all,
Clearly he saw the world and where he was;
For as he gazed around, his eyes did fall
Upon a tree-encompassed plain of grass,
Through which anigh him did a fair stream pass.
He stood and looked, nor a long while did dare
To turn and see what lay behind him there.

At last he did turn, and the cave's mouth, black,
Threatening, and dreadful, close to him did see,
And thither now his first thought drove him back;
A blind hope mingled with the misery
That 'gan to close about him; and yet he
Had no will left to move his feet thereto.
Yea, vague that passed joy seemed—yea, hardly true.

Again he looked about: the sun was bright,
And leafless were the trees of that lone place,
Last seen by him amid the storm's wild light;
He passed his hand across his haggard face,
And touched his brow; and therefrom did he raise,
Unwittingly, a strange-wrought golden crown,
Mingled with roses, faded now and brown.

The cold March wind across his raiment ran
As his hand dropped, and the crown fell to earth;
An icy shiver caught the wretched man
As he beheld his raiment of such worth
For gems, that in strange places had their birth,
But frail as is the dragon-fly's fair wing
That down the July stream goes flickering.

Cold to the very bone, in that array
He hugged himself against the biting wind,
And toward the stream went slow upon his way;
Nor yet amidst the mazes of his mind
The whole tale of his misery might he find,
Though well he knew he was come back again
Unto a lost world fresh fulfilled of pain.

But ere he reached the rippling stony ford,
His right foot smote on something in the grass,
And, looking down, he saw a goodly sword,
Though rusted, tangled in the weeds it was;
Then to his heart did better memory pass,
And in one flash he saw that bygone night,
Big with its sudden hopes of strange delight.

For, to you, now his blanched and unused hand
Clutched the spoiled grip of his once trusty blade!
There, holding it point downward, did he stand,
Until he heard a cry, and from a glade
He saw a man come toward him; sore afraid
Of that new face he was, as a lone child
Of footsteps on a midnight road and wild.

There he stood still, and watched the man draw near;
A forester, who, gazing on him now,
Seemed for his part stayed by some sudden fear
That made him fit a shaft unto his bow,
As his scared heart wild tales to him did show
About that haunted hill-side and the cave,
And scarce he thought by flight his soul to save.

Now when he saw that, out into the stream
The knight strode, with a great and evil cry,
Since all men suddenly his foes did seem:
Then quailed the man, yet withal timidly
His bowstring drew, and close the shaft did fly
To Walter's ear, but the carle turned and fled,
E'en as he drew the bowstring to his head.

But the knight reached the other side, and stood
Staring with hopeless eyes through that cold day;
And nothing that he now might do seemed good:
Then muttered he: "Why did I flee away?
My tears are frozen, and I cannot pray;
Nought have I, God, for thee to take or leave,
Unless that last faint hope thou didst receive."

But as he spake these words unwittingly,
He moaned; for once again the moonlit place

Where last he said them did he seem to see,
And in his heart such longing did that raise,
That a bright flush carne o'er his haggard face,
And round he turned unto the cliff once more,
And moved as if the stream he would cross o'er.

Who shall tell what thought stayed him? who shall tell
Why pale he grew? of what was he afraid,
As, turning, fast his hurried footsteps fell
On the wind-bitten blooms of spring delayed?
What hope his dull heart tore, as brown birds made
Clear song about the thicket's edge, when he
Rushed by their thorny haunts of melody?

Heavily now his feet, so well wont, trod
The blind ways of the wood, till it grew thin,
And through the beech-trunks the green sunlit sod
He saw again; and presently did win
Into another cleared space, hemmed within
A long loop of the stream, and midmost there
Stood the abode of some stout wood-dweller.

Now as he came anigher to the sun,
Upon his glittering, gauzy, strange array
The bough-flecked, dazzling light of mid-day shone,
And at the wood's edge made he sudden stay,
And, writhing, seemed as he would tear away
The bright curse from him, till he raised his face,
And knew the cottage midmost of the place:

Knew it, as one a-dying might behold
His cup made joyous once with wine and glee,
Now brought unto him with its ruddy gold,
Stained with the last sad potion scantily;
For he, a youth, in joyous company,
Maying or hunting, oft had wandered there,
When maiden's love first known was fresh and fair.

He moaned, and slowly made unto the door,
Where sat a woman spinning in the sun,
Who oft belike had seen him there before,
Among those bright folk not the dullest one;
But now when she had set her eyes upon
The wild thing hastening to her, for a space
She sat regarding him with scared white face;

But as he neared her, fell her rock adown.
She rose, and fled with mouth that would have cried
But for her terror. Then did Walter groan:
"O wretched life! how well might I have died
Here, where I stand, on many a happy tide,

When folk fled not from me, nor knew me cursed,
And yet who knoweth that I know the worst?"

Scarce formed upon his lips, the word "Return"
Rang in his heart once more; but a cold cloud
Of all despair, however he might yearn,
All pleasure of that bygone dream did shroud,
And hopes and fears, long smothered, now 'gan crowd
About his heart: nor might he rest in pain,
But needs must struggle on, howe'er in vain.

Into the empty house he passed withal;
As in a dream the motes did dance and grow
Amidst the sun, that through the door did fall
Across its gloom, and on the board did show
A bag of silver pieces, many enow,
The goodman's market-silver; and a spear
New-shafted, bright, that lay athwart it there.

Brooding he stood, till in him purpose grew;
Unto the peasants' coffer, known of old,
He turned, and raised the lid, and from it drew
Raiment well worn by miles of wind-beat wold.
And, casting to the floor his gauzy gold,
Did on these things, scarce thinking in meanwhile
How he should deal with his life's new-born toil.

But now, being clad, he took the spear and purse,
And on the board his clothes begemmed he laid,
Half wondering would their wealth turn to a curse,
As in the tales he once deemed vainly made
Of elves and such-like—once again he weighed
The bright web in his hand, and a great flood
Of evil memories fevered all his blood,

Blinded his eyes, and wrung his heart full sore;
Yet grew his purpose among men to dwell,
He scarce knew why, nor said he any more
That word "Return:" perchance the threatened hell,
Disbelieved once, seemed all too possible
Amid this anguish, wherefrom if the grain
Of hope should fall, then hell would be a gain.

He went his ways, and once more crossed the stream,
And hastened through the wood, that scantier grew
Till from a low hill he could see the gleam
Of the great river that of old he knew,
Which drank the woodland stream: 'neath the light blue
Of the March sky, swirling and bright it ran,
A wonder and a tale to many a man.

He went on wondering not; all tales were nought
Except his tale; with min of his own life,
To ruin the world's life, hopeful once, seemed brought;
The changing year seemed weary of the strife
Ever recurring, with all vain hope rife;
Earth, sky, and water seemed too weak and old
To gain a little rest from waste and cold.

He wondered not, and no pain smote on him,
Though from a green hill on the further side,
Above the green meads set with poplars slim,
A white wall, buttressed well, made girdle wide
To towers and roofs where yet his kin did bide:—
His father's ancient house; yea, now he saw
His very pennon toward the river draw.

No pain these gave him, and no scorn withal
Of his old self; no rage that men were glad
And went their ways, whatso on him might fall;
For all seemed shadows to him, good or bad;
At most the raiment that his yearning clad,
Yearning made blind with misery, for more life,
If it might be, love yet should lead the strife.

He stood a space and watched the ferry-boat
Take in its load of bright and glittering things;
He watched its head adown the river float,
As o'er the water came the murmurings
Of broken talk: and as all memory clings
To such dumb sounds, so dreamlike came back now
The tale of how his life and love did grow.

He turned away and strode on, knowing not
What purpose moved him; as the river flowed
He hastened, where the sun of March blazed hot
Upon the bounding wall and hard white road,
The terraced blossoming vines, the brown abode
Where wife and child and dog of vine-dressers
With mingled careless clamour cursed his ears.

How can words measure misery, when the sun
Shines at its brightest over plague and ill?
How can I tell the woe of any one,
When the soft showers with fair-hued sweetness fill,
Before the feet of those grief may not kill,
The tender meads of hopeful spring, that comes
With eager hours to mock all hopeless homes?

So let it pass, and ask me not to weigh
Grief against grief:—ye who have ever woke
To wondering, ere came memory back, why day,

Bare, blank, immovable, upon you broke—
Untold shall ye know all—to happy folk
All heaviest words no more of meaning bear
Than far-off bells saddening the summer air.

But tells my tale, that all that day he went
Along the highway by the river side,
Urged on by restlessness without intent;
Until when he was caught by evening-tide,
Worn out withal, at last must he abide
At a small homestead, where he gat him food
And bed of straw, among tired folk and rude.

A weary ghost within the poor hall there,
He sat amid their weariness, who knew
No whit of all his case, yet half with fear
And half with scorn gazed on him, as, with few
And heavy words, about the fire they drew,
The goodman and goodwife, both old and grey,
Three stout sons, and one rough uncared-for may.

A ghost he sat, and as a ghost he heard
What things they spoke of; but sleep-laden night
Seemed to have crushed all memory of their word,
When on the morrow, in the young sun's light,
He plodded o'er the highway hard and white;
Unto what end he knew not: though swift thought
Memory of things long spoken to him brought.

That day he needs must leave the streamside road,
Whereon he met of wayfarers no few;
For sight of wondering eyes now 'gan to goad
His misery more, as still more used he grew
To that dull world he had returned unto;
So into a deep-banked lane he turned aside,
A little more his face from men to hide.

Slowly he went, for afternoon it was,
And with the long way was he much foreworn;
Nor far between the deep banks did he pass,
Ere on the wind unto his ears was borne
A stranger sound than he had heard that morn,
Sweet sound of mournful singing; then he stayed
His feet, and gazed about as one afraid:

He shuddered, feeling as in time long past,
When mid the utter joy of his young days
The sudden sound of music would be cast
Upon the bright world with the sun ablaze,
And he would look to see a strange hand raise
The far-off blue, and God in might come down

To judge the earth, and make all hid things known.

And therewithal came memory of that speech
Of yesternight, and how those folk had said,
That now so far did wrong and misery reach,
That soon belike earth would be visited
At last with that supreme day of all dread;
When right and wrong, and weal and woe of earth,
Should change amid its fiery second birth.

He hastened toward the road as one who thought
God's visible glory would be passing by,
But, when he looked forth tremblingly, saw nought
Of glorious dread to quench his misery;
There was the sky, and, like a second sky,
The broad stream, the white road, the whispering trees
Swaying about in the sound-laden breeze.

For nigher and nigher ever came the song,
And presently at turning of the way
A company of pilgrims came along,
Mostly afoot, in garments brown and grey:
Slowly they passed on through the windy day,
Led on by priests who bore aloft the rood,
Singing with knitted brows as on they strode.

Then sank his heart adown, however sweet,
Pensive and strange, their swinging song might be,
For nought like this he had in heart to meet;
But rather something was he fain to see,
That should change all the old tale utterly;—
The old tale of the world, and love and death,
And all the wild things that man's yearning saith.

Nathless did he abide their coming there,
And noted of them as they drew anigh,
That in that fellowship were women fair,
And young men meet for joyous company,
Besides such elders, as might look to die
In few years now, or monks who long had striven
With life desired and feared, life for death given.

Way-worn they seemed, yet many there strode on,
With flashing eyes and flushed cheeks, as though all
Within a little space should be well won:
Still as he gazed on them, despair did fall
Upon his wasted heart; a fiery wall
Of scorn and hate seemed 'twixt their hearts and his;
While delicate images of bygone bliss

Grew clear before his eyes, as rood and saint

Gleamed in the sun o'er raiment coarse and foul,
O'er dusty limbs, and figures worn and faint:
Well-nigh he shrieked; yet in his inmost soul
He felt that he must ask them of their goal,
And knew not why: so at a man he clutched,
Who, as he passed, his shoulder well-nigh touched.

"Where goest thou then, O pilgrim, with all these?"
"Stay me not!" cried he; "unto life I go,
To life at last, and hope of rest and peace;
I whom my dreadful crime hath hunted so
For years, though I am young—O long and slow
The way to where the change awaiteth me—
To Rome, where God nigh visible shall be!

"Where He who knoweth all, shall know this too,
That I am man—e'en that which He hath made,
Nor be confounded at aught man can do.—
And thou, who seemest too with ill down-weighed,
Come on with us, nor be too much afraid,
Though some men deem there is but left small space,
Or ere the world shall see the Judge's face."

He answered not, nor moved; the man's words seemed
An echo of his thoughts, and, as he passed,
Word and touch both might well be only dreamed.
Yea, when the vine-clad terraced hill at last
Had hid them all, and the slim poplars cast
Blue shadows on the road, that scarce did show
A trace of their passed feet, he did not know

But all had been a dream; all save the pain,
That, mingling with the palpable things around,
Showed them to be not wholly vague and vain,
And him not dead, in whatso hard bonds bound,
Of wandering fate, whose source shall ne'er be found.
He shivered, turned away, and down the same
Deep lane he wandered, whence e'en now he came.

He toward the night through hapless day-dreams passed,
That knew no God to come, no love: he stood
Before a little town's grey gate at last,
And in the midst of his lost languid mood,
Turned toward the western sky, as red as blood,
As bright as sudden dawn across the dark,
And through his soul fear shot a kindling spark.

But as he gazed, the rough-faced gate-warder,
Who leaned anigh upon his spear, must turn
Eyes on him, with an answering anxious fear,
That silent, questioning, dared not to learn,

If he too deemed more than the sun did burn
Behind the crimson clouds that made earth grey—
If yet perchance God's host were on its way.

So too, being come unto his hostelry,
His pain was so much dulled by weariness,
That he might hearken to men's words, whereby
It seemed full sure that great fear did oppress
Men's hearts that tide, that the world's life, grown less
Through time's unnoted lapse, this thousandth year
Since Christ was born, unto its end drew near.

Time and again, he, listening to such word,
Felt his heart kindle; time and again did seem
As though a cold and hopeless tune he heard,
Sung by grey mouths amidst a dull-eyed dream;
Time and again across his heart would stream
The pain of fierce desire whose aim was gone,
Of baffled yearning loveless and alone.

Other words heard he too, that served to show
The meaning of that earnest pilgrim train;
For the folk said that many a man would go
To Rome that Easter, there more sure to gain
Full pardon for all sins, since frail and vain,
Cloudlike the very earth grew 'neath men's feet:
Yea, many thought, that there at Rome would meet

The half-forgotten Bridegroom with the Bride,
Stained with the flushed feast of the world; that He,
Through wrack and flame, would draw unto His side
In the new earth where there is no more sea.
So spake men got together timorously;
Though pride slew fear in some men's souls, that they
Had lived to see the firm earth melt away.

Next morn were folk about the market cross
Gathered in throngs, and as through these he went
He saw above them a monk's brown arms toss
About his strained and eager mouth, that sent
Strong speech around, whose burden was 'Repent;'
He passed by toward the gate that Romeward lay,
Yet on its other side his feet did stay.

Upon a daisied patch of road-side grass
He cast himself, and down the road he gazed;
And therewithal the thought through him did pass,
How long and wretched was the way he faced.
Therewith the smouldering fire again outblazed
Within him, and he moaned: "O empty earth,
What shall I do, then, mid thy loveless dearth?"

But as he spake, there came adown the wind
From out the town the sound of pilgrims' song,
And other thoughts were borne across his mind,
And hope strove with desire so hopeless strong,
Till in his heart, wounded with pain and wrong,
Something like will was born; until he knew
Now, ere they came, what thing he meant to do.

So through the gate at last the pilgrims came,
Led by an old priest, fiery-eyed and grey;
Then Walter held no parley with his shame,
But stood before him midmost of the way.
"Will one man's sin so heavy on you weigh,"
He cried, "that ye shall never reach your end?
Unto God's pardon with you would I wend."

The old man turned to him: "My son," he said,
"Come with us, and be of us! turn not back
When once thine hand upon the plough is laid;
The telling of thy sin we well may lack,
Because the Avenger is upon our track,
And who can say the while we tarry here,
Amid this seeming peace, but God draws near?"

The. crowd had stayed their song to hear the priest,
But now, when Walter joined their company,
Like a great shout it rose up and increased,
And on their way they went so fervently
That swept away from earth he seemed to be;
And many a thought o'er which his heart had yearned
Amid their fire to white ash now seemed burned.

For many days they journeyed on, and still
Whate'er he deemed that he therein should do,
The hope of Rome his whole soul seemed to fill;
And though the priest heard not his story through,
Yet from him at the last so much he knew,
That he had promised when they reached the place,
To bring him straight before the Pope's own face.

Through many a town they passed; till on a night
Long through the darkness they toiled on and on
Down a straight road, until a blaze of light
On the grey carving of an old gate shone;
And fast the tears fell down from many an one,
And rose a quavering song, for they were come
Unto the threshold of that mighty Rome.

They entered: like a town of ghosts it seemed
To Walter, a beleaguered town of ghosts;

And he felt of them, little if he dreamed
Amid his pain of all the marshalled hosts
That lay there buried mid forgotten boasts;
But dead he seemed as those his pleasures were,
Dead in a prison vast and void and drear.

Unto a convent that eve were they brought,
Where with the abbot spake the priest for long,
Then bade the hapless man to fear him nought,
But that the Pope next day would right his wrong;
"And let thy heart," quoth he, "O son, be strong,
For no great space thou hast to sin anew:
The days of this ill world are grown but few."

Night passed, day dawned, and at the noon thereof
The priest came unto Walter: "Fair my son,
Now shalt thou know," he said, "of God's great love;
Moreover thou shalt talk with such an one
As hath heard told the worst deeds man hath done,
And will not start at thine or mock at thee:
Be of good heart, and come thy ways with me."

Amid the tumult of his heart, they went
Through the calm day, by wonders wrought of old;
And fresh young folk they met, and men intent
On eager life; the wind and the sun's gold
Were fresh on bands of monks that did uphold
The carven anguish of the rood above
The wayfarers, who trusted in God's love.

But no more dead the grey old temples seemed
To him than fresh-cheeked girl or keen-eyed man;
And like a dream for some dim purpose dreamed,
And half forgotten, was the image wan
Nailed on the cross: no tremor through him ran,
No hope possessed him, though his lips might say,
"O love of God, be nigh to me to-day!"

For surely all things seemed but part of him;
Therefore what help in them? Still on he passed
Through all, and still saw nothing blurred or dim,
Though with a dread air was the world o'ercast,
As of a great fire somewhere; till at last,
At a fair convent door the old priest stayed,
And touched his fellow's shoulder, as he said:

"Thou tremblest not; thou look'st as other men:
Come then, for surely all will soon be well,
And like a dream shall be that ill day, when
Thou hangedst on the last smooth step of hell!"
But from his shoulder therewith his hand fell,

And long he stared astonished in his place,
At a new horror fallen o'er Walter's face.

Then silently he led him on again
Through daintily wrought cloisters, to a door,
Whereby there stood a gold-clad chamberlain:
Then, while the monk his errand to him bore,
Walter turned round and cast a wild look o'er
Fair roof, and painted walls, and sunlit green,
That showed the slim and twisted shafts between.

He shut his eyes and moaned sore, for as clear
As he beheld these, did he now behold
A woman white and lovely drawing near,
Whose face amidst her flower-wreathed hair of gold,
Mocked the faint images of saints of old;
Mocked with sweet smile the pictured mother of God,
As o'er the knee-worn floor her fair feet trod.

Through his shut eyes he saw her still, as he
Heard voices, and stepped onward, as he heard
The door behind him shut to noisily,
And echo down the cloisters, and a word
Spoke by a thin low voice: "Be not afeard!
Look up! for though most surely God is nigh,
Yet nowise is he with us visibly."

He looked up, and beside him still she stood,
With eyes that seemed to question; What dost thou,
What wilt thou say? The fever of his blood
Abated not, because before him now
There sat an old man with high puckered brow,
Thin lips, long chin, and wide brown eyes and mild,
That o'er the sternness of his mouth still smiled.

"Wilt thou kneel down, my son?" he heard him say,
"God is anigh, though not to give thee fear;
Folk tell me thou hast journeyed a long way,
That I the inmost of thine heart might hear;
It glads me that thou holdest me so dear.
But more of this thy love I yet would win,
By telling thee that God forgives thy sin."

He knelt down, but all silent did abide
While the Pope waited silent; on the ground
His eyes were fixed, but still anigh his side
He knew she stood; and all the air around
Was odorous with her, yea, the very sound
Of her sweet breath, moving of hair and limb,
Mixed with his own breath in the ears of him.

Outside the sparrows twittered; a great tree
Stirred near the window, and the city's noise
Still murmured: long the Pope sat patiently
Amid that silence, till the thin weak voice
Spake out and said: "O son, have the world's joys
Made thee a coward? what is thy degree?
Despite thy garb no churl thou seem'st to me."

Fearfully Walter raised his eyes, and turned,
As though to ask that vision what to say,
And with a bitter pain his vexed heart burned,
When now he found all vanished clean away:
Great wrath stirred in him; shame most grievous lay
Upon his heart, and spreading suddenly
His hands abroad, he 'gan at last to cry:

"Look at me, father! I have been a knight,
And held my own mid men: such as I kneel
Before thee now, amidst a hopeless fight
Have I stood firm against the hedge of steel,
Casting aside all hope of life and weal
For nought—because folk deemed I would do so,
Though nought there was to gain or win unto.

"Yet before thee an old man small and weak
I quail indeed: not because thou art great,
Not because God through thy thin pipe doth speak,
As all folk trow: but, rather, that man's hate,
Man's fear, God's scorn shall fall in all their weight
Upon my love when I have spoken out—
Yea, let me bide a minute more in doubt!

"Man hates it and God scorns, and I, e'en I—
How shall I hate my love and scorn my love?
Weak, weak are words—but, O my misery!
More hate than man's hate in my soul doth move;
Greater my scorn than scorn of God above—
And yet I love on.—Is the pain enow
That thou some hope unto my heart mayst show?—

"Some hope of peace at last that is not death?
Because with all these things I know for sure
I cannot die, else had I stopped my breath
Long time agone—thereto hath many a lure
Drawn on my hand; but now God doth endure,
And this my love, that never more shall bring
Delight to me or help me anything."

Calm sat the Pope, and said: "Hope, rather, now;
For many a sinner erewhile have I shriven
As utterly o'erwhelmed in soul as thou,

Who, when awhile with words his mouth had striven,
Went forth from me at peace and well forgiven.
Fall we to talk; and let me tell thee first,
That there are such as fain would be the worst

"Among all men, since best they cannot be,
So strong is that wild lie that men call pride;
And so to-day it is, perchance, with thee—
Cast it aside, son; cast it clean aside,
Nor from my sight thy utmost vileness hide;
Nought worse it makes thy sin, when all is done,
That every day men do the same, my son!"

The strained lines of the kneeling wretch's face
Were softened; as to something far away
He seemed a-listening: silent for a space
The two men were—who knows what 'twixt them lay,
What world of wondrous visions, of a day
Passed or to come?—to one lost love so clear,
God's glory to the other present there.

At last the Pope spake; well-nigh musical
His voice was grown, and in his thin dry cheek
There rose a little flush: "Tell of thy fall,
And how thy weak heart its vain lust must seek,
Cursing the kind and treading down the weak!
Tell all the blindness of thy cruelties,
Thy treason, thine unkindness and thy lies!—

"And be forgiven—these things are of earth:
The fire of God shall burn them up apace,
And leave thee calm in thy pure second birth;
No sin, no lust forgotten, in the place
Where, litten by the glory of God's face,
The souls that He hath made for ever move
Mid never-dying, never-craving love.

"How fair shall be the dawning of that day
When thy cleared eyes behold the thing thou wast,
Wherefore, and all the tale: hate cast away,
And all the yearning of thy love at last
Full satisfied, and held for ever fast!
O never-dying souls, how sweet to hear
Your laughter in the land that knows no fear!

"All this thou gainest if to God thou turn,
Since nought but with thy fellows hast thou dealt,
And well He wotteth how vexed hearts may yearn,
Who in the very midst of them hath dwelt,
Whose own soul, too, the world's hard wrong hath felt,
The serpent's burning clutch upon his heel—

Speak, then, and pray, and earn unending weal!"

A strange look crossed the knight's face as he said:
"Surely all these shall love their God full well;
Good to be one of these; yet have I read
That other things God made, and that they dwell
In that abode He made, too, men call hell.
If every man that will become God's friend
Shall have great joy that nevermore shall end,

"Yet is it so that evil dureth still,
Unslain of God—what if a man's love cling,
In sore despite of reason, hope, and will,
Unto the false heart of an evil thing?—
O me!" he cried, "that scarce heard murmuring
Beside me, and that faint sound of thy feet!
Must thou be wordless this last time we meet?"

Then the Pope trembled, for, half-risen now,
Walter glared round him through the empty air;
"O man," he said, "speak out: what seest thou?
What ill thing 'twixt thy God and thee stands there?"
"Ah, me!" cried Walter, "kind thou wert and fair
In the past days, and now wilt thou be gone,
And leave me with this cruel God alone?

"Is it then so as I have deemed erewhile,
That thou fear'st God too, even as I fear?
That I shall see the death of thy kind smile,
When, hand in hand, amid the unshadowed air,
Unto God's face forgot we draw anear?
O mocking lie, that told me while ago,
One minute's bliss was worth unending woe!"

The Pope caught at the staff across his knees,
And, rising, stood, leaned heavily thereon,
And said: "Why kneelest thou mid words like these;
Rise up, and tell me swift what thou hast done,
E'en as one man speaks to another one;
Or let me go, lest I begin to deem
That I myself spake thus in some ill dream!"

But, cowering down again, cried out the knight:
"Nay, leave me not! wait, father; thou shalt hear!
Lo, she is gone now!—surely thou said'st right;
For the whole world is trembling with my fear
And tainted with my sin—I will speak clear
And in few words, and know the end at last.
Yea, though e'en now I know myself outcast.

"Hast thou not heard about the gods, who erst

Held rule here where thou dwellest? dost thou think
That people 'neath their rule were so accurst
That they forgot in joy to eat and drink,
That they slept not, and loved not, and must shrink
From the world's glory?—how if they loved these
Thou tallest devils and their images?

"And did God hate the world, then, for their sake,
When fair the sun rose up on every day,
And blade and bloom through the brown earth did break,
And children were as glad as now?—nay, nay,
Time for thy wrath yet—what if these held sway
Even now in some wise, father?—Nay, say then,
Hast thou not heard, from certain Northern men,

"Of lonely haunters of the wild-woods there,
Not men, nor angels, soulless as men deem,
But of their bodily shape most wondrous fair?
What—thinkest thou I tell thee of some dream,
Some wandering glimmer of the moon's grey beam,
Seen when men's hearts sink mid black-shadowed trees,
And unknown words are in the tangled breeze?

"Belike I dreamed then! O belike some shade
Of nought that is I saw with these mine eyes!—
I saw her feet upon the blossoms laid,
The flowers o'er which no God-made sun shall rise!-
Belike I am a mad fool mid the wise,
But nothing therefor of God's wrath need fear,
Because my body and soul I gave her there.

"What!—must I name her, then, ere thou mayst know
What thing I mean? or say where she doth dwell—
A land that new life unto me did show
Which thou wilt deem a corner cut from Hell,
Set in the world lest all go there too well?
Lo, from THE HILL OF VENUS do I come,
That now henceforth I know shall be my home!"

He sprang up as he spoke, and faced the Pope,
Who through his words had stood there trembling sore,
With doubtful anxious eyes, whence every hope
Failed with that last word; a stern look came o'er
His kind vexed face: "Yea, dwell there evermore!"
He cried: "just so much hope I have of thee
As on this dry staff fruit and flowers to see!"

Walter laughed loud, and knew not who was there,
And who was gone, nor how long he abode
Within that place, or why his feet must fare
Round about Rome that night—or why that load

Was on his heart; or why next morn the road
Beneath his hurrying feet was white and dry,
And no cloud flecked the sunny April sky.

He knew not—though he wondered at all these,
And where he went—but nought seemed strange to him,
And nought unknown, when the great forest-trees
Around a cleared space of the wood were dim
In windless dawn, with white mist that did swim
About a pine-clad cliff, above a stream
Dark, scarcely seen, and voiceless as a dream.

No ignorance, no wonder, and no hope
Was in his heart, as his firm feet passed o'er
The shallow's pebbles, and the flowery slope,
And reached the black-mouthed cavern, the dark door,
Unto the fate now his for evermore,
As now at last its echoing stony dearth,
And dull dark closed betwixt him and the earth.

And what more would ye hear of him? Meseems
It passes mind of man to picture well
His second sojourn in that land; yet gleams
There might be thence, if one had heart to tell,
In sleepless nights, of horrors passing hell,
Of joys by which our joys are misery;
But hopeless both, if such a thing may be.

Let us be silent then, but hear at least
What the old tale tells: that the morrow morn
The Pope was busy at the Holy Feast;
Then through the ancient solemn streets was borne,
Where stood the folk as thick as summer corn;
Then o'er their bowed heads and their weeping stilled,
With his small blessing voice the hushed air thrilled:

And, many other things being said and done,
Unto his own house came back at the last,
And in his quiet garden walked alone
Pondering, his mind perplexed and overcast,
Not with the hurry of the day late past;
Rather that haggard face, those hopeless eyes,
Despite himself would still before him rise.

The shadows fell their longest; a great flood
Of golden light glowed through the peaceful place;
The Pope sat down; the staff of olive-wood
Cursed, as it were, at ending of that case,
Fell from him as he turned his weary face
Unto the western glory: close beside
A babbling conduit, from its stone did glide.

Well sang the birds; all was so sweet and fair,
It melted those dull troublous thoughts within
The old man's heart, transmuted all his care
Into a loving peace right hard to win:
He murmured in his faded voice and thin,
Mid the full sweetness of the spring; "Would God
That man and I this peace together trod!

"For he mayhap had things to say to me
He could not say then, knowing not what I was;
And I—God wot that there are things I see,
To tell of; if the words my lips would pass:
Things dimly seen, indeed, as in a glass—
Woe's me! for who shall help me if I erred!
Yet God, I deemed, had given me that last word.

"O God, if I have done thee deadly wrong,
And lost a soul thou wouldst have saved and blessed,
Yet other words thou knowest were on my tongue,
When 'twixt that soul and mine thine image pressed:
Thou wilt remember this and give him rest!
And as for me, thou knowest I fear thee nought,
Since this my body and soul thine own hand wrought."

The sun was sunken now, the west was red,
And still the birds poured forth their melody,
A marvellous scent about him seemed to spread,
Mid strange new bliss the tears his eyes drew nigh;
He smiled and said; "Too old to weep am I;
Unless the very end be drawing near,
And unimagined sounds I soon shall hear.

"And yet, before I die, I needs must go
Back to my house, and try if I may write,
For there are some things left for me to do,
Ere my face glow with that ineffable light."
He moved and stooped down for his staff; still bright
The sky was, as he cast his eyes adown,
And his hand sought the well-worn wood and brown.

With a great cry he sprang up; in his hand
He held against the sky a wondrous thing,
That might have been the bright archangel's wand,
Who brought to Mary that fair summoning;
For lo, in God's unfaltering timeless spring,
Summer, and autumn, had that dry rod been,
And from its barrenness the leaves sprang green,

And on its barrenness grew wondrous flowers,
That earth knew not; and on its barrenness

Hung the ripe fruit of heaven's unmeasured hours;
And with strange scent the soft dusk did it bless,
And glowed with fair light as earth's light grew less,
Yea, and its gleam the old man's face did reach,
Too glad for smiles, or tears, or any speech.

Who seeth such things and liveth? That high-tide
The Pope was missed from throne and chapel-stall,
And when his frightened people sought him wide,
They found him lying by the garden wall,
Set out on that last pilgrimage of all,
Grasping his staff—"and surely," all folk said,
"None ever saw such joy on visage dead."

Sad eyes there were the while the tale was told,
And few among the young folk were so bold
As to speak out their thoughts concerning it,
While still amidst that concourse they did sit.
But some when to the fresh bright day they turned,
And smooth cheeks even in that freshness burned,
'Neath burning glances might find words to speak,
Wondering that any tale should make love weak
To rule the earth, all hearts to satisfy;
Yet as they spake, perchance, some doubt went by
Upon the breeze, till out of sight and sound
Of other folk, their longing lips had found,
If but a little while, some resting-place,
On hand, on bosom, on bright eager face.
But the old men learned in earth's bitter lore,
Were glad to leave untouched the too rich store
Of hapless memories, if it might be done;
And wandered forth into the noonday sun,
To watch the blossoms budding on the wall,
And hear the rooks among the elm-trees call,
And note the happy voices on the breeze,
And see the lithe forms; making out of these
No tangled story, but regarding them
As hidden elves upon the forest's hem
Gaze on the dancers through the May-night green,
Not knowing aught what troubled looks may mean.


EPILOGUE

So is a year passed of the quiet life,
That these old men from such mishap and strife,
Such springing up, and dying out of dreams
Had won at last. What further then? Meseems
Whate'er the tale may know of what befell
Their lives henceforth I would not have it tell;

Since each tale's ending needs must be the same:
And we men call it Death. Howe'er it came
To those, whose bitter hope hath made this book,
With other eyes, I think, they needs must look
On its real face, than when so long agone
They thought that every good thing would be won,
If they might win a refuge from it.

Lo,
A long life gone, and nothing more they know,
Why they should live to have desire and foil,
And toil, that overcome, brings yet more toil,
Than that day of their vanished youth, when first
They saw Death clear, and deemed all life accurst
By that cold overshadowing threat,—the End.

That night, when first they 'gan their way to wend,
And each dash in the moonlight of the sweep,
That broke the green bay's little-resting sleep,
Drew their stern further from the plague-cursed shore,
Did no cold doubt their gathering hope cross o'er
Of sweet rest fled from? Or that day of days,
When first the sun the veil of mist did raise,
And showed the new land real before them there,
Did no shame blot the victory over fear,
(Ah, short-lived victory!) that, whate'er might grow
And change, there changeless were they fettered now,
And with blind eyes must gaze upon the earth,
Forgetting every word that tells of birth,
And still be dead-alive, while all things else
Beat with the pulse that mid the struggle dwells?

Ah, doubt and shame they well might have indeed.
Cry out upon them, ye who have no need
Of life to right the blindness and the wrong!
Think scorn of these, ye, who are made so strong,
That with no good-night ye can loose the hand
That led you erst through love's sweet flowery land!
Laugh, ye whose eyes are piercing to behold
What makes the silver seas and skies of gold!
Pass by in hate, ye folk, who day by day
Win all desires that lie upon your way!

Yet mid your joyous wisdom and content,
Methinks ye know not what those moments meant,
When ye, yet children, mid great pleasure stayed,
Wondering for why your hearts were so downweighed;
Or if ye ever loved, then, when her eyes
In happiest moments changed in sudden wise,
And nought ye knew what she was thinking of;
Yet, O belike, ye know not much of love,

Who know not that this meant the fearful threat,
The End, forgotten much, remembered yet
Now and again, that all perfection mocks.

"And yet the door of many a tale unlocks,
Makes love itself," saith one, "with all its bliss."
Ah, could I speak the word that in me is!—
I dare not, lest to cursing it should turn.
But hearken—if Death verily makes Love burn,
It is because we evermore should cry,
If we had words, that we might never die:
Words fail us: therefore, "O thou Death," we say,
"Thus do we work that thou mayst take away!
Look at this beauty of young children's mirth,
Soon to be swallowed by thy noiseless dearth!
Look at this faithful love that knows no end
Unless thy cold thrill through it thou shouldst send!
Look at this hand ripening to perfect skill
Unless the fated measure thou didst fill;
This eager knowledge that would stop for nought,
Unless thy net both chase and hunter caught!
O Death! with deeds like these 'gainst thee we pray,
That thou, like those thou slewest, mayst pass away!"

And these folk—these poor tale-tellers, who strove
In their wild way the heart of Death to move,
E'en as we singers, and failed, e'en as we,—
Surely on their side I at least will be,
And deem that when at last, their fear worn out,
They fell asleep, all that old shame and doubt,
Shamed them not now, nor did they doubt it good,
That they in arms against that Death had stood.

Ah me! all praise and blame, they heed it not
Cold are the yearning hearts that once were hot;
And all those images of love and pain,
Wrought as the year did wax, perfect, and wane,
If they were verily loving there alive,
No pleasure to their tale-tellers could give.
And thou, O tale of what these sleepers were,
Wish one good-night to them thou holdest dear,
Then die thyself, and let us go our ways,
And live awhile amid these latter days!


L'ENVOI

Here are we for the last time face to face,
Thou and I, Book, before I bid thee speed
Upon thy perilous journey to that place

For which I have done on thee pilgrim's weed,
Striving to get thee all things for thy need—
I love thee, whatso time or men may say
Of the poor singer of an empty day.

Good reason why I love thee, e'en if thou
Be mocked or clean forgot as time wears on;
For ever as thy fashioning did grow,
Kind word and praise because of thee I won
From those without whom were my world all gone,
My hope fallen dead, my singing cast away,
And I set soothly in an empty day.

I love thee; yet this last time must it be
That thou must hold thy peace and I must speak,
Lest if thou babble I begin to see
Thy gear too thin, thy limbs and heart too weak,
To find the land thou goest forth to seek—
Though what harm if thou die upon the way,
Thou idle singer of an empty day?

But though this land desired thou never reach,
Yet folk who know it mayst thou meet or death;
Therefore a word unto thee would I teach
To answer these, who, noting thy weak breath,
Thy wandering eyes, thy heart of little faith,
May make thy fond desire a sport and play,
Mocking the singer of an empty day.

That land's name, say'st thou? and the road thereto?
Nay, Book, thou mockest, saying thou know'st it not;
Surely no book of verse I ever knew
But ever was the heart within him hot
To gain the Land of Matters Unforgot—
There, now we both laugh—as the whole world may,
At us poor singers of an empty day.

Nay, let it pass, and hearken! Hast thou heard
That therein I believe I have a friend,
Of whom for love I may not be afeard?
It is to him indeed I bid thee wend;
Yea, he perchance may meet thee ere thou end,
Dying so far off from the hedge of bay,
Thou idle singer of an empty day!

Well, think of him, I bid thee, on the road,
And if it hap that midst of thy defeat,
Fainting beneath thy follies' heavy load,
My Master, GEOFFRY CHAUCER, thou do meet,
Then shalt thou win a space of rest full sweet;
Then be thou bold, and speak the words I say,

The idle singer of an empty day!

"O Master, O thou great of heart and tongue,
Thou well mayst ask me why I wander here,
In raiment rent of stories oft besung!
But of thy gentleness draw thou anear,
And then the heart of one who held thee dear
Mayst thou behold! So near as that I lay
Unto the singer of an empty day.

"For this he ever said, who sent me forth
To seek a place amid thy company;
That howsoever little was my worth,
Yet was he worth e'en just so much as I;
He said that rhyme hath little skill to lie;
Nor feigned to cast his worser part away
In idle singing for an empty day.

"I have beheld him tremble oft enough
At things he could not choose but trust to me,
Although he knew the world was wise and rough:
And never did he fail to let me see
His love, his folly and faithlessness, maybe;
And still in turn I gave him voice to pray
Such prayers as cling about an empty day.

"Thou, keen-eyed, reading me, mayst read him through,
For surely little is there left behind;
No power great deeds unnameable to do;
No knowledge for which words he may not find;
No love of things as vague as autumn wind—
Earth of the earth lies hidden by my clay,
The idle singer of an empty day!

"Children we twain are, saith he, late made wise
In love, but in all else most childish still,
And seeking still the pleasure of our eyes,
And what our ears with sweetest sounds may fill;
Not fearing Love, lest these things he should kill;
Howe'er his pain by pleasure doth he lay,
Making a strange tale of an empty day.

"Death have we hated, knowing not what it meant;
Life have we loved, through green leaf and through sere,
Though still the less we knew of its intent:
The Earth and Heaven through countless year on year,
Slow changing, were to us but curtains fair,
Hung round about a little room, where play
Weeping and laughter of man's empty day.

"O Master, if thine heart could love us yet,

Spite of things left undone, and wrongly done,
Some place in loving hearts then should we get,
For thou, sweet-souled, didst never stand alone,
But knew'st the joy and woe of many an one —
By lovers dead, who live through thee, we pray,
Help thou us singers of an empty day!"

Fearest thou, Book, what answer thou mayst gain
Lest he should scorn thee, and thereof thou die?
Nay, it shall not be.—Thou mayst toil in vain,
And never draw the House of Fame anigh;
Yet he and his shall know whereof we cry,
Shall call it not ill done to strive to lay
The ghosts that crowd about life's empty day.

Then let the others go! and if indeed
In some old garden thou and I have wrought,
And made fresh flowers spring up from hoarded seed,
And fragrance of old days and deeds have brought
Back to folk weary; all was not for nought.
No little part it was for me to play—
The idle singer of an empty day.

THE END.

William Morris - A Short Biography

British poet, author, thinker and publisher William Morris was born in 1834 in Walthamstow, Essex. The eldest son of wealthy Londoners Emma Shelton Morris and William Morris, the younger Morris would become one of the most influential people in the cultural landscape of Victorian England.

Educated at home and at a nearby preparatory school, Morris's childhood was one of privilege, with books, leisurely excursions and ponies for personal use. The idyll ended (to an extent) with the sudden death of Morris Senior in 1847 when the younger Morris was just 14 years old. The next year, Morris began his formal studies at Marlborough College in Wiltshire. After three years of bullying and homesickness, Morris returned to his family home and was thereafter privately tutored.

In 1852, Morris entered Oxford University to study the Classics. While there he also became interested in medieval-era history and architecture. Morris would come to identify with medievalist ideals, as did a growing socio-political movement in England that rejected the values of the prevailing Victorian capitalist system. Morris would become even more politically active later in life, embracing the socialist values that he had recognized in medievalism as an undergraduate.

Morris made several important and life-long friends while at Exeter College at Oxford, most notably the artist and designer Edward Burne-Jones. Morris and Burne-Jones became part of a group of Oxford thinkers (most of them from the industrial city of Birmingham) who would be known historically as "The Birmingham Set." The group included divinity student William Fulford, poet and theologian Richard Watson Dixon, mathematician Charles Faulkner and scholar Cormell Price – internally they called themselves "The Brotherhood." The members of the group shared literary interests as well as values and were huge fans of Alfred Lord Tennyson, art critic John Ruskin, the Arthurian legends and William Shakespeare.

In 1856, Morris helped fund and start up the *Oxford and Cambridge Magazine*, the first of many cooperative projects in which he took an active role. Twelve issues were published. Also in 1856 – upon completion of his Bachelor of Arts degree - Morris was apprenticed briefly to the Oxford based Gothic revival architect George Edmund Street. Morris would use lessons learned from Street, and supervising architect Philip Webb, during the design process for his own Red House in Kent. Morris lived there with his new family – wife Jane Burdon, who he married in 1859, and daughters Jenny and Mary – until 1865.

In 1858 Morris published *The Defence of Guenvere*, an innovative volume of lyric and dramatic verse, which nonetheless was not well received critically. Morris would not publish again until 1867 when Bell and Dandy published the epic romantic poem *The Life and Death of Jason*. The printing was financed by Morris himself; happily, the book was well received and Morris received a fee for the second edition.

From 1861 Morris commuted from The Red House to London where he had opened a decorative arts firm with Burne-Jones, Webb, Faulkner and other friends: the Pre-Raphaelite painter Dante Gabriel Rossetti, Ford Madox Brown and Peter Paul Marshall. The company – known publicly as Morris, Marshall, Faulkner & Co. and privately as "The Firm" – specialized in locally produced fabrics, furniture, tapestries, wallpaper, architectural carving and stained glass windows. In 1875, Morris assumed total control of the company, now named Morris & Co. Though known in his lifetime chiefly for being a poet, Morris would also achieve posthumous acclaim as a chief architect of the "Arts and Crafts" British design movement.

In 1865, Morris sold The Red House and moved to Bloomsbury in London with his family. By 1870, he was a cultural fixture in that city and a celebrity of some stature.

From 1865 to 1870, Morris worked on another epic poem, *The Earthly Paradise*. Designed as homage to Chaucer, it consists of 24 stories, each with a different narrator from a different cultural background. Set in the late 14th century, it is about a group of Norsemen who flee the Black Death by sailing away from Europe, on the way discovering an island where the inhabitants continue to venerate an ancient Greek god. Published in four parts by F. S. Ellis, the epic gained a cult following and established Morris' reputation as a major poet.

Greatly influenced by his friendship with Icelandic theologian Eiríkr Magnússon and several visits to Iceland, Morris produced a series of English-language translations of the Icelandic Eddas and Sagas (old Norse poems and stories). Morris also taught himself calligraphy and created hand written copies of Nordic tales in translation, including *Frithiof the Bold* and *Halfden the Black*. It was the continuation of a life-long devotion to craft, a feature of many of his subsequent works, including the poetic drama *Love is Enough*, published in 1872 with woodcut illustrations by Burne-Jones.

Though leading a rich life in London, Morris did find the city unhealthy for his young family. He came across and fell in love with a 16th century manor house in Oxfordshire. The Morris family would share Kelmscott Manor with Morris' friend Rossetti (who, it is said, had developed a close relationship with Morris' wife Jane) until their friendship eventually disintegrated. Kelmscott also lent its name to another of Morris' achievements – the Kelmscott Press, which he co-founded, with Emery Walker, in 1891. The bespoke publishing house was dedicated to publishing limited edition, illuminated style fine art books, in keeping with Morris' devotion to the craft of making books as beautiful objects. The Press dovetailed with Morris' continuing design work with Morris & Co. Over the next seven years, it would publish 66 volumes, the first of which was Morris' own novel, *The Story of the Glittering Plain*, in 1891. The Kelmscott Press would go on to publish 23 of Morris' books, but also editions of works by Keats, Shelley, Ruskin, and Swinburne, as well as copies of various Medieval texts. Kelmscott's magnum opus would turn out to be the Kelmscott Chaucer, published in 1896; it took several years to complete and included 87 illustrations and decorative borders from Burne-Jones.

In 1883, Morris joined England's first socialist organization, the Democratic Federation, later renamed the Socialist Democratic Federation (SDF). This was the beginning of years of overt activism on behalf of workers and the poor. In 1884, Morris and a large group of SDF members seceded in order to form the brand new Socialist League (SL). For the rest of the decade, Morris worked tirelessly for the cause; he met several times each week with his comrades from the SL and delivered hundreds of lectures. He was arrested in 1885 for disorderly conduct at the trial of several Socialist protesters, wrote for and edited SL's newspaper, *The Commonweal* and wrote a long series of socialist literary works, including the song collection *Chants for Socialists* (1884); a narrative poem, *The Pilgrims of Hope* (1885); the historical meditation *A Dream of John Ball* (1887); and his most influential work, *News from Nowhere* (1890), a pastoral utopian communist vision of England in the twenty-first century.

Morris also continued as a poet and prose writer. In December 1888, the Chiswick Press published his *The House of the Wolfings*, a fantasy story set in Iron Age Europe, which provides a reconstructed portrait of the lives of Germanic-speaking Gothic tribes. The book contains both prose and poetic verse and was followed by a two-volume sequel, *The Roots of the Mountains*, in 1899.

Morris also embarked on a translation of the quintessential Anglo-Saxon tale, *Beowulf*. Because he could not fully understand Old English, his poetic translation was based largely on that already produced by A.J. Watts. *The Tale of Beowulf* was not well received.

In the last nine years of his life, Morris wrote a series of imaginative fictions usually referred to as the "prose romances." These novels – including *The Wood Beyond the World* and *The Well at the World's End* (1896) – have been credited as important milestones in the history of fantasy fiction, because, while other writers wrote of foreign lands, or of dream worlds, or the future (as Morris had already done in the utopian *News from Nowhere*), Morris's works were the first to be set in an entirely invented neo-medieval fantasy world.

By 1896, Morris was an invalid, not working much but being visited by friends and family at his home. The great man died of tuberculosis on October 4th, 1896. Morris' funeral was held on October 6th, his corpse carried from Kelmscott House, his home in Hammersmith, to Paddington rail station, where it was transported to Oxford, then to Kelmscott, where it was buried in the churchyard of St. George's Church.

Morris lives on with the legacy of the Arts and Crafts movement, in his many fine literary works, essays and translations and through his homes, which have been preserved by the UK's National Trust and the William Morris Society as monuments to the man and the epic period of cultural history in which he flourished.

William Morris - A Concise Bibliography

Collected Poetry, Fiction, and Essays

The Hollow Land (1856)
The Defence of Guenevere, and other Poems (1858)
The Life and Death of Jason (1867)
The Earthly Paradise (1868–1870)
Love is Enough, or The Freeing of Pharamond: A Morality (1872)
The Story of Sigurd the Volsung and the Fall of the Niblungs (1877)
Hopes and Fears For Art (1882)
The Pilgrims of Hope (1885)
A Dream of John Ball (1888)
A Tale of the House of the Wolfings, and All the Kindreds of the Mark. In Prose and in Verse (1889)
The Roots of the Mountains (1890)
Poems By the Way (1891)
News from Nowhere (or, An Epoch of Rest) (1890)
The Story of the Glittering Plain (1891)
The Wood Beyond the World (1894)
Child Christopher and Goldilind the Fair (1895)
The Well at the World's End (1896)
The Water of the Wondrous Isles (1897)
The Sundering Flood (1897)
A King's Lesson (1901)
The World of Romance (1906)
Chants for Socialists (1935)

Translations
Grettis Saga: The Story of Grettir the Strong with Eiríkr Magnússon (1869)
The Saga of Gunnlaug the Worm-tongue and Rafn the Skald with Eiríkr Magnússon (1869)
Völsung Saga: The Story of the Volsungs and Niblungs, with Certain Songs from the Elder Eddawith Eiríkr Magnússon (1870) (from the Volsunga saga)
Three Northern Love Stories & Other Tales with Eiríkr Magnússon (1875)
The Odyssey of Homer Done into English Verse (1887)
The Aeneids of Virgil Done into English (1876)
Of King Florus and the Fair Jehane (1893)
The Tale of Beowulf Done out of the Old English Tongue (1895)
Old French Romances Done into English (1896)

Published Lectures and Papers
Lectures on Art delivered in support of the Society for the Protection of Ancient Buildings (Morris lecture on The Lesser Arts). London, Macmillan, 1882
Architecture and History & Westminster Abbey". Papers read to SPAB in 1884 and 1893. Printed at The Chiswick Press. London, Longmans, 1900
Communism: a lecture London, Fabian Society, 1903